PHILOSOPHICAL ASPECTS OF MODERN SCIENCE

PHILOSOPHICAL ASPECTS OF MODERN SCIENCE

C. E. M. JOAD

GYAN

Published by

GYAN

Gyan Publishing House
5, Ansari Road
Daryaganj, New Delhi-110002
Phone: 011-47034999, 9811692060
E-mail: books@gyanbooks.com

Distribution Network
gyanbooks.com
India, USA, Canada, UK, Australia

ISBN: 978-93-6920-551-6 (PB)

First Published, 1932

2nd Impression 2025

Printed at: Gyan Press, Delhi.

PHILOSOPHICAL ASPECTS OF MODERN SCIENCE
Author: C. E. M. JOAD

PHILOSOPHICAL ASPECTS
OF
MODERN SCIENCE

C·E·M·JOAD

PHILOSOPHICAL ASPECTS OF MODERN SCIENCE

LONDON
GEORGE ALLEN & UNWIN LTD
MUSEUM STREET

CONTENTS

NOTE

The bulk of Chapter VII first appeared as an article in *Mind*, and my thanks are due to the editor for permission to reprint it.

Part of the matter contained in Chapters VIII and IX originally formed part of a paper read to the Aristotelian Society under the title "Modern Science and Religion," in January 1931.

INTRODUCTION

It is often said that current developments in physical science have no bearing upon philosophical problems, and that the metaphysician may ignore them as lying outside his province. There are, no doubt, good reasons for this view. There is, it is obvious, a sense in which the precise formula for the analysis of matter which happens to be current among physicists at the moment, has little or no metaphysical significance. There is, however another sense in which the work of scientists such as Professor Eddington and Sir James Jeans seems to me to have an important bearing upon metaphysical problems. I will try to make clear what this sense is.

The conceptions of the physical universe sponsored by modern science are changing with extreme rapidity, but the various pictures with which we are presented have at least this feature in common, that they are all extremely remote from the world of common sense, and the later ones are more remote than the earlier. Being different from the world we know, they are imaginatively difficult to conceive. Hence the question arises, What is the real status of these world pictures? Are the objects which physics affirms in any sense independent of the mind of the physicist who conceives them, and, if they are, what is their relation to the objects of the common-sense world? Is a chair, for instance, a square piece of wood resting on four wooden legs, or is it a dance of atoms and electrons which are neither square nor wooden; or is it in some mysterious fashion both at once? And, if it is both at once, what is the relation of the one description to the other?

These questions are, I think, strictly philosophical. For it is the business of philosophy to correlate the evidence collected by the special sciences, and to try to fit it into a coherent scheme of the universe as a whole. Nor is it only the special sciences which afford data for the philosopher, for the vision of the artist, the religious consciousness of the saint, and the day-to-day experience of the plain man are equally facts of which philosophy must take cognizance. If they conflict, he should try to harmonize them, even if the attempt involves, as it so often has done, the necessity of stigmatizing some of them as in some sense illusory. It is this task of correlation and harmonization which, as it seems to me, the changing conceptions of modern physics urgently demand. They have simply got to be fitted into some more or less coherent scheme of the universe as a whole. If the titles of papers read at philosophical congresses may be taken as an index of the interest of philosophers, most philosophers appear to be of the same opinion. An increasing number of the papers read at these congresses deal explicitly or implicitly with the metaphysical implications of modern science, and physics is the centre of interest. It cannot be said that this growing preoccupation with the problems set by modern science has been attended up to the present with very satisfactory results. Theories there are in plenty, but there is no agreement among the theorists. The position at the moment seems to be that the facts (if facts they be) discovered by the physicists are outrunning the capacity of human schematization to embrace them, while conceptions of the physical universe are following one another with a rapidity which has overtaxed the accommodation provided by philosophers for their reception.

Hence to the question, "What, if the statements made by physicists are true, is the external world like?" there is no sort of agreed answer. The situation is admittedly difficult, nor has it been made less so by the efforts of the scientists to come to the assistance of the philosophers by sketching universes on their own account. Scientists, indeed, and especially physicists, have shown in recent years an increasing disposition to enter the domain of philosophy; regrettably, I cannot help thinking, for the metaphysical interpretations which they have been led to place upon their results cannot but have seemed to the philosophers somewhat elementary. In particular the physicists have been making a belated discovery of the uses of Idealism. The physical world, they have seen reason to suppose, is not a something lying out there waiting to be discovered by scientists, a something which is unaffected by the process of discovery and exhibits features which it possessed prior to the process; it is modified, it may even be partially constructed, by the mind of the investigating scientist. The activity of the physicist's mind is not, it seems, exclusively revelatory; it is at least partly contributory to the features it appears to reveal. Thus there is an increasing tendency to emphasize the rôle played by mind in determining the characteristics of the scientific world, and philosophically minded scientists, discovering for themselves the commonplaces of idealist philosophy, accord a somewhat naïve recognition to what the philosophers could always have told them, and would have told them with some unanimity until the last few years.

One of the most important movements in philosophy in recent years has been the realist reaction from the dominant Idealism of the last century. It was the object of this reaction to save at least some part of the common-sense world from infection by the mind of the knower, and in so doing to guarantee the objective and independent reality of the objects it contained. Of this reaction Professor Moore and Mr. Bertrand Russell were in this country the chief protagonists. Of recent years it has admittedly become increasingly difficult to maintain the common-sense Realism of the earlier movement in all its integrity—its authors have themselves considerably modified, and Mr. Russell in particular has largely abandoned it—and the neo-realists' world of correlated sense data has borne less and less resemblance to the common-sense world of physical objects, which realism began by trying to preserve. In spite, however, of these later complexities I still feel that the realist reaction was on the right lines, and that its vindication of an external world existing in independence of knowledge was largely successful.

Of this movement in philosophy the philosophically minded scientist takes little or no account. For what, if the modern physicist is right, becomes of the objective status of a chair? Between the dance of atoms and electrons into which its physical reality is analysed and the ideal qualities of brownness, 'shinyness,' hardness, and so forth, which are said to be bestowed upon the physical reality by the mind (or sense organs) of the observer, the chair, as we know it in everyday life, has completely vanished. The modern physicist, in fact, first destroys the everyday world of common-sense objects, and, when confronted by the fact that the world of scientific objects which he proceeds to substitute for it has no affinity with anything that we actually experience, proceeds to attribute the difference between the two worlds to the constructive agency of the mind. Thus between physics on the one hand and Idealism on the other, the common-sense world is dissolved utterly away.

It is the desire to try to rehabilitate it which is partly responsible for the essay in theory of scientific knowledge, which forms the main part of this book. Partly, but not wholly; for I cannot claim—nor, indeed, did I expect—that, so far as the vindication of the common-sense world is concerned, the attempt has met with much success. Chairs and tables do not, I fear, exist in the way in which in everyday life we suppose them to exist; but it does not follow that the physicist's analysis of them into atoms and electrons invested with secondary qualities projected upon them by the mind is therefore correct. So much, at least, I hope that I have shown.

But the attempt to clear up the muddle of the relation between the worlds of science and of common sense, important as the task undoubtedly is, would not in itself have constituted a sufficient motive for the writing of this book. The problem of sense perception is altogether too difficult for me to have hoped to tackle it with any great measure of success, and, if this were the only issue which modern physics raises, I should not have attempted it.

But another question is involved, a question which, more practically important than the purely logical issue to which I have hitherto referred, is also one upon which, as it seems to me, it is easier to speak with some degree of confidence. This is the question of value. I use the term "value" generically to include moral, æsthetic and religious value. I also wish to imply by it such value as is associated with the word 'truth.' What is the relevance of this question to modern developments in physics? Suppose that we conceive of value as an objectively real factor, or as including a number of objectively real factors, residing in and characterizing the universe. The universe, we shall say, is such as to contain, among other things, this element, or these elements, of value. The suggestion that value is, in fact, of this character, an objectively real and independent element in the universe, is, of course, highly controversial; the issues which it involves are familiar and the discussions to which it gives rise are traditional in the history of philosophy. The relevance of modern developments in physics to these familiar issues may be seen by contrasting the nineteenth- and twentieth-century scientific attitudes to value. If the picture of the universe presented by nineteenth-century science was in essentials accurate, then the supposition I have made with regard to value is inadmissible; for the framework of nineteenth-century science was such as to assign to value only a subjective status. A marked change has characterized the attitude of modern scientists, and to-day science is no longer inclined to dismiss the deliverances of the moral and religious consciousness as necessarily illusory.

Now this change of front is due not so much to any positive grounds which science has supplied for regarding them as veridical—it is doubtful, indeed, whether science by its very nature could supply such grounds—as to the recognition of the fact that it has removed the grounds, which it had itself supplied, for dismissing them as necessarily subjective. This result has come about in the following way. Science until recent years has been dominated by the notion that to be real a thing must be of the same nature as that which we can, or theoretically could, see and touch. Hence, to enquire into the nature of the things we saw and touched, to analyse them into their elements and atoms, was to deal directly with reality; to apprehend values or to enjoy religious experience was to wander in a world of shadows. Common sense, under the influence of science, took the same view; to use the eye of the body to view the physical world was to acquaint oneself with what was real; to use that of the soul to see visions was to become the victim of illusion. And the views of the universe to which the visions led had, it was urged, no objective reality. Parallel with this belief that the real must be a substance tangible and visible was the belief that it must be subject to the laws which were observed to operate in the physical world—that it must work, in short, like a machine. As Eddington puts it, nineteenth-century science was disposed, as soon as it scented a piece of mechanism, to exclaim, "Here we are getting to bedrock. This is what things should resolve themselves into. This is ultimate reality." The implication was that whatever did not show itself amenable to mechanistic causation—value, for example, or the feeling of moral obligation, or the sense of Deity—was not quite real.

The present position is different. Science in abandoning the conception that to be real a thing must be like the entities which physics studies, and the conception that to be real is to work like a machine has removed the grounds, such as they were, for treating the worlds revealed in religious and aesthetic experience as something less than real, or as owing such reality as they possess to their dependence upon the knowing mind. The result is that moral experience and the religious consciousness are alike rehabilitated as modes of directly apprehending an objective reality revealed as external to apprehension. It is no longer the case that, if science is true, religion is not, and we are, therefore, free to consider the claims to objectivity of the religious, the moral and the aesthetic consciousness on merits.

It is important that we should realize this change in the intellectual climate of our day; it is equally important that we should not make too much of it. I say this because the reaction against the claim of nineteenth-century science to be the sole legitimate avenue for the exploration of reality does not stop here. The wheel has turned full circle, and in their enthusiasm for idealistic interpretations of phenomena many scientists seem anxious to deny the revelatory character of science altogether. It is not about the universe, they seem to assert, that science gives us information; it merely introduces us to ourselves. "Where science has progressed the farthest, the mind has but regained from nature that which the mind has put into nature." So Professor Eddington, who seems to conceive of the scientist as one who fares through the uttermost confines of the universe to discover himself. Nor, as is sometimes alleged, is this tendency confined to leading English scientists, to such writers as Professor Eddington, Sir James Jeans, and Sir Oliver Lodge. These admittedly are the leaders of what I may venture to call the idealist movement in modern science. Moreover, they have set forth their views in considerable detail, a fact of which I have taken advantage to subject them to a critical examination.

The views of Continental physicists are not so well known in this country, but from a series of interviews with them, accounts of which have from time to time been contributed by Mr. J. W. N. Sullivan to the *Observer*, there seems considerable reason to suppose that on the Continent also there is a tendency to take what might be broadly described as an idealist view of the universe. This, at least, is true of Einstein and Max Planck. Einstein's views are sufficiently well known, but the following quotation from an interview with Max Planck is not without interest in this connection.

In answer to the question, "Do you think that consciousness can be explained in terms of matter and its laws?" he is reported to have answered that he did not. "Consciousness," he continued, "I regard as fundamental. I regard matter as derivative from consciousness. We cannot get behind consciousness. Everything that we talk about, everything that we regard as existing postulates consciousness."[1] Statements of this kind suggest, if they do not presuppose, an idealist view of the universe, which is further regarded as having important religious implications.

In so far as modern physics is thought to provide justification for such a view, the reaction against materialism and mechanism has, as I shall try to show, gone too far. If science is no longer a useful stick with which to beat religion, it does not follow that religion is appropriately employed for the castigation of science. It may be the case, as indeed I think it is, that science and religion are each of them legitimate avenues for the exploration of reality, but of different orders of reality. And not only science and religion, but the knowledge of the common-sense world which forms part of our day-to-day experience.

I should hold, then, that the researches of the scientist are, equally with the perceptions of the plain man, the moral consciousness of the good man, the sensitivity of the artist and the religious experience of the mystic, revelatory of reality. Epistemologically they stand on equal terms. Such arguments as there are for supposing that any of these forms of experience is *merely* subjective, apply also to the others; but equally if any of them gives us information about a world external to ourselves, so also do the others. In other

[1] J. W. N. Sullivan, "Interview with Max Planck," *Observer*, January 25, 1931.

words, I can see no ground for claiming objectivity for the one form of experience while denying it to the others. It is this view which the following pages are designed to support.

From the survey of the philosophical views of contemporary scientists with which the book begins, there is one important omission. There should, it is obvious, be a chapter on Professor Whitehead's philosophy. Such a chapter I had fully intended to include but, when I came to the writing of it, I was brought up short by my inability to state clearly to myself what Professor Whitehead's views were. Up to the time of the issue of his most recent book, I believed with a fair measure of confidence that I had followed, although with difficulty, the development of his thought. *Process and Reality*, however, baffled me. Such parts of it as I could understand seemed to suggest that some of what I had concluded to be Professor Whitehead's views, as set forth in the last half of *Science and the Modern World*, had either been abandoned or, so far at least as I am concerned, had been completely misunderstood. In these circumstances, I no longer had that assurance of comprehension upon which the exposition, still more the criticism of a writer's philosophy should be based.

That Professor Whitehead's views are important, I am convinced; I know, too, that they are highly relevant to the theme of this book, but I hesitate to embark upon their detailed examination, lest the exposition of any particular position should be rendered valueless and criticism of it frustrated by a statement to the effect that the position in question was not, and never had been, Professor Whitehead's.

In the circumstances I can only apologize for an omission of the seriousness of which nobody is more sensible than myself.

PHILOSOPHICAL ASPECTS OF MODERN SCIENCE

CHAPTER I

THE IDEALISM OF PROFESSOR EDDINGTON

Of the various interpretations of the physical world which have been advanced by modern scientists, none has obtained a wider currency than that put forward by Professor Eddington. It provides, or purports to provide, not only an account of the physical world, but a comprehensive scheme of the universe as a whole. The account of the physical world is markedly idealist in character, and has undoubtedly been largely responsible for the current belief that modern physics favours an idealist interpretation of the universe as a whole.

I shall first summarize very briefly the main features of Professor Eddington's scheme, and then suggest certain criticisms. These I put forward with the less diffidence in that, while it would be presumptuous for a philosopher to criticize Professor Eddington's science, the latter part of *The Nature of the Physical Universe*, and the whole of the smaller book, *Science and the Unseen World*, consist not of an account of the conclusions of modern physics but of an attempt by the author to interpret these conclusions, and to gauge their significance from the point of view of our conception of the universe as a whole. These writings are, therefore, not science but philosophy, and may legitimately be subjected to the ordinary methods of philosophical analysis.

According to Professor Eddington, the world contains three different sorts of constituents: (*a*) Mental images which are "in our minds and not in the external world," (*b*) "some kind of counterpart in the external world which is of inscrutable nature," (*c*) "a set of pointer readings which exact science can study and connect with other pointer readings."[1] The statement that this set of pointer readings has substantive existence as a constituent of the real world must, as will shortly appear, be accepted with reserve. The evidence for it is discussed on pages 32 and 33.

The question immediately arises, how, given these materials, are we to account for the appearance of the world of everyday experience? Professor Eddington's answer seems to be, 'It is the product of the mind's operations upon the material constituted by (*b*).' It is the result, in other words, of a process of "world building" by mind. I say that it is (*b*) which provides the raw material for world building and not (*c*), because it is obvious, from what Professor Eddington says about (*c*), that (*c*), the world which science explores, although in one sense it is a part of the external universe, is also in another and an important sense a product of the operations of the mind. This sense, in which the scientist's world (*c*) is a product of the operations of the mind, is, however, different from the sense in which the everyday world is a mental product; for, while the world of everyday experience is the product of mind's constructive powers, the world of science is the result of a process of mental *abstraction*. If, then, (*c*), being abstracted from something else, only comes into separate existence where there is a scientist's mind to abstract it, it cannot, it is obvious, be that which is initially given to mind as raw material for the construction of the everyday world.[2]

What, then, is the precise status of (*c*), and whence is it derived? It is the answer which he gives to this question that forms the most distinctive feature of Professor Eddington's scheme. Physics, he says, gives us knowledge not of what things are in themselves, but of the responses which are made

[1] Eddington, *The Nature of the Physical World*, p. 254.

[2] See, however, page 33 for a qualification of this statement.

to things by various measuring machines. He instances the case of an elephant sliding down a grassy hillside, and considers the account which the ordinary physicist would give of this phenomenon. He wishes, we will suppose, to know how long it will take the elephant to get to the bottom. For the elephant he proceeds to read a weight of two tons, for the sloping hillside an angle of 60°, for the soft yielding turf a coefficient of friction. Replacing the material objects, the elephant, the hillside and the turf, with these pointer readings, namely two tons, 60° and a coefficient friction, he makes certain calculations and produces an answer in terms of seconds—that is to say, in terms of another pointer reading as measured on the dial of his watch. But the answer, it is clear, is not an answer which tells us anything about the elephant or about the hillside, the objects with which the problem started, but merely about the relation between certain abstracted features of the elephant and the hillside, those features, namely, which are susceptible of exact quantitative measurement.

The instance is typical of the procedure of physics which, Professor Eddington proceeds to point out, deals not with things in themselves, but with the quantitative aspects of things. Hence the information it gives is not information about things, but consists of sets of pointer readings which show the responses made to these quantitative aspects by various measuring machines. Physics thus deals with a closed world, the boundaries of which are the quantitative and measurable aspects of phenomena which have been selected as being alone amenable to treatment by the methods of the physicist. In fact "the whole subject-matter of exact science consists of pointer readings and similar indications."[1] Professor Eddington frequently warns us against the mistake of envisaging the real world in the likeness of these "indications." "Although we seem to have very definite conceptions of objects in the external world, those conceptions do

[1] Eddington, *The Nature of the Physical World*, p. 252.

not enter into exact science and are not in any way confirmed by it."[1]

And if we ask the question, 'After what model, then, are we to envisage the external world?' Professor Eddington replies that the answer to that question is not the physicist's business. His results do not apply to noumenal reality, but only to the aspects of it which his mind has selected for treatment. As to the nature of the something which underlies the 'indications,' that which the indications indicate, the physicist does not know, nor, apparently, in his capacity as physicist, care. "And if to-day you ask a physicist what he has finally made out the ether or the electron to be, the answer will not be a description in terms of billiard balls or flywheels, or anything concrete; he will point instead to a number of symbols and a set of mathematical equations which they satisfy. What do the symbols stand for? The mysterious reply is given that physics is indifferent to that; it has no means of probing beneath the symbolism."[2]

Scientific objects, then, are symbols. What they symbolize is an unknown something, the underlying (*b*) in fact, whose quantitative aspects have been abstracted to constitute (*c*). Even the atom, the fundamental constituent of contemporary matter, is, we are told, like everything else in the physical world, only a schedule of pointer readings. Presumably, therefore, it too is only a mind-selected or mind-abstracted 'indication' of something, the reality of which evades us. "Science has nothing to say as to the intrinsic nature of the atom. The physical atom is, like everything else in physics, a schedule of pointer readings."[3] (*c*) is thus in some sense indicative of and in some sense an abstraction from (*b*).

Nevertheless, there is no way, at any rate, for the physicist, from (*c*) to (*b*). For (*c*), the world of physics, is a closed

[1] Eddington, *The Nature of the Physical World*, p. 253.
[2] Id., *Science and the Unseen World*, p. 20.
[3] Id., *The Nature of the Physical World*, p. 259.

circle. In a famous essay in *Science, Religion and Reality*, the substance of which appears again in *The Nature of the Physical World*, Professor Eddington emphasizes the cyclic method of physics. The entities with which physics deals are, he points out, ultimately definable in terms of each other. Each physical expression is translatable into some other expression; inevitably, since each expression is the product of the same process of mental abstraction. But it is translatable *only* into some other physical expression; it is not translatable into anything else, into the so-called physical objects of the perceptual world, for instance, or into a reality which underlies the pointer readings and exists independently of the mind of the physicist. And it is precisely this property which the entities[1] belonging to the world of physics possess, of being translatable in terms of each other, but not translatable in terms of anything else, which leads Professor Eddington to speak of the world of physics as a closed circle.

In order to enforce his point he takes an illustration from the general theory of relativity. In its analytical form the theory is a statement to the effect that in empty space *potentials* obey certain differential equations. What are potentials? Quantities derived from certain more fundamental quantities called intervals in space-time. What are intervals in space-time? Relations between events measured by scales or clocks. What are scales or clocks? They are pieces of matter. What is matter? There are two answers to this question: I will give the first, the scientist's answer, and reserve the second. "Confining ourselves to mechanics, which is the subject in which the law of gravitation arises, matter," says Professor Eddington, "may be defined as the embodiment of three related physical quantities—mass (or energy), momentum and stress."[2] What are mass, momentum and stress? They are expressions containing *potentials*

[1] I use the words 'entities' and 'expressions' interchangeably, following Professor Eddington.

[2] *The Nature of the Physical World*, p. 262.

and their derivatives; and in reintroducing *potentials* we have returned to our starting-point.

All other physical definitions are, according to Professor Eddington, characterized by the same kind of interlocking. "Electric force is defined as something which causes motion of an electric charge; an electric charge is something which exerts electric force."[1] The only way to break the circle is to give the second of the two answers to the question, "What is matter?" and define matter as what mind knows. The only property of matter which escapes the closed circle of the physicist's definitions is thus the property of 'knowability' by mind.

We are now within sight of the foundations of Professor Eddington's Idealism. For if we ask whence the world of everyday experience, the world which contains matter as a palpable substantial thing, arises, the only possible answer on Professor Eddington's premises is from the constructional operations of the human mind. Something which is like neither the world of physics nor the world of sense impinges upon the sense organs and stimulates the mind to a process of world building, from which the worlds both of physics and of sense result. This something, as I said at the beginning, can only be the mysterious (*b*), that which the scientist's symbols symbolize. Of this world (*b*) we are told that it is "the background in which" the schedule of pointer readings "have their being—their actuality."[2] The "background" is also spoken of as that in which the pointer readings are "embedded."[3]

Postponing for further consideration the question of the nature of the background (*b*), I will begin with an account of the process of world building to which it stimulates the mind. The process is really a twofold process, and it results in the construction of the worlds not only of science (*c*) but also of sense. Let us consider each process separately.

[1] Eddington, *The Nature of the Physical World*, p. 264.

[2] Ibid., p. 282.

[3] Ibid., pp. 259-260.

(1) To begin with the construction of the world of sense, it is perhaps not without significance that it is chiefly by means of similes and metaphors that Professor Eddington indicates the sort of process which he conceives to have resulted in the familiar world of everyday experience. The similes are those of the procedure of the palaeontologist reconstructing an extinct monster from its foot-prints,[1] and of an editor receiving messages from a number of different reporters and, with the aid of a good deal of invention, piecing them together into a story.[2] Of the metaphors I will mention three. We are told that the "fibres of the external world run into our consciousness,"[3] and that "code messages" are "transmitted along the nerves into its" (the mind's) "sanctum."[4] These code messages the mind *interprets* in order to read the physical world. The mind is also said to "weave an impression out of the stimuli" travelling along the nerves to the brain.[5]

The material reaching the brain along these channels, the material which the mind must utilize for its world building is of the scantiest. It is not only the familiar secondary qualities of Locke, colour and temperature, sound and texture, that are "fancies" projected by the mind into the external world; most of the so-called primary qualities are also "fancies," and "permanence," the "structure" of familiar things, and their "substantiality" are all said to be the products of the mind's faculty of "world building." The treatment of "substance," is particularly instructive. Physicists, says Professor Eddington, "have chased the solid substance from the continuous liquid to the atom, from the atom to the electron, and there they have lost it."[6] "Substance," then, is not something which is discovered by the physicist in the external world; yet "substance" certainly belongs to the world of our everyday

[1] Eddington, *The Nature of the Physical World*, p. 278.
[2] Ibid., p. 100.
[3] Ibid., p. 278.
[4] Ibid., p. 240.
[5] Ibid., p. 317.
[6] Ibid., p. 318.

experience. The inference is inescapable; substance belongs to the everyday world because mind has put it there; it is "a fancy projected by the mind into the external world."[1]

Thus the familiar world is "subjective" through and through, in the sense that it owes the features which are discerned in it to the activity of the same mind as that which discerns them. And in this sense in which the familiar world is subjective, the world of science is said to be "objective."[2]

(2) Nevertheless, the scientist's world, in so far as the scientist is a mathematical physicist, is also the result of a process of world building. The materials for the construction of the world of field physics are "relations" and "relata." It is a little difficult for the layman to understand what these "relations" and "relata" are; in particular, the difference between them is a little obscure, relata being defined as the meeting points of relations and relations as performing the function of unifying the relata.

The relata are distinguished from each other by the number and nature of the co-ordinates assigned to each. The relations are described in terms of numerical coefficients, 256 of which are required to "give a numerical measure of the structure surrounding the initial relatum."[3] Later, most of the coefficients are jettisoned as 'useless lumber,' and in the end we are left with sixteen coefficients for each relation, ten of them symmetrical from which geometry and mechanics are constructed, and six of them asymmetrical from which is derived the science of electro-magnetism. The result of the operations of the mathematical physicist's mind upon the selected coefficients, the relations and the relata is the construction of "a physical world which will

[1] Eddington, *The Nature of the Physical World*, p. 318.

[2] Ibid., p. 94. "In general we should describe the familiar world as subjective and the scientific world as objective," a passage in which Professor Eddington seems to be speaking for himself.

[3] Ibid., p. 234.

give a shadow performance of the drama enacted in the world of experience."[1]

I am a layman in mathematics, and I cannot pretend to understand this argument, but the upshot of it, which is the construction of another mental world, is sufficiently clear. It is important, however, to note that the world in question, which is identical with the world of pointer readings to which I have already referred, covers the realm of field physics only. It is not by these methods that the physics of discontinuity is reached, such entities as quanta and electrons not being constructed by the mind out of numerical coefficients, relations and relata, but being apparently discovered by the empirical methods of the laboratory. If we do not exactly see the atoms through the microscope, it is through the microscope that we obtain the data which enable us to infer them. Thus, although we are told that the atom, too, consists of pointer readings, it now appears that it is at any rate not *mere* pointer readings; that, in fact, it *belongs* to the physical world in some sense in which the entities of field physics, which are *merely* schedules of pointer readings, do not belong to it.

We are now in a position to return to the mysterious background (*b*) of the world studied by physics, the background to which the schedule of pointer readings, which the physicist has substituted for physical entities, must be attached, since otherwise it would lack "actuality." Two questions arise: (1) After what manner are we to conceive it? (2) What reasons are there for so conceiving it?

(1) The answer to the first question can be given without hesitation. Professor Eddington envisages the background in which the world of physics is embedded as a "spiritual substratum."[2] He fully realizes that "experience . . . comprises more than can be embraced in the physical world, restricted as it is to a complex of metrical symbols,"[3] and

[1] Eddington, *The Nature of the Physical World*, p. 230.
[2] Ibid., p. 282.
[3] Ibid., p. 288.

that "more" must have "a nature capable of manifesting itself as mental activity."[1] It is not, however, itself mental activity, at any rate it is not consciousness, but is conceived as a "mind stuff," something which, more generalised than our individual conscious minds, is nevertheless not altogether foreign to consciousness. It is, as it were, the raw material of mind, below the level of consciousness—it is only here and there in scattered "islands" that it "rises to the level of consciousness"[2]—but essentially continuous with it. "We must postulate something indefinite, but yet continuous with our mental nature."[3] The word "stuff" must not, however, be allowed to mislead us with its suggestions of substance; its use "has reference to the function it has to perform as a basis of world building."[4]

(2) For this view of (*b*) three rather different reasons are assigned: (i) If matter, in the sense of material substance, is eliminated from the world, spiritual existence is the only kind of model for reality which is left. Thus reality is likened "to our conscious feeling because, now that we are convinced of the formal and symbolic character of the entities of physics, there is nothing else to liken it to."[5]

(ii) Since the human mind evinces itself as so eminently creative, as, for example, by its construction of the worlds, both of sense and of science, from the scanty materials that reach it along the nerve fibres, there is some justification for regarding the background itself as of a piece with our own human minds, so that consciousness will be, rightly conceived, the avenue of approach not only to our knowledge of reality, but to the nature and significance of that reality itself. On this view the greater the activity of the human mind, as, for example, in science, the more closely will the mind be brought into touch and the more vividly will its affinity be realized with an underlying reality which is, in fact, continuous with itself. To think about reality

[1] Eddington, *The Nature of the Physical World*, p. 260.
[2] Ibid., p. 277. [3] Ibid., p. 280. [4] Ibid., p. 280. [5] Ibid., p. 280.

will be to realize that thinking is of the essence of reality. "All through the physical world runs an unknown content, which must really be the stuff of our own consciousness," and, what is more, the more vigorously our consciousness is exercised, the more is its part in the construction of the unknown content revealed to it, for "we have found that, where science has progressed the farthest, the mind has but regained from nature that which the mind has put into nature."

(iii) There is one kind of knowledge which, as Eddington frequently points out, escapes the symbolic frameworks both of sensory experience and scientific knowledge. This is the knowledge which we have of ourselves. "Mind," he says, "is the first and most direct thing in our experience; all else is remote inference."[1] That is to say, we know our own natures as units of spiritual experience directly, in a sense in which we only know the familiar world of everyday objects and the schematized world of physics indirectly, since these worlds, as we have seen, are the products of processes of mental abstraction and mental construction. What more natural than to suppose that a similarly direct knowledge of the nature of anything else would reveal it as similarly experienced and similarly spiritual? "Surely, then, that mental and spiritual nature of ourselves, known in our minds by an intimate contact transcending the methods of physics, supplies just that interpretation of the symbols which science is admittedly unable to give."[2] The point is important, and Professor Eddington emphasizes it by means of another line of argument. In the case of the schedule of pointer readings which is our brain, we know that it is attached to a spiritual background which is our own consciousness. Hence we may not unreasonably conclude of other schedules of pointer readings, that the background to which they too are attached is of the same stuff as spirit and the same stuff as consciousness. In other words, our own

[1] Eddington, *Science and the Unseen World*, p. 24. [2] Ibid., p. 24.

spiritual experience, which is the one thing we know otherwise than as a schedule of pointer readings, gives us a clue to the nature of that underlying substratum to which science never penetrates—that is to say, to the inner reality of the universe. In so far as we are justified in conceiving at all of that which we cannot know, we must conceive it after the likeness of that experience. Hence reality is fundamentally spiritual.

The idealistic implications of Professor Eddington's interpretation of science are sufficiently obvious. I will summarize five of the most important.

(*a*) Reality, the unknown something which underlies the worlds both of sense and of science, in which both are embedded and from which both are derived, is spiritual in nature. It follows that the worlds both of sense and science are phenomenal only; they are appearances of a noumenal reality whose character they belie.

(*b*) The world of sense experience is the result of a process of mental construction, in the course of which the meagre and fragmentary messages received by our sense organs from the external world are woven into the rich and varied patterns of the perceptual world. For Professor Eddington, too, to quote a famous passage of Professor Whitehead's, "The poets are entirely mistaken. They should address their lyrics to themselves, and should turn them into odes of self-congratulation on the excellency of the human mind. Nature is a dull affair, soundless, scentless, colourless."[1]

(*c*) The same may be said of the world of science. This, too, is the product of the categories of our minds, the features we discern in it being the features we ourselves have put there.

(*d*) Mind knows itself with intimacy and certainty; but it is not thus that it knows external objects, or, indeed, any other objects. There are passages, indeed, in which Professor Eddington even goes so far as to suggest that

[1] Whitehead, *Science and the Modern World*, p. 69.

mind knows *nothing at all* but itself. For example, we are told that "the *only* subject presented to me for study is the content of my consciousness."[1] But I doubt if he would wish seriously to maintain this view.

(*e*) There is one important passage in which Professor Eddington defines actuality as "knowableness to mind."[2] He considers the hypothesis of a number of different worlds, each of which obeys the laws of physics but none of which actually exist. What, he asks, is the feature which distinguishes the world that actually exists from all the others that might exist but do not? He comes to the conclusion that the distinguishing property is that the one gets known; it is that with which "consciousness interacts."[3] Mind, then, is the final guarantor of reality, and to be real is to be known by a mind.

Positions (*a*), (*b*) and (*c*) are distinctly Kantian in type; (*d*) is perhaps more reminiscent of Descartes; (*e*) is pure Berkeley.

CRITICISM

A. Questions Relating to the Status of the Physicist's World

The first point that calls for attention is the ambiguous language which, following Professor Eddington, I have been compelled to use in speaking of the status of the physicist's world. I have spoken of it as:

(*a*) Abstracted by the mind of the scientist, presumably from the underlying background or counterpart;

(*b*) Constructed by the mind of the scientist from relations and relata (the second of the two processes of world building);

(*c*) Given as embedded in the background or counterpart which is reality. On the basis of (*c*), I included it in

[1] Eddington, *The Nature of the Physical World*, p. 283.

[2] Ibid., p. 265.

[3] Ibid., p. 266.

Professor Eddington's inventory of the constituents of the world.

It is, I think, clear that the physicist's world cannot be all these things; clear that, if it is actually given as embedded, it cannot be constructed by the mind from relations and relata; clear that, if it is constructed by mental activity from relations and relata, it cannot be a scheme or framework of the measurable aspects of things abstracted by the same mental activity from their total content. My excuse for using all these different expressions to describe the physicist's world is that they do all occur in Professor Eddington's writings, and the fact that they do all occur indicates, I cannot help thinking, a certain confusion in Professor Eddington's mind.

Three rather different conceptions may, I think, be distinguished in a careful reading of his work. (1) That Professor Eddington regards the physicist's world as the result of a process of mind building is, I think, in view of the argument summarized above,[1] abundantly clear. As such its status is that of a mentally constructed world, which is then known by the mind that has constructed it. It is, in fact, an *object of knowledge.*

(2) When, however, he speaks of the world of physics as being a world of symbols, or pointer readings; when, in particular, he speaks of the atom as "a schedule of pointer readings," what, I think, he has in mind and is purporting to describe is not the nature of a world, but the nature of *our knowledge of a world.* We are continually warned against confusing physical nature with the abstract scheme of quantitative relations which form the content of science. Mathematical and scientific formulae are, we are constantly told, to be regarded in the light of symbolic descriptions of a non-mathematical world. Thus on this view it is *scientific knowledge* which is *symbolic* and constructed, not the *objects* which the scientist knows.

[1] P. 26

(3) Frequently, however, Eddington writes as if the scientist's world of symbols had an independent reality of its own. There are many passages which suggest that the features which he notes as characteristic of science are characters not of a way of knowing, but of objects known, and known as given. As already stated, it was on the authority of such passages that I included the world of pointer readings as (*c*) in my summary of Professor Eddington's catalogue of the constituents of the universe. And herein is a most potent source of confusion.

When Professor Eddington speaks of "the formal and symbolic character of the *entities* of physics"[1] (my italics), or of "the *physical world*" as "restricted to a complex of metrical symbols,"[2] it is clear that he is wishing to designate a characteristic not of the physicist's knowledge, but of what he knows. And, that these expressions are not metaphorical merely, the descriptions given of the relation of the physicist's world to the background or underlying substratum are sufficient evidence. The language constantly used about "*embedding*" the schedule of pointer readings, "in some kind of background,"[3] or "*extracting* it" from a "broader reality," which is the "spiritual substratum,"[4] or knowing that pointer readings "are *attached* to a background of consciousness,"[5] implies, in fact it necessitates, that what is so embedded and extracted is not a piece of knowledge, but a piece of what is known. The suggestion is, in short, that the world of science has a kind of separate being of its own as a realm or sphere of reality—we are, in fact, told that "the cycles" of physics "cannot from their very nature trench on the background in which *they have their being*"[6] (my italics)—and the language used would be grossly inappropriate if this "being" were that merely of a selected aspect.

Now this confusion between knowing mind and object known seems to me to run right through Professor Edding-

[1] Eddington, *The Nature of the Physical World*, p. 280. [2] Ibid., p. 288.
[3] Ibid., p. 260. [4] Ibid., p. 282. [5] Ibid., p. 259. [6] Ibid., p. 282.

ton's treatment of the physicist's world. Such a confusion has, it is obvious, many disadvantages; chief among them is the fact that we are left in doubt as to whether the world which science studies and affirms is adjectival in the sense of being a state of the scientist's mind, or a content of his knowledge, or whether it has substantive existence as an aspect of, or a realm of, or a constituent of, a real objective world. And this, surely, is a very serious disadvantage indeed.

B. Questions Relating to the Nature of the Raw Materials with which the Processes of World Building are Performed

It is serious, if only because Professor Eddington makes use of each conception in turn as the development of his argument proceeds; and not only does he do this, but it is absolutely necessary that he should do it, if the argument is to proceed.

I will take two examples to show how different conceptions of the physicist's world are necessitated in turn by the argument.

(1) From the second kind of world building, that of the mathematical physicist, the entities of discontinuous physics, atoms, quanta of energy and so forth were expressly excluded. Our only method of knowing them is empirically through the microscope, or rather by inferences from entities observed through the microscope. We know them, therefore, in terms of and by inference from the world directly apprehended in sensory experience. But the world of sensory experience is itself the product of a process of world building, the process, namely, which is undertaken by the mind of the ordinary man. It is, therefore, ideal or mainly ideal. Therefore the entities known as part of it, or inferred from those known as part of it, must be ideal or mainly ideal; therefore atoms and quanta of energy cannot

be constituents of the real world, but must be mental constructs.

(2) Nevertheless, there are other parts of the argument which require that they should be independently real, in the sense of being objective and found, and not subjective and constructed. Something there must be to start the set of mental processes which result in the process of world building by the ordinary man. And this something surprisingly turns out to be not the underlying background in which the world of physics is embedded, but the entities which belong to the physicist's world. The process of world building by the plain man involves, it will be remembered, the transmitting of code messages from the sense organs to the brain, which pieces them together to make a picture of the everyday world. What, then, is it that impinges upon the sense organs to start the messages? Apparently scientific objects, or, if not scientific objects, objects remarkably like them. Our bodies, we are told, are "being continuously and vigorously buffeted" by rapidly moving molecules.[1] "Stress" in our muscles—and stress, it will be remembered, is one of those entities that formed the physicist's closed circle of entities that are defined in terms of each other—is something that we "feel."[2] Even the atoms are spoken of as if they were real entities, which live their independent lives in the external world unaffected by the fact that, as I have already pointed out, we have elsewhere been warned against thinking of them as possessing any being other than that of "pointer readings," and, as such, presumably owing their existence to the abstracting operations of the physicist's mind. We are even said to see them—"We see the atoms with their girdles of circulating electrons, darting hither and thither, colliding and rebounding"[3]—although this language may be largely metaphorical and should not, perhaps, be stressed.

[1] Eddington, *The Nature of the Physical World*, p. 113.
[2] Ibid., p. 240.
[3] Ibid., p. 290.

And I suggest that Professor Eddington does from time to time attribute to scientific objects an independent existence in the external world, because the process of world building which he imputes to the mind of the ordinary man positively requires some such conception; and this for two reasons. (*a*) Even when all allowance is made for the part played by the mind in projecting colour, temperature and similar qualities into the world that it perceives, something is required to set going the projecting process which precedes and results in the act of perception. The process begins, or so Professor Eddington asserts, with the stimulation of our sense organs. Sense organs can be stimulated neither by mind stuff nor by pointer readings, but only by qualitatively differentiated physical material. In other words, there is implied in the mere fact that our sense organs are stimulated at all, the existence of entities in the physical world the nature and characteristics of which fall outside the purely quantitative scheme, which Professor Eddington regards as constituting and comprising the world of physics. Sir James Jeans, whose general attitude to the world of physics is not dissimilar from that of Professor Eddington, also writes as if the objects, which in the ultimate analysis physics seems prepared to affirm, were objective constituents of reality. "The ethers and their waves," he says, "are the most real things of which we have any knowledge or experience, and so are as real as anything can possibly be for us."[1]

(*b*) Furthermore, Professor Eddington attributes to our own sense organs and nerves functions which necessarily rule them out of the purely quantitative scheme. The sense organs and nerves are essential elements in Professor Eddington's process of world building by the mind. They cannot, therefore, be the products of the process of world building. It follows that they must be independent constituents of the physical world—that is, of the world with

[1] Sir James Jeans, *The Mysterious Universe*, p. 80.

which physics deals. Yet the part assigned to them is clearly not such as can be played by abstractions or by quantitative pointer readings. The "fibres," the "nerve endings" that run into the brain, "the brain" itself, are all described as if they possessed an objective reality which is other than that of schedules of pointer readings. They are frequently spoken of as if they were endowed with physical qualities in their own right; and not only the sense organs and nerve endings, but entities such as air waves and light rays which, although they do not form part of the body, are nevertheless essential constituents of the physical machinery of perception. These, too, must presumably be endowed with substantive existence as qualitatively and not merely quantitatively differentiated entities, before the process of "interpreting code messages" by the mind "in its sanctum" can begin. They cannot, therefore, be regarded as an outcome of this process, and the various Eddingtonian conceptions of the physical world as consisting exclusively of "embedded" pointer readings, or of measurable, quantitative aspects abstracted by mind, or of entities constructed by mind, must be abandoned.

C. Questions Relating to the Process of Building or Constructing the Familiar World

I have objected that the process of world building presupposes the prior existence of at least some entities in that very physical world which it is said to construct. But what are we to say of the process itself? The whole conception of mind as constructing a picture of the external world from messages travelling along the nerve fibres into the brain, and the theory of knowledge in which it issues, seem to me to be self-contradictory and untenable. Of the many objections to which Professor Eddington's theory seems to be open I will mention four.

(1) It is a form of Representationalism, and as such is

exposed to the classical objections to Representationalism. It presupposes three different entities which play their part in perception: (*a*) A mind which knows and proceeds to construct or to weave or to edit; (*b*) the messages from the external world which form the raw material from which it constructs or which it weaves or edits, these messages being delivered by the terminals of certain nerve fibres which incidentally are also said to be known: (*c*) some sort of external world which, impinging on the sense organs, sends the messages.

But if (*a*) always knows (*b*), whether (*b*) be messages or brain fibres, and never (*c*), it cannot know anything about (*c*). Should it attempt to obtain knowledge of (*c*), it will only succeed in obtaining more knowledge of (*b*)s, and the attempt must therefore fail. But if we cannot know (*c*), we cannot know any of its properties; we cannot, therefore, know that it has the property of being able to cause (*b*). Therefore we cannot know that it exists as a cause of (*b*). We are thus cut off from all contact with the external world, shut up within the closed circle of 'messages' for which we can only invent, since we can never know, a sender. Or, to revert to another of Professor Eddington's metaphors, code messages are meaningful only if we know the source from which they come or the entities to which they refer. If we know only the messages, as Professor Eddington implies, they must be meaningless.

(2) To speak of the mind as knowing the ends of "fibres" of the external world which "run into consciousness" is surely wrong. Speaking personally, I am convinced that I do not know anything of the sort. The fibres are presumably nerve fibres running into the brain, the "sanctum" into which the "code messages are transmitted"; indeed, Professor Eddington says that when I feel things, e.g. stress in the muscles, sensations of warmth, and so on, "the feeling . . . is located in a certain corner of the brain."[1] But, as far as

[1] Eddington, *The Nature of the Physical World*, p. 240.

my observation of myself goes, I know less about my own brain and what happens in it than about any other part of my physical or mental make-up.

(3) If, however, what I know are code messages which travel into the brain along the nerve fibres from the outside world, how can I also be said to know my mind as "the first and most direct thing in my experience"? Introspection, which is knowledge of the mind by itself, certainly does not reveal messages travelling along nerve fibres, or any occurrence remotely resembling those suggested by the other metaphors and similes I have quoted. The statement about the mind's immediate and direct knowledge of itself is, therefore, inconsistent with the language used about nerve fibres and code messages, which would be, I should imagine, more appropriate to a knowledge of the brain, if such knowledge were available. For if, as Professor Eddington occasionally suggests, I only know the contents of my own *consciousness*, then the whole account of the machinery of perception which I have outlined must be given up.

(4) Is it, however, in any sense true, as Professor Eddington asserts, that my mind knows itself as "the first and most direct thing in my experience"? I should answer that it is not true in any sense. Not only do I feel fairly certain as the result of introspection that I do not know my own mind simply, intimately and directly, but I find my certainty supported by any textbook on psychology. What I do know intimately and directly is neither mind nor brain, neither mental events nor terminals of nerve fibres, but physical objects such as tables and chairs and people. Nor, I think, would it ever occur to anyone outside a philosophical classroom or a physicist's laboratory to assert that I know anything but physical objects. Certainly I do not, in the brief and uncertain glimpses I do get of my own mind, observe it weaving secondary qualities out of messages reaching the brain, and then projecting them into the external world, which is one of the things which, on Professor

Eddington's theory of world building, my mind is constantly doing.

I cannot, in fact, find any introspective evidence for world building, and the account of the process given by Professor Eddington bristles with difficulties as I have tried to show. It confuses mind with brain, brain with sense organs, and sense organs with objects which impinge upon them. And these objects it represents at one moment as starting-points of a process of world building, which at other moments it makes responsible for their production.

D. The Underlying Substratum, Mind Stuff or Reality

We are now in a position to consider Professor Eddington's conception of reality as being in its fundamental nature mind stuff. Against this conception the following objections may be urged:

(i) There are, I think, three main reasons which are advanced by Professor Eddington for believing in the existence of this mind stuff. If the considerations adduced in (*C*) above are valid, two of these main reasons disappear.

The two in question are as follows: (*a*) In one case, that, namely, of "the pointer readings of his own brain," the physicist knows that "they are attached to a background of consciousness."[1] Therefore, he may not unreasonably conclude of other schedules of pointer readings that they, too, are so attached. This argument clearly implies that the physicist knows the pointer readings of his own brain, or, more precisely, since his brain is, presumably, only a schedule of pointer readings, that he knows his own brain. This, I have argued in (*C*)(2), is not the case, and there cannot, I think, be any reasonable doubt that it is not. Our knowledge of our own brains, such as it is, is inferred from our knowledge of other people's brains. But we do not know that other people's brains are attached to a background of

[1] Eddington, *The Nature of the Physical World*, p. 259.

consciousness, since it is only our knowledge *of our own consciousness* which is said to be unique in the sense of being exempt from the symbolic limitations of scientific knowledge in general, our knowledge of other people being presumably infected with the same symbolism as our knowledge of other external objects. Hence it is only knowledge of the pointer readings of our own brains or that *are* our own brains that will supply the required evidence of "attachment," and this knowledge we do not possess.

(*b*) We know our own minds as the first and most direct thing in our experience; also we only know the contents of our own minds. The inference is that a similarly direct (i.e. non-symbolic) knowledge of anything else would reveal it as similarly mental; therefore properly viewed—viewed, that is to say, from inside—everything *is* probably mental.

This argument, in so far as it asserts that we *only* know our minds, is clearly inconsistent with *D*(i) (*a*), since, if we do only know our own minds, we cannot also know our brains as schedules of pointer readings. Waiving this point, I have argued in *C*(4) that we do not have the direct and intimate acquaintance with our minds which Professor Eddington postulates. If this argument is correct, the inference with regard to the spiritual nature of the inner reality of any other thing, an inference which is based upon the suggestion that we have this direct and intimate knowledge, can no longer be drawn. Thus, if I am right, the first two reasons for believing in the spiritual nature of the underlying reality are based upon an incorrect psychology.

(*c*) The third main reason is as follows: the physical world of pointer readings must have a "background." Since consciousness is the avenue of approach to reality, the background of the physical world must be of a piece with our own human consciousness. What this argument, if it is valid, shows is that the background of the physical world must be conscious and continuous with human consciousness. If it is not, it will not serve the purpose for which Professor

Eddington invokes it. Yet we are explicitly told that it is not "conscious" but below the level of consciousness, and that it "rises to the level of consciousness" only in the form of those "islands" which are human minds.[1] But if it is below the level of consciousness, if it is correctly distinguished from human consciousness because it is below that level, it cannot be of a piece with it.

Still less can it be of a piece with consciousness, if it is quantitative 'relations' and 'relata.' Yet it is in such terms that Professor Eddington on occasion describes it: "The mind stuff is the aggregation of relations and relata which form the building material for the physical world"[2]; and, since these relations and relata constitute, as we have seen, the raw material of the mathematician's world[3] building, since they are the only entities which in general Professor Eddington seems prepared to accept as somehow 'given' and not constructed, there must clearly be a sense in which they are legitimately included in the category of things which are objectively real.

Either, then, the real universe consists of quantitative relations and relata as well as of mind stuff, or quantitative relations and relata somehow are mind stuff. The first alternative suggests a dualistic universe, and it is clear that Professor Eddington does not hold it. The second, apart from its intrinsic difficulty, is open to the objection that quantitative relations and relata are *not* of a piece with consciousness.

(ii) One further criticism of the conception of the mind stuff may be urged. I have already pointed out, when summarizing Professor Eddington's description of world building by the mathematician, that it is the world of field physics only which is constructed out of the quantitative materials of relations and relata. The objects with which the physics

[1] Eddington, *The Nature of the Physical World*, p. 277. [2] Ibid., p. 278.
[3] I say "in general" because of the suggestion to which I have already referred that atoms and quanta are also objectively real.

of discontinuity deals, atoms and quanta of energy, are, apparently, not so constructed; indeed, they seem to be not constructed at all but given. "We see the atoms with their girdles of circulating electrons darting hither and thither, colliding and rebounding."[1] Moreover, as I have already pointed out, there must be qualitatively and not merely quantitatively differentiated entities in the external world, to act as the starting-points of that process of building, which results in the construction of the plain man's world. Something which is not completely analysable in terms of quantitative pointer readings must, in fact, stimulate our sense organs to set the process of familiar world building going, a fact which Eddington seems to recognize when he talks about our bodies being "continuously and vigorously buffeted" by rapidly moving molecules.

It seems clear, then, that some entities must be presupposed as existing in the external world independently of mind, and that these entities must be discrete and qualitatively differentiated one from another. They will, in fact, be particle-like and not continuous in character. Atomicity, therefore, appears to be no less a character of reality than continuity. What, then, is the relation of these particles to the underlying mind stuff? Can they conceivably be regarded as particles of the mind stuff? Clearly not, since the mind stuff is not spatial; we are told that it is not "spread in space and time,"[2] and, indeed, if it is continuous with consciousness, it cannot be. The atoms, however, *are* spatial, since they bombard and buffet our bodies.

Again the mind stuff is continuous, but the distinguishing feature of atoms and quanta is their discrete and discontinuous plurality. It is, indeed, because of this very characteristic of discontinuity that they are not included as mere schedules of pointer readings within the closed circle of field physics. It follows that the atom exists in the real world side by side with the relations and relata and the

[1] Eddington, *The Nature of the Physical World*, p. 290. [2] Ibid., p. 277.

mind stuff, and reality is not homogeneous but plural. It contains, that is to say, as objective features several different kinds of entities which are in no sense mind dependent.

E. The Multiplicity of Worlds

A serious objection to Professor Eddington's scheme of interpretation is, to my mind, the complexity of the world, or rather of the number of worlds which it appears to involve. Professor Eddington continually warns us against attributing independent objective existence to the entities with which physics deals. "Essentia non sunt multiplicanda praeter necessitatem"; one can almost hear him saying it, as he exhibits matter and mass, momentum and stress, intervals and potentials, as merely pointer readings, thereby seeking to deny them substantive existence. Yet it would be difficult to imagine a universe which called more insistently for the operation of Occam's razor than the one with which he, in fact, presents us.

Putting together all the intimations of different worlds which may be found scattered up and down his writings, and ignoring for the moment incompatibilities between them, some of which I have tried to point out, we get the following list.

(1) There is the world of everyday experience, the result of world building by the mind of the ordinary man.

(2) There is the world of pointer readings, the result of world building by the mind of the mathematical physicist.

(3) There is the world of pointer readings which is *given* as "embedded in" a background with which it requires to be supplemented and to which it is attached.

(4) There is a purely quantitative structure of relations and relata which are the raw material from which world (2) is built.

(5) There is the world of discontinuous physics, electrons, quanta and so forth, not constructed from relations and

relata, containing qualitative differences, and presumably performing the function of a stimulus to start the process of world building which results in world (1).

(6) There is the human mind which performs the world buildings.

(7) There is the spiritual substratum for all the rest, an underlying mind stuff, which is in some way continuous with (6).

I have tried to show that the status of some of these worlds is, to say the least of it, equivocal, that the relations between them are not and cannot be satisfactorily worked out, and that some of them at least are represented to us in ways which are fundamentally inconsistent. The world of pointer readings, for example, if it is the product of world building (2), cannot also and at the same time be regarded as embedded in the mind stuff, while worlds (4) and (5) which are objectively real are yet quite clearly not continuous with or part of that mind stuff which is represented as the sole type of objective reality, and after the model of which the universe as it is prior to and independently of processes of world building is to be conceived. That the universe may be and probably is exceedingly complicated is no doubt true. But I find it difficult to believe that it has the particular kind of complexity that Professor Eddington suggests, or that the richness and variety of the familiar world we know could not be accounted for by a more economical use of materials.

F. THE FAMILIAR WORLD PRESUPPOSED

There is in my view one criticism of a general type to which a number of current interpretations of the universe based on modern science are exposed, and to which I shall have occasion to recur in succeeding chapters. From this criticism Professor Eddington's scheme is not exempt. The criticism in its general form may be stated as follows. Modern science starts, as it must needs do, from the world of everyday experience, and proceeds to analyse this world into certain constituents which are alleged to be in some sense more fundamental than the world with which it starts. It then endeavours, on the basis of these constituents, which it uses as raw materials, to account for the emergence of the everyday world, or perhaps I should say for the appearance of the everyday world. In other words, the world of everyday experience is presupposed as the starting-point of a process of analysis and construction which results in the world of everyday experience.

This procedure, I cannot help feeling, must be mistaken. Professor Eddington's account of the universe exemplifies it in at least two respects. In the first place, the abstract scheme of structures and relations which forms the basis of the mathematical physicist's process of world building is suggested by the everyday world. The question which of the various measures of structure will be ultimately selected for world building by the mathematical physicist and which rejected as lumber is decided by reference to the everyday world, the test which is applied to them being that of helping to form a world which will "shadow the things of common experience." Thus the world of common experience is the datum from which the physicist starts and the criterion by which he determines the validity of the structure he raises. It is, therefore, presupposed as real and objective throughout.

In the second place, the world building of the ordinary man is a process which begins with and proceeds from the messages which reach his brain along his nerve fibres. These messages originate—I am taking what is, I think, on the whole Professor Eddington's main view—from the impact of something upon his sense organs. This something appears to be the entities of discontinuous physics, atoms, quanta of energy and so forth. From the process thus started the everyday world results. But how are the atoms and quanta reached? By a process of inference and deduction from the world which the physicist observes. No physicist has seen an atom; what he does see is the world of everyday experience, from which he infers atoms and quanta. It is into entities of this type that, he asserts, the external world, or at least the discontinuous part of it, really resolves itself. Thus atoms and quanta are the result of a process of inference based upon observation of the everyday world, while at the same time they originate a process which ends in the construction of the everyday world. Thus the everyday world must be presupposed before the process which results in its construction can take place.

CHAPTER II

THE IDEALISM OF SIR JAMES JEANS

I. Introductory

No work dealing with the philosophical aspects of modern science would be complete without some account of the views of Sir James Jeans. Sir James Jeans's books, like those of Professor Eddington, have a considerable popular vogue; they also conclude with chapters, the matter of which belongs strictly speaking to philosophy rather than to science. This is particularly true of Sir James Jeans's book, *The Mysterious Universe*, an expansion of the Rede lecture delivered at Cambridge in November 1930, the last chapter of which, entitled, "Into the Deep Waters," is devoted to an exposition of the author's view of the nature of the universe as a whole, and more particularly of his belief with regard to its origin. This chapter is admittedly a confession of faith rather than a statement of fact; at the same time it is based directly upon the conclusions of the scientific part of the work, the reasons for which are given at length in the author's larger book, *The Universe Around Us*, and it presents a picture of the universe which not only reflects, but, in the author's view, is to some extent necessitated by, the conclusions of modern physics and modern astronomy.

Sir James Jeans's views are entitled, therefore, to inclusion within the scope of the survey of this book, which seeks to examine and to evaluate, from the point of view of philosophy, the metaphysical views which are held to be indicated by recent developments in the physical sciences, even if they did not merit consideration for their intrinsic interest.

As in the chapter on Professor Eddington, I shall confine myself to a consideration of Sir James Jeans's philosophical views, the clearest and most complete expression of which is found in the chapter above referred to. As with Professor

Eddington, so with Sir James Jeans, the occasion for metaphysical speculation is afforded by the break-up of the mechanistic scheme of the physical universe which was drawn up by the scientists of the last century. It is this break-up of mechanism which constitutes his starting-point and orientates his approach. Sir James Jeans's pronouncements on this subject are no less decisive than those of Professor Eddington quoted in the first chapter. "In a completely objective survey of the situation the outstanding fact would seem to be that mechanics has already shot its bolt and has failed dismally on both the scientific and philosophical side. If anything is destined to replace mathematics, there would seem to be specially long odds against it being mechanics."[1] "To-day there is a wide measure of agreement, which on the physical side of science approaches almost to unanimity, that the stream of knowledge is heading towards a non-mechanical reality."[2] These quotations could be paralleled from many similar passages in Sir James Jeans's work, and to him, as to Professor Eddington, the break-up of mechanism seems to suggest that the only possible alternative to the universe being like a machine is that it should be like a thought. "The universe," he continues, "begins to look more like a great thought than like a great machine."[3] Reading the books of Professor Eddington and Sir James Jeans a person having some acquaintance with philosophical literature finds difficulty in avoiding the impression that their writers have only recently crossed the threshold of philosophical speculation. Great scientists as they are, they have the somewhat naïve air of being struck, as it were for the first time, by the force of considerations which have long been the stock-in-trade of idealist philosophers. To those accustomed to philosophical writings this belated discovery of the uses of Idealism by great scientists is a highly instructive phenomenon.

[1] Sir James Jeans, *The Mysterious Universe*, p. 146.
[2] Ibid., p. 148.
[3] Ibid., p. 148.

But while Sir James Jeans shares with Professor Eddington the idealist tendencies common to many modern physicists, his conclusions are based less upon a critique of the nature of our knowledge of the physical world as revealed by an examination of the physiological machinery of perception and of the limitations of scientific method, than upon certain considerations suggested by physics and astronomy with regard to the evidence of design in the universe as a whole, and the nature of the design which he is thereby led to infer. His concern is less with epistemological than with metaphysical considerations, his procedure, which is to present arguments purporting to show what the universe as a whole must be like, being strikingly reminiscent of the methods of rationalist philosophers of the seventeenth century such as Spinoza and Leibniz.

While Professor Eddington is predominantly empirical, Sir James Jeans's approach to philosophical problems may, therefore, be described as rationalist, in the eighteenth-century sense of the word, and *a priori*, and, as might be expected from the angle of approach, his pre-occupation is primarily with the significance of mathematics. It cannot be said, however, that when he is arguing in the high *a priori* manner about what may be or what must be, Sir James Jeans always shows to the best advantage. Some of his arguments, indeed, are far from convincing, and derive such plausibility as they possess from the circumstance of his overlooking certain fairly obvious considerations. I cite in illustration of this assertion the following suggestion, an argument typical of many, which purports to show that time may not be of the essence of reality. "It may be that time, from its beginning to the end of eternity, is spread before us in the picture, but we are in contact with only one instant, just as the bicycle wheel is in contact with only one part of the road. Then, as Weyl puts it, events do not happen; we merely come across them."[1]

[1] Sir James Jeans, *The Mysterious Universe*, p. 119.

It seems fairly clear that, even if the events we 'come across' do not themselves happen in time, our 'coming across them' is at least a temporal event, preceded and succeeded by earlier and later "comings across." Now there is no suggestion that we are in any sense unreal, or that our doings and experiencings are unreal happenings. Therefore the events which are constituted by our "comings across" are real events, and they are in time. Therefore, some events in the universe, if they occur as Sir James Jeans suggests, must be in time. Yet the object of the simile is to suggest that no events are in time. . . . If, however, it be objected that the events which are constituted by our successive contacts with the 'spread-out' timeless reality are not themselves quite real, then there is no need to take too seriously the suggestion which is based upon them; there is no need, in other words, to suppose that this suggestion really indicates to us the nature of reality.

The writer might, no doubt, urge, and with justice, that this is to break a butterfly on a wheel. I mention the suggestion not because I think Sir James Jeans attaches much importance to it, but because it exemplifies the light-hearted way in which the writer plays (if I may use such a word to indicate the impression which the author's treatment undoubtedly produces) with metaphysical notions. In this respect it is typical of many similar suggestions which are scattered up and down the book, suggestions which are frequently impracticable for some equally obvious reason.

The writer's main metaphysical argument, which I now proceed to consider, starts, however, on a very different footing from these stray suggestions. It falls into two main parts: it asserts, first, that the universe was created by a being with a mind which thinks mathematically or in terms of mathematics; secondly, that the universe is a thought in the mind of such a being. These two assertions are obviously quite different, and it is important to keep them distinct, although the writer does not always do so. I shall, therefore, consider them in turn and summarize, so far as I can, the reasons which the writer gives for them.

II

A (1) The argument for the first position begins by emphasizing two sets of considerations derived from modern science, the first from physics, the second from astronomy.

(*a*) The first set of considerations is advanced with a view to showing that physics does not give us information about the being or nature of material things. It only ascertains facts about the relations between certain of their aspects. In this sense physics deals with abstractions. The ether is an abstraction, the ether waves are abstractions, and the waves which "make-up" an electron exemplify this "quality of abstractness . . . in a far more acute form." As for the electron "isolated in space," it "provides a perfectly eventless universe," while the seven-dimensional space-time in which the wave-mechanics postulates the meeting of two electrons is described as being, in the view of most physicists, "purely fictitious."[1]

The arguments for this view of the nature of the physicist's world are similar to those which I have already considered in the chapter on Professor Eddington, and I shall not attempt to summarize them a second time. It is worth while to point out, however, that Sir James Jeans seems to use the word 'abstractions,' not in Professor Eddington's sense to mean constructions of the physicist's mind, but in its more precise meaning, to denote selected aspects of an independent reality. The conclusion of this set of considerations is that the world which science studies is, in the language of Plato's famous simile, a world of shadows, the shadows which reality throws on the wall of our cave.

(*b*) The second set of considerations is devoted to establishing the familiar point of man's relative insignificance in

[1] Sir James Jeans, *The Mysterious Universe*, pp. 120–121.

the material universe. Facts are marshalled, mainly from astronomy, to show how little we are in time, how little in space. The facts are staggering but by now sufficiently familiar.

(i) There are facts relating to the insignificance of man's planet. There is not, as astronomers used until recently to think, one system of stars, but many. Each of these systems came into being as the result of the gradual break-up of a spiral nebula, to which Sir James Jeans gives the name of "an island universe."

About two million such nebulae are visible through the great 100-inch telescope at Mount Wilson, and Sir James Jeans quotes an estimate to the effect that the whole universe is about a thousand million times as big as the area of space visible through this telescope. Each spiral nebula contains enough matter to make a thousand million of our suns. If a thousand million is multiplied by two million, and that again by a thousand million (the average number of estimated stars in each nebula), the resultant figure gives some indication of the probable number of stars in the universe. It is, Sir James Jeans estimates, "probably something like the total number of grains of sand on all the sea-shores of the world."[1] Now the sun is one such grain of sand; yet the sun is a million times as big as the earth and 300,000 times as massive!

In spite of this immense number of stars, space is almost empty. "If we place an apple at the centre of the Earth and place a grape-fruit, two more apples, two apricots and a currant in the six continents of the Earth's surface, we shall have a fairly good scale model of the arrangement in space of our Sun and its six nearest neighbours."[2] There is no reason to suppose that space as a whole is more directly crowded than the region adjacent to our sun; there is, indeed, some reason to suppose that large areas of space are

[1] Sir James Jeans, *The Mysterious Universe*, p. 1.

[2] Id., "The Birth of the World," *Harmsworth's Universal History*, p. 66.

less crowded. With regard to the size of space as a whole, we are told that light, which takes a seventh of a second to travel round the earth, takes "probably something like 100,000 million years to travel round the universe."[1]

(ii) Secondly, there are facts showing the fortuitous character of life, and the rarity in the universe of the conditions in which alone we can suppose it to be possible. Life, as we know it, can occur only on those tiny specks of burnt-out ash which are plants. According to the tidal theory of the formation of planets, a necessary condition of the occurrence of a planetary system is the close approach of two stars in a certain condition of development. The odds against such an approach are very great. "Exact calculation demonstrates that, with the stars moving as they now are in the neighbourhood of the Sun, in a period of seven million years only about one star in a hundred thousand will approach near enough to another for the birth of a solar system to be possible, and even then there are odds of, perhaps, ten to one against a solar system actually being formed."[2] Thus the occurrence of a planetary system is an exceedingly rare accident, and the number of planets in the universe on which conditions even remotely approximate to those in which life, as we know it, alone is possible, is exceedingly small. We should have to visit thousands of millions of stars before finding a planetary system as recent as our own. Elsewhere Sir James Jeans estimates that the zones of the universe in which life, as we know it, is possible added together constitute less than a thousand million millionth part of the whole of space.[3]

(iii) A third set of facts which point in the same direction are time facts. The life of our own planetary system, judged in relation to an astronomical time scale, is very short; the period of life upon the earth, judged in relation to a geological time scale, is very short, and the period of human life,

[1] Sir James Jeans, *Eos*, p. 18.

[2] Id., *The Birth of the World*, p. 72.

[3] Id., *The Mysterious Universe*, p. 5.

judged in relation to a biological time scale, is very short. To take the biological time scale alone, the whole past of life upon the earth is reckoned at roughly twelve hundred million years; of human life at about one million!

The cumulative effect of facts of this kind is to suggest that the occurrence of life is an unplanned accident in a fundamentally lifeless universe. Amid the vast immensities of astronomical space and geological time life appears as a tiny glow flickering uncertainly and doomed to ultimate extinction. An incidental and unwanted passenger, it travels across an environment which is fundamentally alien and brutal. But only for a while; one day, when the heat of the sun is no longer such as to maintain conditions suitable to life, it will finish its pointless journey with as little significance as in the person of the amoeba it began it.

Taking the facts collected by science at their face value, the only possible conclusion in Sir James Jeans's view is that "one tiny corner, at least, and possibly several tiny corners of this universe of atoms had chanced to become conscious for a time, but was destined in the end, still under the action of blind mechanical forces, to be frozen out and again leave a lifeless world."[1]

But are we justified in taking them at their face value? The second stage of the argument insists that we are not.

(2) While the first stage demonstrates that science deals with shadows, and that man is insignificant in time and space, the second points out that man can understand the shadows, and deduces that the insignificance is therefore apparent only.

Sir James Jeans points out that all the interpretations of the physical universe put forward by modern scientists, however much they may differ in other respects, have one point in common—they are mathematical in character. "The essential fact is simply that *all* the pictures which science now draws of nature, and which alone seem capable of

[1] Sir James Jeans, *The Mysterious Universe*, p. 148.

according with observational fact, are *mathematical* pictures."[1] "It would now seem to be beyond dispute that in some way nature is more closely allied to the concepts of pure mathematics than to those of biology or of engineering."[2] Nature fits, in fact, into a "mathematical mould," and the explanation of "the shadows" which is fuller and goes farther than any other kind of explanation is the explanation "in terms of the concepts of pure mathematics."[3]

This conclusion is first used as the ground for an important deduction which is then linked up with a further set of considerations.

(3) The deduction is that the universe must have been constructed, or at least designed, by a mathematical mind, or by a Creator who thinks mathematically.

That the universe was created; that, in other words, it came into being as a result of a definite act or series of acts has already been shown by the writer on other grounds. The fact of entropy in the universe may, Sir James Jeans holds, be regarded as fairly well established. The universe is like a clock that is running down. The heavier atoms radiate away their substance in the form of radiant energy, and break down into lighter atoms (the "burnt-out ash" of which our own planet is composed). Sir James Jeans is responsible for the theory that in the centre of the stars the heat is so intense that protons and electrons are actually annihilated; it is this annihilation of protons and electrons which he regards as the source of the recently discovered phenomena known as cosmic rays or cool radiation. Everywhere these processes of annihilation and breaking-down are going on; there is, Sir James Jeans holds, no known example of the contrary process.[4] "The transformation of matter into radia-

[1] Sir James Jeans, *The Mysterious Universe*, p. 127.

[2] Ibid., p. 133.

[3] Ibid., p. 133.

[4] Professor Millikan has put forward a theory which ascribes cosmic rays to a building-up process; but Sir James Jeans does not, I gather, accept this.

tion is a 'one way,' or, as it is technically called, an 'irreversible process. Matter can change into radiation, but under present conditions radiation can never change back into matter."[1]

Ultimately, therefore, the fate of the universe is to dissolve "into radiation; there would be neither sunlight nor starlight but only a cool glow of radiation uniformly diffused through space."[2]

Since the universe bears witness only to processes of energy diffusion, some other process must be postulated for the concentration of the energy diffused. The processes known to cosmic physics are analogous to the gradual diffusion of a drop of ink in a glass of water; an observer of this diffusion would infer that somebody had shaken the drop into the water. Similarly Sir James Jeans infers an act or series of acts of energy storing or energy concentration in the form of matter, which he envisages as acts of creation. "Everything," he says, "points with overwhelming force to a definite event, or series of events, of creation at some time or times, not infinitely remote. The universe cannot have originated by chance out of its present ingredients, and neither can it have been always the same as now."[3] The need for a creator thus established, the further step is next taken of attributing to his mind the property of or capacity for mathematical thinking.

Sir James Jeans has recourse at this point to two similes, to indicate the view he is disposed to adopt of the relation of the creator's mind to the workings of the universe. "Imagine," he says, "a race of blind worms, whose perceptions were limited to the two-dimensional surface of the earth. Now and then spots of the earth would sporadically

[1] Sir James Jeans, *Eos*, p. 52.

[2] Ibid., p. 56. I take it that such a universe would be qualified by the addition of the specks of "burnt-out ash," which is the expression by which Sir James Jeans denotes non-radio-active matter. So far as I understand him, there is no reason to suppose that this, too, diffuses itself in radiation. It is literally dead matter.

[3] Ibid., p. 55.

become wet. We, whose faculties range through three dimensions of space, call the phenomenon a rain-shower, and know that events in the third dimension of space determine, absolutely and uniquely, which spots shall become wet and which shall remain dry. But if the worms, unconscious even of the existence of the third dimension of space, tried to thrust all nature into their two-dimensional framework, they would be unable to discover any determinism in the distribution of wet and dry spots; the worm-scientists would only be able to discuss the wetness and dryness of minute areas in terms of probabilities, which they would be tempted to treat as ultimate truth."[1] And just as the facts discovered by the worm scientists would be the two-dimensional phenomena of a three-dimensional reality, just as shadows on a wall are a representation in two dimensions of a reality which, in fact, occupies three, so, he suggests, the four-dimensional space-time continuum which mathematical physics studies may be merely a phenomenal projection of a reality which occupies more than four dimensions; this reality is subsequently identified with God's mind.

For the introduction of the word "shadows" leads to an extended use of Plato's simile of the prisoners in the cave. We are such prisoners, and the world our science studies is only a reflection on the walls of the cave of a play which is taking place in the sunlight outside, a play which is first identified with nature—Sir James Jeans speaks, for example, of science as studying "the world of phenomena, the shadows which nature throws on the wall of our cave"[2]—and later with the workings of God's mind. And the shadows, as we have seen, work mathematically.

(4) The further set of considerations is derived from an examination of our own capacity for mathematical thinking. Whence, Sir James Jeans asks, is our mathematical knowledge derived? He considers and rejects the notion that

[1] Sir James Jeans, *The Mysterious Universe*, p. 125. [2] Ibid., p. 129.

our knowledge of mathematics is empirical in the sense of being derived from an observation of the external world. He regards mathematics as a creation of pure thought, taking a rationalist (in the philosophical sense of the term 'rationalist') view of the origin and nature of mathematics. He holds, in other words, as Descartes held and as Leibniz held, that mathematical knowledge is *a priori*, being reached by a process of reflection upon the implications or certain given premises, which are seen to be self-evident. The premises may, he admits, have been suggested originally by our sensory experience of the external world, but mathematics is synthetic as well as analytic, and there is more in the completed structure than in the foundations upon which it is reared. This 'more' has been worked out "by the mathematician in terms of abstract thought practically uninfluenced by contact with the outer world, and drawing nothing from experience."[1]

(5) We are now in a position to consider the significance of these considerations in relation to the conclusion reached in (2) (that the physical world is completely interpretable in terms of mathematical concepts), and the deduction based on it in (3) (that it is, therefore, the creation of a mathematical mind). Their significance consists in the fact that the shadows studied by science are not meaningless to us, but are found to obey the laws of mathematics, which we have constructed or discovered for ourselves. Sir James Jeans stresses the significance of this fact; it is, he says, as if, having invented a game for ourselves, and laid down its rules, we suddenly discover that the world outside obeyed the very rules which we had invented.

"And now it emerges that the shadow-play which we describe as the fall of an apple to the ground, the ebb and flow of the tides, the motion of electrons in the atom, are produced by actors who seem very conversant with these purely mathematical concepts—with our rules of our game

[1] Sir James Jeans, *The Mysterious Universe*, p. 130.

of chess, which we formulated long before we discovered that the shadows on the wall were also playing chess."[1]

This link is of great importance in the chain of argument. Considering our insignificance in the cosmic scheme, the natural supposition would, Sir James Jeans thinks, have been that the shadows should be meaningless. The extent of our unimportance in the scheme of things astronomy has already demonstrated. The whole life of our species is but a moment in the day of the universe; the stage on which its drama is played occupies but a pin-head of its extent. Is it not strange, then, that we, insignificant dwellers on a tiny speck of burnt-out ash, whose life upon earth with its pains and pleasures, hopes and fears, raises hardly a bubble on the vast ocean of reality, should be able to understand its phenomenal workings—stranger still that we should be able to divine its inner nature? It is little short of a miracle that this almost invisibly small creature, man, should possess a mind which, looking out upon the universe, maps its geography, measures its moments, and catalogues its contents. How is the miracle accomplished? Man, Sir James Jeans answers, is enabled to do these things because the universe fits with surprising exactitude into the mathematical framework which he has constructed.

What, then, is the inference? That the universe bears witness to the workings of a mind that has kinship with our own. Consider, says Sir James Jeans, the case of a deaf musician confronted for the first time with a pianola: "although he could hear nothing, he would immediately recognize this succession of numbers "(1, 5, 8, 13) "as the intervals of the common chord, while other successions of less frequent occurrence would suggest other musical chords. In this way he would recognize a kinship between his own thoughts and the thoughts which had resulted in the making of the pianola; he would say that it had come into existence through the thought of a musician."[2]

[1] Sir James Jeans, *The Mysterious Universe*, p. 131.
[2] Ibid., pp. 131–132.

Thus, recognizing mathematics in the universe, we must conclude that a mathematical mind constructed it. And is not a further conclusion indicated? Our own knowledge of mathematics derives, as we have seen, in the writer's view, not from a study of nature but from the reasoning reflections of our own minds. Our own minds, then, work mathematically in the sense that the capacity for mathematics is latent in them from the first. Our own minds, then, it is suggested, own the same origin as the universe they study, an origin in the brain of a mathematical thinker. Hence we reach the general conclusion that "the universe shows evidence of a designing or controlling power that has something common with our own individual minds—not, so far as we have discovered, emotion, morality, or aesthetic appreciation, but the tendency to think in the way which, for want of a better word, we describe as mathematical,"[1] or, more shortly, "the universe appears to have been designed by a pure mathematician."[2]

B. But to say that the universe has been constructed by a mathematician is very different from asserting that it *is* a mathematical thought or *is* a thought in the mind of a mathematical thinker. Yet this assertion is also made. If, we are told, it is a fact that science deals with shadows, and that the essence of things is, therefore, unknowable, "then the universe can be best pictured, although still very imperfectly and inadequately, as consisting of pure thought, the thought of what, for want of a wider word, we must describe as a mathematical thinker."[3]

What are the reasons for this further assertion? Such as are given are not, unfortunately, as clear as could be wished. Emphasis is laid on the statement already made that the universe as a whole and in its details works mathematically, and it is then implied, as though it followed from this, that the universe is *exhaustively* analysable in terms of mathe-

[1] Sir James Jeans, *The Mysterious Universe*, p. 149.
[2] Ibid., p. 132.
[3] Ibid., p. 136.

matics. By this is meant that there is literally no aspect of any phenomenon which cannot be described in mathematical terms. "*The final truth* about a phenomenon resides in the mathematical description of it; so long as there is no imperfection in this our knowledge of the phenomenon is *complete*"[1] (my italics). The inference is that, if in any case we are unable to give a complete account of something in mathematical terms, it is because our mathematics is not yet good enough, not that there is anything unamenable to mathematical treatment in the phenomenon itself.

And that Sir James Jeans does not, by statements such as that just quoted, mean merely that the universe can be completely *described* in terms of mathematics is evident from what he proceeds to say about substance and space-time. Science, as we have seen, does not tell us what things are (although apparently it justifies us in saying that "*the final truth*" about things would be mathematical); it merely tells how they behave. Therefore science gives us no knowledge of the "real essence of substances."[2] If we have no knowledge of substances, the line between Realism and Idealism becomes blurred, since there is no longer a brute extraneous given something to resist analysis in mathematical terms.

Similarly with regard to space and time. The attempt to picture imaginatively the space of modern physics must, we are told, be abandoned; it is three, six, seven or more dimensional according to the particular function which, in connection with any given train of reasoning, it is required to perform. Hence to ask *where* the wave system of a group of electrons envisaged by the Schrödinger theory is to be found, or *how* it is to be conceived, is to ask questions which should not be put. "It exists in a mathematical formula; this and nothing else, expresses the ultimate reality."[3] Similarly also with time which, being indissolubly bound

[1] Sir James Jeans, *The Mysterious Universe*, pp. 140–141.
[2] Ibid., p. 137.
[3] Ibid., p. 142.

up with space, is or should be capable of the same mathematical interpretation.

The view that space time is completely mathematical subsequently appears as a ground for the conclusion that it is also mental, in the sense in which to be mental is to be a creation of mind. "On this view," i.e. that space exists as a mathematical formula, "we need find no mystery in the nature of the rolling contact of our consciousness with the empty soap bubble we call space time, for it reduces merely to a contact between mind and a creation of mind—like the reading of a book, or listening to music."[1]

But if the entities of which the universe is on a naïvely realistic view supposed to consist, substance and space-time, turn out to be mathematical, that is completely resolvable into mathematical formulae, and if to be mathematical is to be mental, more will be implied by the various statements asserting the mathematical nature of things than that the universe is describable in terms of mathematics; it will be implied that the universe somehow *is* mathematics. And, since mathematics is thought, to be mathematical will also be to be mathematical thought.

There is, further, a subsidiary argument from the fact of entropy in the universe. This fact, as we have seen, suggests that the universe must have an end; it also implies that it must have had a beginning. Time and space being finite "almost compel us, of themselves, to picture the creation as an act of the thought."[2] Time and space must have come into being as a result of this act. God does not, therefore, Himself work in time and space; He works with them, and they are, therefore, the products of His thinking. The implication is again slipped in that a universe which is a creation of thought must itself be thought.

Sir James Jeans is thus led "by a very different road to a not altogether dissimilar conclusion" from that of Berkeley, whose famous passage to the effect that the "choir of heaven

[1] Sir James Jeans, *The Mysterious Universe*, p. 143. [2] Ibid., p. 144.

and furniture of earth . . . have not any substance without the mind" he quotes with approval.[1] With Berkeley he holds that the apparent objectivity of things is due to their "subsisting 'in the mind of some Eternal Spirit.'"[2] He further adopts the Berkeleyan distinction between imagination and perception. While to be substantial is to be a thought in God's mind, there are, he thinks, degrees of substantiality, "For substantiality is a purely mental concept measuring the direct effect of objects on our sense of touch."[3] Creations of an individual mind are less substantial than creations of a universal mind. Hence, while our private worlds, for example the worlds of our imagination or of our dreams, exist in our minds only, the public world of familiar things, including the "space of everyday life . . . which is the same for us all, is the space of the universal mind."[4]

This constitutes a distinct advance on the earlier position. The entities with which science deals, constituting the public world, "which is the same for us all," are now no longer conceived as shadows of God's thoughts; they *are* God's thoughts. Thus we reach a complete Idealism in the adoption of the "concept of the universe as a world of pure thought."[5]

III

To criticize in detail the various assertions summarized above would be a formidable task. Nor do I propose to attempt it. I shall confine myself to suggesting certain difficulties in the main positions upon which the structure of Sir James Jeans's metaphysic is based. Some of these positions seem to me to involve assertions which are untrue; others to be supported by arguments which are unsound. As before, I shall consider separately the two different stages in Sir James Jeans's argument, namely, (*A*) that the universe was constructed by a mathematical thinker, and (*B*) that the

[1] Sir James Jeans, *The Mysterious Universe*, p. 137. [2] Ibid., p. 137.
[3] Ibid., p. 138. [4] Ibid., p. 140. [5] Ibid., p. 140.

universe is a thought in the mind of a mathematical thinker.

A. In connection with the first of these positions I wish to mention four sets of considerations. The first two sets suggest doubts as to the validity of the arguments adduced in its favour; the second two purport to show that, even if the arguments were valid, the conclusions based upon them are not necessitated and are probably mistaken.

(1) (*a*) Sir James Jeans holds that nature is more closely allied to pure mathematics than to any other science, and more amenable to interpretation in terms of the concepts of pure mathematics than in those of any other science. This leads him to assert that (i) nature, by which he means the supposedly material world which science studies, and (ii) the universe as a whole are exhaustively analysable in terms of pure mathematics. That nature (i) is more amenable to interpretation in terms of mathematics than of any other kind of concept is possibly true. That nature (i) is exhaustively analysable in terms of pure mathematics seems to me to be demonstrably untrue.

Living organisms, for example, are part of nature. But the concepts of biology, by means of which their character as living is investigated and their behaviour studied, are certainly not mathematical. For example, the concept of emergence, which is increasingly employed by biologists, is not only not a mathematical concept, but actually contradicts the fundamental laws of arithmetic by its implication that something can come out of nothing. Oxygen and hydrogen are neither of them wet, but water which is or which emerges upon their combination is wet. If, then, the whole were completely analysable in terms of its parts, it would not—or so upholders of the doctrine of emergence assert—be possible to account for the property of wetness. The inference seems to be that some wholes, at least, are not so analysable. This is said to be more particularly the case with regard to those wholes which are living organisms, the behaviour of which suggests that they can only adequately be treated otherwise than as aggregates of parts. Biologists, at least treat them otherwise, finding in the co-ordination of the various parts to serve the purposes of the whole, the persistent drive to reach a certain form which is the form appropriate to the species, the maintenance of that form when achieved and the maintenance, where possible, of a stable appropriate environment phenomena, which can only be interpreted on the assumption that the organism acts as a unitary whole. The living organism, moreover, grows, and in so doing exhibits itself at any given moment of its growth as more than it was at the preceding moment. Not only does it act as a whole; it seems to be constantly achieving or aiming to achieve a higher degree of wholeness, in the sense of a wholeness which includes and integrates more parts, so that the concept of 'holism,' whatever be its metaphysical validity, is found increasingly serviceable as a methodological postulate.

Now arithmetic asserts that a whole is, and is no more than, the sum of its parts. It also asserts that nothing can come out of nothing, and that there cannot be more in the effect than there is in the cause. To say, therefore, that the concepts of mathematics are those which are most suitable for the purpose of the biologist seems to be the very reverse of the truth. Nor in order that this stricture may be justified is it necessary to raise the question whether the concepts of emergence and 'holism' are valid; it is sufficient to point to the fact that they are methodologically useful.

Again, there seems to be a growing agreement among biologists as to the impracticability of attempts to explain the behaviour of living organisms without introducing the notion of life or mind as a unique concept. I do not mean that biologists have recourse to the idealist methods of interpretation which Sir James Jeans favours—the suggestion that the concept of life must be introduced as a unique concept in biology is, indeed, independent of any metaphysical theory. I wish merely to make the point that the view of the living organism as being *exhaustively* analysable in terms of material, as being, in other words, all body, seems to be increasingly difficult to maintain.

To mention only one consideration of the many which might be raised in this connection, although we can now describe with some exactitude in terms of the arrangement of genes the germinal material which an offspring receives from its parents, and although its physical constitution seems to be completely determined by the reaction of this germinal material to its environmental conditions, there is no reason whatever to suppose, and considerable reason to doubt, that this germinal material exhausts the initial equipment of the living organism. Nobody has yet succeeded in tracing the inspiration of a new symphony to a combination of genes, or in locating the origin of a heresy in a chromosome, nor does it seem likely that anybody ever will. Until some attempt of this kind is successful, it always remains possible that we shall have to supplement the inherited, *material,* substance with the addition of some element of mind or spirit, which although intimately connected with the chemical material, is yet other than it, in order to give a complete account of the initial equipment of the living human organism. But the conception of an initial spiritual or mental equipment is surely not one which lends itself to analysis in mathematical terms.

This last consideration directs attention to the wider assertion (ii), that the universe as a whole is or is exhaustively analysable in terms of the concepts of pure mathematics. I shall return to the implications of this assertion in another connection at the end of this chapter. For the present I am concerned merely with the question of fact, and on the question of fact it is sufficient to point out that if by the universe is meant literally all that there is, there seems to be absolutely no reason to think that the assertion is true.

The consideration last mentioned raises—it is obvious—the mind-body controversy. Without presuming to offer an opinion upon the issues involved, one may, I think, legitimately ask whether it is a fact that the behaviour of living organisms in general and human beings in particular can be satisfactorily explained on the assumption that they are complicated, mechanistic automata? Is it further the case that the facts of our own mental life, the fact of our knowing and doubting and enquiring, the realization that we are conscious and the inner conviction that our consciousness is in some sense a free activity, can be explained on this assumption? Philosophers have in general been inclined to take the view that they cannot, and there seems to be a growing tendency on the part of biologists and psychologists to agree with them. The weight of opinion among biologists and psychologists seems in other words to be at the moment in favour of the view that mechanistic concepts are not adequate to the explanation of the behaviour of living organisms and the facts of mental life. Moreover, scientific opinion favours this view increasingly, and this for a reason which should have weight with Sir James Jeans.

While mechanism reigned supreme in the physical sciences, there was a strong incentive to justify its extension to biology and psychology. If everything in the physical world worked like a machine, it was at least likely that living organisms did so too, so that, even if the application of mechanical concepts to life demanded considerable dialectical ingenuity and involved some straining of the factual evidence, the attempt was at any rate worth making. But, as Sir James Jeans frequently points out, mechanism has broken down in the physical sciences, and the incentive to extend its application to psychology and biology no longer exists. There is no reason, therefore, to deny the legitimacy of the concept of life in the interpretation of biology and of mind in the interpretation of psychology. But with what meaning can it be said that life and mind are analysable or interpretable in terms of mathematical concepts? Mind, we may agree, may *think* mathematically—although there seems good reason to doubt whether the mind of a rabbit, for instance, even does that—but to say that it does so is very different from asserting that mind *is* mathematical, in the sense of being like a formula completely resolvable into mathematical expressions. And that Sir James Jeans realizes the difficulty of supposing that it is so resolvable is suggested by the following quotation, which, although it is designed to support his general view of the exclusively mathematical character of nature, in fact implies the partially non-mathematical character of mind. Nature, he says, "does not model her behaviour . . . on that forced on us by our whims and passions, or on that of our muscles and joints, but on that of our thinking minds."[1] Now the aspect of us that is whimsical and passionate is assuredly an aspect of our psychology; it is, in the general sense of the term, mind. Thus our fanciful and passionate minds, so far from being mathematical in essence, do not even seem to work mathematically. But our fanciful and passionate minds are certainly constituents of what is, and might even with a fair show of plausibility be termed part of nature.

Similarly with regard to universals such as goodness, truth and beauty. Whatever may be the status of these entities, whether they are to be regarded on Platonic lines as discrete, objective features of the universe which, themselves neither mental nor material, are known by mind and in some unexplained way bestow their characteristics on material things, or whether they are more properly to be regarded as mental concepts, there can, I think, be no doubt that they correspond to real aspects of what is, and that ethics, logic, and aesthetics are in some sense expressions of our recognition of these aspects. The tendency to analyse them into mere states of the individual knowing mind, which is to reduce them to the status of merely subjective entities owning no counterpart in the objective world, perceptibly diminishes in recent philosophical literature. Particularly is it absent

[1] Sir James Jeans, *The Mysterious Universe*, p. 135.

from the writings of modern scientists, who are almost over-generous in their readiness to admit the existence of non-scientific factors in the universe; and in recent months I have read in the works of such diverse men of science as Einstein, Professor Whitehead, and J. B. S. Haldane, testimonies to the reality of concepts, as self-subsistent independent entities. Yet avowedly they are not in any sense of the word mathematical. Beauty, indeed, may have some affinity with mathematics, and so, on some views, may truth; but nobody, so far as I am aware, wishes to assert that beauty *is* mathematics, while to call the concepts of Ethics mathematical is simply to misuse terms.

Again I do not wish to imply that the view of universals as independent, objective reals is necessarily true. I suggest merely that, if Sir James Jeans is right, it cannot be true, for the reason that there cannot be universals of any but of a mathematical kind. I should regard it, therefore, as an objection to Sir James Jeans's assertion that everything that is is analysable in terms of mathematical concepts, that, if it were true, it would imply that most of the views which philosophers, and more recently scientists also, have entertained with regard to the nature of universals are false; yet no reason is given by Sir James Jeans for thinking them to be false.

(*b*) The reasons for supposing that the universe has been constructed by a mathematical mind are considerably weakened if our own knowledge of mathematics has not been obtained independently of the observation of nature—if, in other words, mathematics is not entirely *a priori*. Sir James Jeans admits this, and considers, therefore, and rejects the view that our knowledge of mathematics was derived empirically from a study of nature.

I do not wish to assert that Sir James Jeans is not right in this view of mathematical thinking. I wish merely to point out that many competent philosophers have taken a different view, and that a long line of thinkers, stretching from

Berkeley and Hume down, if I am not mistaken, to Mr. Russell to-day has held that the concepts of mathematics were arrived at not *a priori*, by the reflection of the mind upon the implications of certain premises intuitively seen to be necessary, but by generalization from the observed phenomena of nature. If this were, in fact, the case, then the argument from the singularity of the fact that the universe is found to obey the laws of a game which mathematicians have independently formulated in their studies would not apply. The laws of mathematical thought would, on this view, coincide with the laws of things, simply because they had been discovered by a study of the laws of things.

(2) I now propose to assume that the facts are as Sir James Jeans asserts; that is to say, that the universe, or, at any rate, the physical world, is exhaustively analysable in terms of mathematical concepts, and that these have been formulated *a priori*. Are the inferences which he bases upon these facts tenable? We must, I think, agree that they are; at least, they cannot be proved to be untenable. I do not, however, think that they are necessary inferences, and I hope to show that they are not even probable ones. The following considerations seem to me to suggest that they are are not:

(*a*) The natural inference from the view that mathematics is both synthetic and *a priori* is the inference drawn by Kant. The world, on this view, works mathematically because our minds have put mathematics into it. And they have put mathematics into it by the mere process of knowing it. But it is only of the world as known to mind that this is true. The real world, in the sense of the world that exists independently of our knowing minds, does not work mathematically; at least, we have no reason to suppose that it does. On the contrary, since it is in respect of the feeling of moral obligation that we approach most nearly this noumenal world, and since, therefore, it is our capacity for moral experience that forms our one direct link with it, we should be justified, in so far as we are entitled to conceive it at all, in thinking of it in terms of ethical concepts. It is, in fact, more like the obligation to do our duty than it is like a mathematical expression. But, if it is only to the world which our minds have constructed that mathematical concepts are applicable, the only inference which it is legitimate to draw is that it is our minds and not the external world of nature *as it really is* which work mathematically. Mathematics, in other words, is latent in us, and we cannot help imposing its framework upon what we know. Thus, if we follow Kant, the fact that we find mathematics in the world is no evidence whatever for the existence of a mathematical creator other than ourselves.

Now this Kantian view of the mind as imposing its own concepts upon the external world, and in the course of its exploration rediscovering the features which it has itself imputed, is very prevalent in modern scientific literature. Professor Eddington's work, for example, is, as we have seen, pervaded by it. The passage from Professor Eddington, which in another connection I have already quoted, "We have found that where science has progressed the farthest, the mind has but regained from nature that which the mind has put into nature," is a typical statement of this view, and more metaphorical expressions such as "The footprint on the sands of time turns out to be our own" bear witness to its prevalence in the background of Professor Eddington's thought. Nor is it only Professor Eddington's work that exemplifies this attitude. There is, indeed, if we may trust Professor J. B. S. Haldane, a general consensus of opinion among modern scientists that Kant is the philosopher who, more accurately than any other, expresses their instinctive attitude to the universe.[1] Hence the suggestion I am making, that the universe seems to work mathematically only because we have put mathematics into it, so far from being out of

[1] See J. B. S. Haldane, *Possible Worlds*, p. 124 *seq.*, "Kant and Scientific Thought."

accord with the temper of modern science, seems to be one to which many scientists are predisposed.

Now I do not wish to press this suggestion, especially as it is not one of which, as subsequent chapters will show, I can avail myself. It is sufficient to point out that it has a historical past of considerable importance, that it is prevalent as a canon of interpretation among modern scientists, and that it is one which Sir James Jeans's hypothesis of the world as the creation of a single mathematical mind ignores. Unwisely, I cannot help thinking, since, if the suggestion is valid, the hypothesis, to say the least of it, is unnecessary.

(*b*) Let us, however, waive this point and assume that the mathematical behaviour of the universe is discovered by our minds, which play no part in determining the nature of what they discover. Is the inference to a creator who thinks mathematically necessitated?

To return to the question of the nature of universals which I raised in (1) (*a*), the world exhibits beauty; it also exhibits goodness. To what extent is the existence of these factors in the universe a reason for inferring a creator who thinks in terms of beauty and goodness, and has stamped his creation with the impress of his thoughts? Many would answer, 'To a considerable extent.' But the world admittedly also exhibits evil and plurality (I am taking the appearance of things at its face value, and considering only those features and qualities with which our experience indubitably acquaints us). To what extent, then, is the existence of evil and plurality a reason for inferring a creator who thinks in terms of evil and manyness? Most would, I think, answer, 'To a very small extent.' And if I slightly alter the form of the question and enquire to what extent we are entitled to infer from these apparent features of the universe, that the creator *is* evil and *is* many, most people would say that there was no reason whatever for this presumption. In other words, the mere existence, whether real or apparent, of a particular feature in the universe is no ground for attributing its causation to the mental attributes of a creator, still less for assuming that the creator of the universe, if the universe was, in fact, created, exemplifies it or *is* it.

An important distinction must be made here which, as I think, Sir James Jeans overlooks. The fact that a person thinks certain thoughts does not presuppose that the person must be like the thoughts which he thinks, still less that he must *be* them. We do not expect the driver of fat oxen to be himself fat, or a geometrician to look like a triangle, and the good detective who is versed in the ways of criminals is not himself criminal. That the creator thinks in terms of mathematics, if he does, is not, therefore, a reason for supposing that he himself is mathematical, as Sir James Jeans seems to suggest. Nor, to return to the former point, is the presence of mathematical law in the world a reason for supposing that he even thinks in terms of mathematics, unless the presence of beauty and goodness is also a reason for supposing that he thinks in terms of aesthetics and ethics. That he may do so is, of course, possible; but what on this assumption we are to say of evil and plurality I confess I do not know.

And if the argument insists on the universality of mathematics, and suggests that this universality entitles us to say that the creator *is* mathematical, or thinks in terms of mathematics in some sense in which he is not ethical or artistic, or does not think in terms of ethics or aesthetics, the reply would appear to be, first, that, as already pointed out, the universe does not appear to be entirely mathematical, and, secondly, that, even if it did, it also appears to be entirely 'many'; so that 'multiplicity' on the basis of Sir James Jeans's argument would appear to be as truly a characteristic of the Creator as mathematics.

I do not propose to dwell further on this argument, which nevertheless seems to me to have considerable weight, because it is only a particular form of the classical objection to the argument from design. The universe undoubtedly exhibits phenomena pointing to design, and this fact, if it were the only fact to be taken into account, might entitle us plausibly to infer a designer who planned it. But it also exhibits phenomena pointing to lack of design, so much so that an interpretation of the facts of nature in terms of the mechanical operation of non-purposive forces is always possible and may be correct. If we are honest, we must take account impartially of both sorts of phenomena, and not allow our wishes or our hopes to lead us to minimize the second, or to write them off as illusory or partially understood manifestations of the first. That they cannot be so written off, the manifest failure of the attempt to explain, in the sense in which to explain is to explain away, pain and evil on the design hypothesis affords to my mind convincing testimony. For, even if pain and evil are in some sense unreal, the error we make in thinking them to be real must be a real error. Error, then, on this assumption is a basic and fundamental factor of what is, and to argue, as Sir James Jeans does, would convict us, therefore, of attributing to the creator the responsibility for the creation of error.

The upshot of considerations of this kind is purely negative; they point to the untrustworthiness of inferences, based upon the manifestation of this or that character by the world that appears to the nature of a hypothetical reality behind the world that appears. It may, of course, be the case that the creator is a mathematician; I do not wish either to assert or to deny that he is; but the mere fact that some departments of the world that appears exhibit the workings of mathematical law does not constitute a reason for supposing either that there is a creator, or that, if there is, he is pre-eminently, still less exclusively, a mathematician. It suggests merely that, if there is a creator, he must be credited, at least, with the capacity for creating among other things a world which exhibits among other things mathematical law.

B. This last consideration leads us directly to the more extreme idealist position, which asserts not merely that the universe is constructed by a mathematical thinker, but that it is a thought in his mind. The universe, then, is thought. I summarized above, as well as I was able, the arguments for this view; but the arguments were themselves not as clear as could be wished, and my summary reflected their obscurity. The gist of the matter is, I think, as follows: the last vestige of materiality having disappeared from the external world, it can be completely and exhaustively analysed in terms of mathematical laws and concepts; mathematical laws and concepts are mental, at least they are of the nature of thought; therefore the universe is mental and of the nature of thought.

The argument thus depends upon the reduction of the external world to mathematical laws and concepts. It is, I think, important to realize precisely what this reduction involves. The statement of which I have frequently made use in this chapter, "the universe is exhaustively analysable in terms of mathematical concepts," is ambiguous. It may mean merely that everything in the universe behaves in accordance with or *obeys* mathematical law; or it may mean that everything in the universe *is* mathematical law in the sense of being identical with it. And the two meanings are different meanings. To say that the external world obeys mathematical law and to say that it *is* mathematical law is to make two very different assertions. Modern science may provide good reasons for making the first, but to extend these reasons to justify the second is, I hold, a fallacy. Yet it is a fallacy which seems to me to be frequently made. Having given reasons for supposing that everything in the physical universe can be described in terms of mathematical formulae, writers like Eddington and Jeans are presently found to be making the very different assertion that everything in the physical universe is a mathematical formula. The advance from the one position to the other is so gradual that it is difficult to say precisely where the transition takes place. All that one feels justified in affirming is that, whereas at the beginning of their books the writers in question are bringing forward arguments in favour of the first position, in the last chapters they write as if they had somehow demonstrated the second.

In the preceding chapter I have tried to show how Professor Eddington advances from the position that mathematical formulae are symbols, which describe the physical world by symbolizing it, to a position in which he speaks of the physical world as *itself* symbolic. This led him to make the further suggestion that this "symbolic world" of physics, although only "a complex of metrical symbols," possessed a separate being of its own which was, in some sense undefined, embedded in the real world. The difficulties which this suggestion was found to involve arise, I now suggest, from treating what may quite conceivably be a true description of the physical world as if it were an exhaustive definition of it, and then proceeding to identify the physical world with the definition.

To this procedure it may be objected that all description necessarily presupposes that there should be a thing described, and that the thing described should be other than the description given of it. If it is not, the description resolves itself into being a description of itself. Applying this general consideration to the case in point, I should urge that the fact that the universe is completely describable in terms of pure mathematics, if it were a fact, would itself constitute a reason for inferring that the universe could not itself *be* pure mathematics. In other words there must be something which is other than the description to correspond with the description which is given of it; and it is to this something that the description applies.

The point, as I have suggested above, is of considerable importance in the light of the procedure adopted by modern scientists. Modern physics sets out to describe the workings of the physical universe in accordance with a particular set of concepts. The procedure so far is obviously legitimate;

but having made his description as comprehensive as possible, the physicist too often shows a disposition to regard it as constituting not only a description of behaviour but as an analysis or even a definition of the thing behaving; this definition he then proceeds to equate with the thing. Thus matter is eliminated and the reduction of the world to pure concepts or pure thought is facilitated. Apart from doubts which I have suggested as to its logical validity, this attempted identification of description with the thing described seems to me to be unduly optimistic as regards the possibility of a complete account of the physical universe in intelligible terms. It fails, in other words, to apprehend the necessary limits not only of scientific but of *any type* of explanation or interpretation of the physical world. Taking as I do a pluralistic view of the universe, I cannot avoid the conclusion that it must of necessity include an intractable element, which may be regarded as an element of 'otherness,' of contingency or of mere brute given—what, I think, Plato wished to designate by the phrase τὸ μὴ ὄν. And this element, although it is that to which the explanation applies and which the interpretation seeks to interpret, contains an irrational core which can never be analysed away in terms of intelligible concepts.

We are here in sight of a time-honoured controversy, the controversy between dualistic and monistic interpretations of the universe, which in its general aspect lies outside the scope of this book and which I shall not, therefore, pursue here. A word may, however, be added as to the particular form in which the point of view I am suggesting constitutes a difficulty for any attempted reduction of the universe to purely intelligible terms, such as that contemplated by Sir James Jeans.

As I hinted above, such a reduction when undertaken from the standpoint of the physicist seems to rest upon a misapprehension with regard to the procedure of science and the limits of scientific interpretation. The procedure of science is to take the given manifold of sense, and to analyse and correlate it with a view to exhibiting an apparently chaotic diversity of phenomena as exemplifying the workings of law. Success in this undertaking enables us to understand and to predict. The understanding is of the immediate cause of the phenomena; the prediction is of their recurrence, given the same cause, in the future. As it advances, science succeeds in bringing an ever greater area of the given under the aegis of an ever-diminishing number of laws. As its researches are pushed farther and farther back, what was formerly accepted as brute given is shown to be amenable to law and brought within the scientific fold. But science will never succeed in dispensing with the existence of a something which is regarded as that to which at any given moment its laws are applicable, and this something, from the very fact that it is *its consequences* which law determines, must itself be other than the operations of the law. And in saying that it is other than the operations of the law, I mean that it is itself unamenable to and unreachable by the operations of reason at the particular stage which science happens to have reached. Granted that it may subsequently become amenable, yet it can only do so by giving way to a new something which assumes the rôle of brute given in its place. As Professor A. E. Taylor has pointed out in another connection:

"We have to appeal in all our experiences of the actual not only to 'laws' but to 'collocations.' Science, which hates to accept anything whatever as mere 'given fact,' is always trying, with much success, to reduce the 'collocations' with which it starts as given to mere consequences of 'laws.'" Thus it reduces the collocation which appears as brute matter to elements; the collocation of elements to atoms; the collocation of atoms to charges of positive or negative electricity. "But every success in such reduction is achieved at the price of acquiesence in some assumption of an earlier and more ultimate 'collocation.' Without 'collocations' which have to be taken as 'brute fact,' as *there* we do not know how or why, the functional dependences we call 'laws' would reduce to functions without any arguments and would thus become as insignificant as the symbol f or ϕ before a blank. Here we clearly come upon an inevitable limit to the whole work of scientific explanation."[1]

Now in discovering what the something is whose consequences scientific laws determine, sense experience alone will avail. Analyse and formularize the universe as we may, there remains a fundamental element of geography which expresses itself in facts of the type, 'the interval between two events X and Y in space time happens to be A'—facts which are at once contingent and intractable.

With regard to a large number of facts in the universe there seems to be no necessary reason why they should be just as they are; they just are.

There is, for example, no necessity that a substance possessing the specific gravity of gold should be yellow, or that at a certain point on the beach at Margate at 11.30 a.m. on March 7, 1926, there should be one white pebble two inches to the north and one inch to the east of one blue pebble.

A further consideration pointing in the same direction arises in connection with the difference between sense perception and imagination. If there are no external facts given to the senses, facts which are just as they are, and which, being so, constrain and condition the character of our perceptions, there would be no means of distinguishing between what we perceive and what we imagine. Sir James Jeans sees the difficulty and adopts Berkeley's solution by suggesting that, whereas the things we perceive have objective existence in the Creator's mind, those we imagine are subjective in the sense that they exist only in our own. But this solution is open to precisely the same objection as Berkeley's.

[1] A. E. Taylor, "The Freedom of Man," *Contemporary British Philosophy*, Vol. II, p. 298.

Not only does it postulate a Creator to account for a difference the obvious cause of which has been wilfully ignored, and so provoke the retort that it would be simpler to affirm the obvious cause, but, since the things we imagine are usually pleasanter than those which we perceive, which is, indeed, why we imagine them, it suggests that the contents of God's mind are more disagreeable than those of our own. This is an unpleasant view to take of the Creator, and should, if possible, be avoided.

The existence of given facts is thus, I suggest, a presupposition of the difference between perception and imagination. But, if they do exist, then the only way to discover what manner of facts they are is to go and look, to adopt, in other words, the method of physical science; and it is because Sir James Jeans's account of the universe presupposes a stage of analysis at which the methods of science may be superseded, everything being ultimately discoverable by insight or by the method of pure reasoning, that, in my view, it is in the last resort unacceptable. The method of 'going to look,' as the empirical philosophers of the seventeenth and eighteenth centuries successfully established against the rationalists, is the only method by means of which certain aspects of the universe can be known. There is, in other words, if you want to know what these aspects of the universe are like, no alternative to sense perception supplemented by scientific method.

Professor Eddington and Sir James Jeans, when they come to the philosophical interpretation of their results, seem to me to be over-ready to turn their backs upon the methods by which they have reached them. Raised by science to an eminence from which they can look out upon the universe, they show a disposition to make light of, if not to forget, their origins. I do not mean that they forget that there is science or that they are scientists, but that they seem anxious to conceive of the universe in such a way as to make no provision for there being ultimate facts of the kind which, as scientists, they have established, or for the validity of the methods by which they have established them. Yet these facts are the scaffolding upon which their conception of the universe is reared. Unlike Plato's ascending metaphysicians, they do not descend but strike down the ladder by means of which they have climbed; the procedure in my view is, to say the least of it, unwise.

CHAPTER III

MR. RUSSELL'S NEUTRAL STUFF

I. INTRODUCTORY

A philosophical interpretation of modern physics on somewhat different lines from those of Professor Eddington and Sir James Jeans has been advanced by Mr. Bertrand Russell. This interpretation first appeared in *The Analysis of Matter*, and subsequently in the more recent book, *An Outline of Philosophy*; but Mr. Russell's statement of his views on the problems which physics raises is by no means confined to these two books.

Mr. Russell has advocated for some time past a metaphysical view which he calls "neutral monism." It is briefly to the effect that neither mind nor matter is a primitive constituent of the universe, but that both are derivations from a more fundamental homogeneous stuff, the difference between them being, on this view, ultimately reducible to the difference between different forms of arrangement of the fundamental stuff. It is urged in favour of this view that it accords with the implications of modern physics and modern psychology, and *The Analysis of Matter* and, in a lesser degree, *An Outline of Philosophy* are in effect a restatement of the doctrines of neutral monism, in the light of the conclusions reached by modern science and with particular reference to those conclusions. I do not mean to suggest that modern physics is, so to speak, prejudged by Mr. Russell from the point of view of a metaphysical doctrine, because he happened on other grounds to hold the view which he calls neutral monism; merely that he brings to the interpretation of modern science a metaphysical framework which, having been constructed with the express intention of giving due weight to the physicist's view of the world, claims to be peculiarly fitted to accommodate the physicist's results.

Mr. Russell has often censured contemporary philosophy for its neglect of modern science. Modern philosophy is, he holds, too aloof and academic in tendency, and pays insufficient regard to brute fact. Hence, he has urged, its conclusions tend to reflect little more than the minds of the philosophers who have reached them. The inquiry into the extent and nature of brute fact is undertaken by science and especially by physical science, and it is natural, therefore, that Mr. Russell's philosophy should aim at giving an interpretation of the world and of our experience of the world which, while it is in accordance with what the physicist has discovered about brute fact, is careful not to go beyond what has been discovered. In achieving this aim it is, I think, at first sight successful, so successful as to lend countenance to Mr. Russell's own assertion that most of what he writes is not philosophy at all—philosophy, in fact, in the traditional sense of the word, ought not, he holds, to exist—but is simply science.

That Mr. Russell does in reality go beyond brute fact, that he enters the realm of speculative interpretation, and that what he writes is to this extent and in this sense truly philosophy, I shall try to show. I shall also try to show that in certain respects the process of 'going beyond' the facts leads him to make inadmissible because self-contradictory assertions, so that although what Mr. Russell writes is truly philosophy, some of the philosophy cannot be true.

I propose first to give a brief summary of Mr. Russell's main views in so far as they are relevant to the metaphysical interpretation of modern science, and, secondly, to offer certain criticisms of these views.

II. Exposition of Mr. Russell's Views

It will be convenient to divide the expository section into three parts. There is (*A*) an account of the nature of the physicist's knowledge of a piece of matter, there is (*B*) the bearing of the conclusions derived from a consideration of (*A*) upon the theory of perception, and there is (*C*) the general metaphysic of neutral monism which the theory of perception illustrates.

(*A*) The question of the way in which the physicist knows a piece of matter does not strictly belong to philosophy at all, but to physics; I only refer to it here because Mr. Russell devotes considerable attention to it in his book, *An Outline of Philosophy*, and apparently regards it as having an important bearing upon our knowledge of the external world. What he is chiefly concerned to emphasize is the indirect character of the physicist's knowledge of a piece of matter. This does not mean merely that the physiological machinery of perception is such that we never know any external thing directly, although Mr. Russell does in fact hold this view (see (*B*) below); it means also that the nature of a piece of matter is such that it cannot be known directly by any human observer. Physics is said to have demonstrated this truth in the following way: Physicists have succeeded in analysing a piece of matter into its constituent atoms. Now we never know an atom directly; we only know the effects of changes in the alleged atom on the surrounding spatio-temporal field. So long as the atom neither loses nor absorbs energy, we know nothing about it. But when, as the result of an apparently spontaneous electronic jump from an outer to an inner orbit, the atom radiates energy, we observe certain effects in its neighbourhood. In other words, events in a certain neighbourhood will be such as are compatible with and can be calculated on the assumption that there is an electric charge of a certain magnitude in the middle of the neighbourhood. Energy, in fact, spreads out from a particular centre. We may, if we like, conceive that there is at the centre an arrangement of electrons rotating round a proton which is the source of the energy radiation. But the conception is by no means necessitated. "The idea that there is a little hard lump there, which *is* the electron or proton, is an illegitimate intrusion of common-sense notions derived from touch. For aught we know, the atom may consist entirely of the radiations which come out of it."[1] "It is not," said Lotze, "in virtue of a substance contained in them that things are; they are, when they are qualified to produce an appearance of there being a substance in them."[2] The grounds for Lotze's assertion were *a priori* and metaphysical. Yet, if Mr. Russell is right, his remark exactly expresses the view of the modern physicist; and the physicist's reasons for it are empirical and scientific. The atom, in fact, has become an underlying *noumenon*, in which the phenomena which are known may inhere, or from which they may emanate, but which is never itself known. Now matter is composed of atoms, and what is true of atoms is true of matter. "Matter," therefore, to quote an epigram of Mr. Russell's, has become "a convenient formula for describing what happens where it isn't."[3]

If the atom resolves itself into the effects which the atom, if it existed, would produce, when it changed in the surrounding spatio-temporal field, what are we to say of the surrounding spatio-temporal field? Precisely what we have said about the atom. In so far as there are effects in that field, they take the form of occurrences or events. These occurrences or events are physical; therefore they will ultimately be susceptible of the same analysis as that which is applicable to the atom.

To quote Mr. Russell again, "there is a certain air of taking in each other's washing about the whole business. Events in empty space are only known as regards their abstract mathematical characteristics; matter is only an abstract mathematical characteristic of events in empty space."[4] In other words, we describe what is happening at

[1] Russell, *An Outline of Philosophy*, p. 163.
[2] Lotze, *Metaphysics* (English translation), Vol. I, p. 100.
[3] Russell, *An Outline of Philosophy*, p. 165.
[4] Ibid., p. 153.

place A in terms of the events at place B; we describe what is happening at place B in terms of the events at place C, and so on indefinitely.

In so far, then, as the conception of matter has historically connoted the notion of substance, we must conclude that modern matter is not material. The concept of material substance, in fact, has faded out of modern physics, and has been replaced by that of emanations from a locality. For substance X being defined in terms of its effects on substance Y, substance Y in terms of its effects on substance Z, and so on indefinitely, matter (if the mixture of metaphors may be forgiven) is perpetually dangled like a carrot before the nose of the enquiring mind. It is a something to which the mind is ever being led, but which it never reaches. It may be asked what bearing this analysis has upon the metaphysical question of the nature of the external world. The bearing admittedly is not very direct, the implications of the analysis being mainly negative in character. We are shown how little we really know about the ultimate constituents of matter, and a certain caution is thereby introduced into our statements, or, if it is not, at least, the implication runs, it ought to be. What I conceive Mr. Russell to be saying is something of this nature. To the nineteenth-century scientist matter offered no problems; or rather, such problems as it suggested were not epistemological. It was a hard, tangible something lying out there in space upon which the horse sense of the materialist could base his irrefragable convictions. The materialist was not slow to take advantage of the opportunity, and the familiar closed world of nineteenth-century science was the result. We now know that this notion of matter was unduly simple. Our knowledge of matter, it seems, is not straightforward and direct; it is inferential and therefore indirect. In particular it never gives us information about a piece of matter; it only tells us about some of the effects of its supposed behaviour. Physics, in short, "tells us nothing as to the intrinsic character of matter."[1] So little do we know about the intrinsic characteristics of a piece of matter that the modern preference for the interpretation of phenomena in terms of mind is little more than a preference for working in terms of the less unknown rather than of the more. Not that this preference is Mr. Russell's, who is very far from wishing to explain things in terms of mind. So far as the analysis has hitherto proceeded he would, I imagine, be content to point out that the conception of the universe as made of a simple homogeneous material stuff must be given up. We do not know what material stuff is like, since no mind has ever experienced such a thing. It follows that the conception of matter as being a material stuff is, at least, not fundamental. Thus far, then, as I have said, the result is mainly negative. The next step is an analysis of the process of perception.

(*B*) Mr. Russell's account of this process, as it presents itself to the physicist and the physiologist, may be illustrated by an example which he himself gives. Let us suppose that we are looking at a star—Sirius, for example—on a dark night. Sirius presumably is a highly complicated set of physical processes, of which, if we are to take Sir James Jeans's view, the most characteristic are the stripping off of the rings of electrons from the nuclei of the protons, and the actual annihilation of electrons and protons to produce radiation. From this complicated set of physical processes there is generated another physical process which we call the propagation of light rays, which may also, at any rate from certain points of view, be analysed into movements of protons and electrons. After a specified length of time which astronomers calculate this 'travelling' physical process reaches the retina of the eye, where it is changed into another physical process. This process in the retina causes yet another physical process in the optic nerve, which in its turn is followed by or produces an effect in the brain

[1] Russell, *An Outline of Philosophy*, p. 154.

about which we know very little, but which presumably takes the form of movements in the cells of which the matter of the brain is composed, and is therefore analysable in terms of physics. As a result of this last series of movements, those namely in the matter composing the brain, there ensues something which, if we take the ordinary view, can only be regarded as a mystery, namely the psychological experience of seeing a yellow patch. As the result of this experience we say that we are looking at the star Sirius.

As I am a layman in such matters, I give Mr. Russell's summary of the process in his own words. "I conceive what happens when we see an object more or less on the following lines. For the sake of simplicity, let us take a small self-luminous object. In this object a certain number of atoms are losing energy and radiating it according to the quantum principle. The resulting light-waves become superposed according to the usual mathematical principles; each part of each light-wave consists of events in a certain region of space time. On coming in contact with the human body, the energy in the light-wave takes new forms, but there is still causal continuity. At last it reaches the brain, and there one of its constituent events is what we call a visual sensation. This visual sensation is popularly called seeing the object from which the light-waves started—or from which they were reflected, if the object was not self-luminous."[1] Thus the process known as seeing a star involves a double inference. First, there is the inference from the fact of the movements in the cells of the brain to the conclusion that I am seeing a yellow patch. But the belief that there is a yellow patch which is a constituent of the external world, and which is, so to speak, *there* for me to see, may be mistaken; all we are entitled to say is that the brain is being stimulated in a certain way. Hence to infer from the physical events in the brain to the existence of other physical events in the external world, which may be supposed to have

[1] Russell, *An Outline of Philosophy*, pp. 154, 155.

caused the brain events, is to run the risk of error. The nearer this supposed causal event is to the brain, the smaller the risk.

"We are less likely to be mistaken if we say that the surface of the eye is being stimulated in a certain way, and still less likely to be mistaken if we say that the optic nerve is being stimulated in a certain way. We do not eliminate the risk of error completely unless we confine ourselves to saying that an event of a certain sort is happening in the brain; this statement may still be true, if we see Jupiter in a dream."[1]

The second inference is from the yellow patch, which is what we actually observe, to the star. We suppose, let us say, that the yellow patch is caused by or is an appearance of Sirius, a star of a certain size, whose attributes astronomers catalogue, which several months ago sent out the light rays as a result of which we are now seeing the yellow patch. But in this inference, too, we may be mistaken; the yellow patch might be caused by or be an appearance of a lamp hanging on the mast of a ship; we are also said to "see stars" as the result of a blow on the nose.

Hence our knowledge of so-called external objects is at best inferential; the inferences involved are precarious and may be mistaken. The event which actually causes us to have the psychological experience of seeing something occurs in our brains. Mr. Russell emphasizes the fact that the chain of physical events leading up to the movements in the brain as a result of which we "see" something is continuous. There is, therefore, he suggests, no ground for arbitrarily selecting any particular set of events in the chain, as, for example, the set which constitutes the star or the patch, and asserting that these events constitute the object of the psychological experience of seeing. If any event or set of events can properly be said to be *the* cause of our

[1] Russell, *An Outline of Philosophy*, p. 138.

experience, it must be the last set of events in the chain, namely, those which occur in the brain.

The principle of causal continuity is cited in confirmation of this view. Mr. Russell takes the case of a physiologist observing a brain, and asks where is the actual thing, entity or event which the physiologist sees? He answers that, if we are speaking of physical space, the actual event, which Mr. Russell calls a percept, which constitutes the physiologist's seeing and which also constitutes what the physiologist is observing, must be in his *own* brain.

"Light-waves travel from the brain that is being observed to the eye of the physiologist, at which they only arrive after an interval of time, which is finite though short. The physiologist sees what he is observing only after the light-waves have reached his eye; therefore the event which constitutes his seeing comes at the end of a series of events which travel from the observed brain into the brain of the physiologist. *We cannot, without a preposterous kind of discontinuity, suppose that the physiologist's percept, which comes at the end of this series, is anywhere else but in the physiologist's head*" (my italics).[1]

What, then, we actually observe of the physical world are percepts in our brains[2]; these percepts are also "the events which constitute" (our) "seeing."

What, then, is the nature of the percept? Clearly, one would be tempted to reply, if it is in the brain, it must be physical. But this is not in fact the answer that Mr. Russell gives. For the physical phenomena that happen in the brain, which are the events which constitute our seeings, are elsewhere described by him as "sensations." Indeed, all physical phenomena are probably of the nature of sensations. "We now realize that we know nothing of the intrinsic quality of physical phenomena except when they happen to be

[1] Russell, *An Outline of Philosophy*, p. 146.

[2] See for confirmation of this *An Outline of Philosophy*, pp. 147, 148, quoted on page 93.

sensations, and that therefore there is no reason to be surprised that some are sensations, or to suppose that the others are totally unlike sensations."[1] And if the reader feels disposed to make the obvious comment that a sensation is a psychological event, to point out that it is absurd to speak of what happens in the brain as 'psychological,' that, since what happens in the brain is causally continuous with what happens in the stars, the view seems to involve a greater absurdity still, and to ask whether the explanation is that Mr. Russell is after all evincing a leaning to idealist views, Mr. Russell retorts that the absurdity only serves to illustrate the difficulty of the ordinary dualistic hypothesis which asserts that the brain is one kind of thing, and that the mind is another, and supposes that when we see something the two in some mysterious way interact, so that the physiological event becomes transformed into the psychological event. Such a view, Mr. Russell thinks, presupposes that the process of perception is nothing short of miraculous. "We" are, he says, required by it to "suppose that a physical process starts from a visible object, travels to the eye, there changes into another physical process, causes yet another physical process in the optic nerve, finally produces some effect in the brain, simultaneously with which we see the object from which the process started, the seeing being something 'mental,' totally different in character from the physical processes which precede and accompany it. This view is so queer that metaphysicians have invented all sorts of theories designed to substitute something less incredible." . . . "We first identify physical processes with our percepts, and then, since our percepts are not other people's thoughts, we argue that the physical processes in their brains are something quite different from their thoughts."[2]

The whole difficulty arises, in Mr. Russell's view, from our habit of thinking of mind and brain as two different things,

[1] Russell, *An Outline of Philosophy*, p. 154. [2] Ibid., p. 147.

the former containing mental and the latter physical events, the former sensations and the latter the objects of the sensations. In fact, however, there is only one class of event, the class of percepts, which, while in themselves they are neither mental nor physical, may be treated as either according to the context in which they are taken. Taken in one context a percept is a sensation; taken in another it is the object of the sensation. But the sensation and its object are not two events but one considered in two different relations. "Everything that we can directly observe of the physical world happens inside our heads, and consists of 'mental' events in at least one sense of the word 'mental.' It also consists of events which form part of the physical world."[1] This brings me to Mr. Russell's neutral monism.

(*C*) This position has been exhaustively discussed in recent philosophical literature, and is by now sufficiently familiar. I shall, therefore, summarize its main features in a few words, and then indicate its bearing upon the particular questions under discussion, that is to say upon the nature of scientific objects, the nature of the objects actually apprehended in sensory experience, and the nature of the mind which apprehends. Roughly Mr. Russell's conclusion is that each of these three apparently different types of entity is susceptible of analysis in the same terms.

(1) There is first the view of the physical object as a system of sense data. Physical objects are not, in Mr. Russell's view, constituents of the external world, what we actually meet with when we have sensory experience of, say, a table being sense data, that is to say, entities such as raps of sound, patches of colour, hard objects and cool objects. "Instead of supposing that there is some unknown cause, the 'real' table behind the different sensations of those who are said to be looking at the table, we may take the whole set of these sensations . . . as actually *being* the table. That is to say, the table . . . is the set of all those particulars

[1] Russell, *An Outline of Philosophy*, pp. 147, 148.

which would naturally be called 'aspects' of the table from different points of view."[1]

(2) No two persons ever experience the same sense data. This conclusion depends upon a variety of considerations, but chiefly on the fact that each individual inhabits a private space, from which he obtains a special and peculiar view of the world which Mr. Russell calls a 'perspective.' A perspective is a view of the world from a particular place, and there are as many perspectives as there are places from which to view the world. No perspective contains any place in common with that contained by any other perspective. Every mind is associated with (I am deliberately using a non-committal expression to denote the relationship) a brain. A brain occupies a place; therefore no two minds have the same view of the world, and no entity that is experienced by one mind is the same as that experienced by any other. The "world seen by one mind contains no place in common with that seen by another, for places can only be constituted by the things in or around them."[2] Hence the world of perceptual experience is a private world of private sense data. The physical world consists of innumerable private worlds of private data, as many, in fact, as there are places from which to view it. If, and only if, there is a brain and nervous system in one of these places will the sense data be experienced.

(3) A consideration of psychology leads Mr. Russell to the view that the mind consists of discrete atomic constituents, which he divides into sensations and images. He gives reasons for dispensing with the notion of consciousness as a special entity, containing or expressing itself in acts of consciousness which are unique, mental existents. Moreover, he denies the distinction between act and content of consciousness postulated by Brentano and Meinong, and is inclined to merge the former in the latter. There are sensa-

[1] Russell, *The Analysis of Mind*, p. 98.
[2] Id., *Our Knowledge of the External World*, p. 87.

tions and images, some of which have the quality of being conscious; there is not a consciousness which contains or is conscious of, among other things, sensations and images.

(4) The physical world being composed of series of sense data, and a mental biography of series of sensations and images, the next step is to run the two series together. Mr. Russell frequently emphasizes the fact that modern psychology and modern physics are "coming together." Under the influence of modern physics matter has become less and less 'material'; under the influence of modern psychology mind has become less and less 'mental.' Physicists, as has already been pointed out, have succeeded in divesting so-called 'material' events of the quality of substance, and Behaviourists have divested so-called 'mental' events of the quality of consciousness, at least as an essential attribute. Material substance and consciousness are, therefore, no longer specific, discrete kinds of things. As matter becomes less material and mind less mental, the gap between mind and matter closes up. Thus the way is open for a view which regards the distinction between mind and matter as illusory. Such a view is in fact suggested by Mr. Russell, and the essence of it may be most conveniently conveyed by his remark: "The stuff of the world may be called physical or mental, or both or neither, as we please; in fact, the words serve no purpose,"[1] a circumstance which doubtless explains some of the otherwise puzzling and apparently confusing language which I have been obliged to use in describing Mr. Russell's theory of percepts which are both sensations and sense data, and are at once in our heads and in our minds and in the external world.

Mr. Russell's solution of the apparent difficulty is to insist on the absolute identity of the entities so variously described. The identity is not achieved by representing sensations as sense data, or vice versa, but by exhibiting both sensations and sense data as derivatives from a more

[1] Russell, *An Outline of Philosophy*, p. 148.

fundamental type of entity, to which Mr. Russell gives the name of "neutral particulars," each such particular, when it is experienced by a mind, being called non-committally a percept. A percept is thus at once the sense datum which the mind experiences, and the sensation which is the mind's experience of it. But the 'mind' is only the series of such sensations suitably related,[1] just as the physical object is only a series of sense data.

Mr. Russell illustrates the conception by a celebrated analogy. If a photographic plate is exposed to a star on a clear night, it reproduces the appearance of the star. We are accordingly forced to conclude that at the place where the plate is, and at all places between it and the star, something is happening which is specially connected with the star. Similarly at every place to which the star is presented something is happening which is specially connected with the star, although, unless at the place in question there is an object akin to a photographic plate, that happening is not recorded.

The complete system of all these happenings, or, in other words, the system of all the appearances of the star at different places, constitutes the momentary star. Let us now return to the photographic plate. Many other things are happening at the place where the plate is besides the presented appearance of the star. Among these are the appearances of other stars, and doubtless also of numerous other objects whose impression is too faint for the plate to record. It follows, then, that, besides the happenings which consist of the collected system of all the appearances or aspects of our original star at different places, we can also collect together at a given moment another system of happenings which are occurring at the place where the plate is. One particular or member of this second system, namely,

[1] This statement is qualified in *The Analysis of Mind*, where the mind is spoken of as being composed also of images which, presumably, are not also sense data.

the appearance of the original star, will belong also to our first system of particulars, which constitutes the star. Thus, every particular belongs to two distinct series or systems of particulars, namely, that series which together with itself constitutes the physical object, and that series which together with itself constitutes the appearances of all objects at a given place.

Now let us suppose that the place at which the appearance of the star is presented is occupied not by a photographic plate but by a mind. The appearance of the star at that place will now be called a sensation, and will belong to the series of sensations which, taken together, at any one moment constitute what is called a mind at that moment. It remains, however, all the time a member of the other series to which it belongs, namely, the series which constitutes the star, and as a member of this series it forms one of the sense data which are presented to mind.

The conclusion is that the sensation and the sense datum are simply the same neutral particular taken in two different contexts; and the neutral particular is also the percept.

The difference between what is called a mind and what is called an object presented to a mind is, therefore, a difference not of substance but of arrangement. Thus we arrive at the following conclusions:

(1) A perception of an object is the appearance of the object at a place where there is a brain with sense organs and nerves forming part of the intervening medium. (2) An object is the sum-total of the appearances (of which the appearance which is a perception is one) presented by it at all places at a given moment. (3) A mind is the sum-total of all the appearances presented at a place at which at a given moment there is a brain with sense organs and nerves forming part of the intervening medium; a mind is, in fact, the view of the world from a particular kind of place.

If mind at any given moment is completely analysable

in terms of the percepts which at that moment would normally be said to be the percepts *of the mind*, the notion of mind as an activity expressing itself in acts of apprehension must be abandoned. An act of apprehension, on this view, is a member of a particular set of neutral particulars arranged in a certain context, and the entity apprehended is the same member arranged in another context.

Now since there would *prima facie* appear to be a difference between the proposition "this sense datum is one of a number of sense data which are to be found in the same visual perspective" and the proposition "this sense datum is being apprehended," between saying, in other words, that a particular cross-section of the world appears from a particular place, and saying that this cross-section is being perceived by, is or appearing to, a mind, it follows that the characteristic of "being apprehended by" must involve a relation which holds between the sense datum and something else, and the relation must be such that the sense datum can either have it or not have it. And the view of the relation which Mr. Russell, so far as I understand him, suggests, involves the corollary that to say that "sense datum X is apprehended" and to say that "sense datum Y belongs to a certain visual perspective" is to say precisely the same thing in two different ways. In other words, the relation which the sense datum has to something else when it is apprehended is precisely the same as its relation to the visual field or perspective to which it belongs. In this event the 'something else' must be not a mind but "a perspective or visual sense field," to which the mind is from this point of view apparently equivalent. The mind is thus merely a cross-section of a non-mental world, and being experienced by a mind is equivalent to standing in a relation of a particular sort to the set of neutral particulars to which the entity which is 'experienced' belongs.

III. Criticism

The criticism which I wish to offer of the theories outlined above falls under three heads; there is, first, the question of the alleged privacy of the objects of perception; secondly, the legitimacy of the application of concepts derived from physics to problems of epistemology; and, thirdly, the elimination of the act of apprehension, which 'perceiving' would normally be said to involve, with a view to avoiding the difficulties of dualism.

(1) The short objection to the theory of the alleged privacy of the objects of perception is that it leads to physiological solipsism. Berkeley's view is commonly criticized because, when purged of inconsistencies such as the notions of God and of the self, it reduces itself to the statement that only ideas in the mind of the knower are known. Mr. Russell substitutes brain for mind, and asserts that only events in the knower's brain are known.

As a general rule he is not afraid to accept this conclusion; in fact, he boldly avows it. For example, he criticizes Behaviourism because, although it is a psychology which bases itself upon the observation of external behaviour, that is to say, upon the behaviour of living organisms other than the observer, it overlooks the fact that no such behaviour can be observed. It can only be inferred from events taking place in the observer. "When," says Mr. Russell, "Dr. Watson watches rats in mazes, what he knows, apart from difficult inferences, are certain events in himself."[1] These inferences, as has already been pointed out, are liable to error. "Physics," we are told, "gives reason to expect that percepts will, in certain circumstances, be more or less deceptive if taken as signs of something outside the brain."[2] Mr. Russell's position, then, is clear. What we know are events in our own brains; so much is explicitly avowed, the example of the physiologist who imagines him-

[1] Russell, *An Outline of Philosophy*, p. 140. [2] Ibid., p. 141.

self to be observing the brain of his patient concluding with the clear statement: "if we are speaking of physical space what the physiologist sees is in his own brain."[1] We are, however, able to infer from the private events in our brains and bodies to events happening outside them; and, although these inferences may be mistaken, in general they are not. Apparently we can know in a general sort of way when they are not mistaken. Physics itself is the outcome of this knowledge, and "Physics," says Mr. Russell, "is true in its broad outline."[2]

Again the events in ourselves, which are what we know when we believe ourselves to be perceiving something, "are connected, in a manner not quite invariable, with the movements of matter."[3] Also, surprisingly, when commenting upon the behaviourist definition of knowledge, Mr. Russell assures us that "from the first we know external objects."[4]

If we waive the doubts suggested by this last quotation, the position is, I think, fairly clear. If we take science seriously, what we "see must count as inside the body; what goes on elsewhere can only be inferred."[5] Nevertheless the inference may justifiably be made, and things do, therefore, go on elsewhere. The short and to my mind overwhelming objection is that, if we never have any direct knowledge of anything outside our own bodies, we have absolutely no right to infer anything outside. The objection may be stated in two forms.

First, Mr. Russell says that some of our inferences to outside events may be mistaken, although most are not; also, he implies that it is possible to know when they are mistaken, since, if it were not possible, there would be no reason for trusting physics. But in order that we may know that an inference to outside events is not mistaken, it must be possible for us to have direct knowledge of the outside events. We could then compare the outside events as inferred with the

[1] Russell, *An Outline of Philosophy*, p. 146.
[2] Ibid., p. 136.
[3] Ibid., p. 140.
[4] Ibid., p. 137.
[5] Ibid., p. 146.

outside events as directly known, and checking the former in the light of our direct knowledge of the latter, conclude that the inference was correct. But, according to Mr. Russell, we never have such direct knowledge of outside events; therefore the inference must remain a guess with no evidence to support it and no means of verifying it.

Secondly, to the question "Where are the events which we know?" Mr. Russell answers, as we have seen, "inside our heads." The events have, we are told, a relation to, in that they are "connected in a manner not quite invariable with," the movements of "matter," by which Mr. Russell means the matter of the external world which physics investigates. The relation is one of causal continuity, the events in our brains being the end events of a chain which may stretch back to a star. The position is, then, that we know events A in our brains; these events A are causally related to events B in the external world; these events B we do not know. But if we do not know events B, we cannot know any of their properties; we cannot, therefore, know that they have the property of being causally continuous with events A, and we cannot know that they exist.

The difficulty here is precisely that traditionally urged against Locke's Representationalism, with the occurrence of events of the kind which physics postulates in the external world taking the place of Locke's external objects possessing primary qualities. Like Locke's view, Mr. Russell's is logically reducible to Solipsism, but the Solipsism in which Mr. Russell's view issues is not psychological but physiological.

Like psychological Solipsism, physiological Solipsism is, I suppose, logically irrefutable; but, as Mr. Russell has himself said of psychological Solipsism, there is no reason to think that it is true. And compared with psychological Solipsism, physiological Solipsism seems to me to suffer from one serious disadvantage. It affirms that we only know events happening in our own brains; do we, then, know our own brains? We do not. On the contrary, if Mr. Russell is right, we only know private sense data (Mr. Russell's percepts). Why, then, postulate the existence of a brain at all? The answer to this question brings me to the second main criticism I wish to urge against Mr. Russell's view.

(2) We do not, we are told, observe other people's brains, but only our own private sense data. The question which immediately suggests itself is, do we know that these sense data are in our brains, and, if we do know it, how do we know it? We do not after all know our own brains, in the sense of directly apprehending them, and the attempt to obtain such knowledge would probably prove fatal. Mr. Russell's answer presumably is that physics gives us this knowledge, and physics, as we have seen, he regards as true in the main. The whole of his theory, indeed, might be regarded as a sustained attempt to apply the knowledge gained by physics to the problem of perception. Our question then becomes, how does Mr. Russell know that physics is true?

On this question the following observations may be offered.

(*a*) Physics, it is clear, presupposes a public world of common objects. Whatever may be the proper analysis of this world, there can, I think, be no reasonable doubt that an external world of real things, which are also public things, is in fact assumed by every working physicist. If there were no common public facts for physicists to investi gate, if no two physicists had ever thought about the same thing, but each was always exclusively concerned with the private world of his own experience, then physics, I suggest, would not be possible, if only because physicists could not intelligibly communicate with each other.

These observations are reinforced by a consideration of the process by which the world of physics has gradually emerged from the common-sense world of public objects.[1] But if the structure of physics presupposes the existence of a

[1] Set .or a further account of this Chapter VII, pp. 175–179.

common world of public objects which are known, physics cannot be invoked as an authority for the view that we only know private data. And if physics cannot be made responsible for the view that we only know private data without destroying the foundations upon which physics is based, there can be no justification, so far, at least, as physics is concerned, for the assertion that the data which we know are in our own brains.

(*b*) (i) The immediately preceding argument affords a particular example of a general criticism which might be urged against Mr. Russell's position as a whole, which is that Mr. Russell's line of argument involves a continual putting of the cart before the horse.

(α) Taking physics as valid in the main, he argues in the light of the knowledge which physics has obtained, that what we know are private sense data, which are events in our own brains. The argument is here from physics to private sense data.

(β) Starting from these private sense data (events in our brains), he embarks upon a process of world building, and with the aid of certain assumptions about other perceivers, unperceived sense data and correlations (not invariable) between the sense data perceived and the movements of external matter, he reaches the public world of common facts which physics studies. The argument here, then, is from private data to public facts.

(γ) From a study of the world of public facts, the study of physics is gradually built up. The argument here, then, is from public facts to the world of physics.

On the three stages of this argument the following comments may be made. The fact that sense data are private is certainly not itself a datum of my experience; still less is it a datum of my experience that sense data are or are identical with events in my brain. Therefore the belief that sense data are private, and the belief that they are identical with events in my brain, can only be grounded in a knowledge of physics. It is only if physics is true in the main that these views about the nature of sense data suggest themselves. But how, if we only know private data, we can ever know the public facts which physics presupposes is not clear. Thus we reach the result that the belief that we only know private data is an inference from the facts of physics which, if it is in fact true that we only know private data, cannot themselves be known.

(ii) A further difficulty arises from Mr. Russell's insistence that physics does not give us knowledge of things in themselves, but merely informs us of the relations between their mathematical properties. This point of view is urged with considerable force in *The Analysis of Matter*, and is, I imagine, held in one form or another by many if not most mathematical physicists. Some of the reasons for it have been glanced at in the first chapter in connection with Professor Eddington's views. The emphasis which Mr. Russell lays upon the indirect nature of our knowledge of the atom affords a further ground for the same conclusion, namely, that physics gives us no knowledge of the nature of things. But if it does not, I do not see how it can be invoked to justify the assertion that what we know are private data, and that these are in our heads. These facts, if they are facts, are neither abstract nor mathematical, and it is difficult, therefore, to see how knowledge of the relations between the abstract mathematical properties of events can justify us in asserting them. Yet, as I have pointed out, Mr. Russell's view of perception derives its main authority from physics.

(iii) Of course, if we may take seriously Mr. Russell's statement already quoted that "from the first we know external objects," the word "know" being used in the sense in which a Behaviourist would use it, it is possible to see how the world of physics has been reached. But if it is the case that we do know external objects, it cannot also be true that we only know private sense data or that we only know events in our heads.

(*c*) A difficulty of a rather different kind arises in connection with the non-mathematical qualities of common objects. Whence, it may be asked, do these arise, and what is their status? The question is an important one and it is a defect which appears to me to be common to a number of theories of perception which base themselves upon modern physics, that they do not satisfactorily answer it. I shall attempt an answer to this question in the ensuing chapters. For the present I confine myself to pointing out that, if we insist that the external world consists of entities possessed only of mathematical properties, the answer is far from clear. Water, for example, is not for physics wet, since for physics water consists of atoms of hydrogen and oxygen which are themselves neither wet nor dry. If, then, we ask how the wetness of water is to be explained, the physicist's answer must take the form of suggesting that wetness is emergent upon a combination of entities including nerves, sense organs and brains, which are themselves devoid of it. It is on these lines that, so far as I understand him, Mr. Russell seeks to give an account of wetness. Certain atoms impinge upon our sense organs and create a disturbance which travels along the neural paths to the brain, as a result of which we perceive a wet datum, or more strictly a wet percept occurs. Something which is wet it thus produced by the impact of non-wet atoms upon non-wet sense organs, nerves and brain.

But this explanation postulates the existence of nerves and sense organs which are conceived after the model of ordinary physical objects. It implies that we see with eyes that are brown and spherical, feel with skin that is pink and sensitive, and that cilia ranged along the cochlea of the inner ear are involved in our hearing. Thus the analysis by means of which the quality of wetness is reduced to a number of component physical events characterized exclusively by mathematical properties is not applied to the brownness and 'sphericality' of eyes and the pinkness and sensitivity of skin.

In other words, an analysis of the objects of perception in terms of physics can only be given provided that we refrain from applying it to the sense organs by and through which we perceive them. If, however, we push the analysis in terms of physics to its logical conclusion, and resolve eyes and skin and ears into their atomic components, it seems impossible to explain how the "wetness" of water ever comes to be perceived. For, if we confine ourselves strictly to physics, the process of perception is in the last resort one in which immense numbers of electrically charged atoms exert forces of attraction and repulsion upon one another, as a result of which they are caused to move in different ways. The process of perception, in other words, is simply the movement of material, and material of which only mathematical properties can be predicated. As a result of this movement there is a perception of something that is wet, or, perhaps I should say, a percept occurs which is wet. In other words, the perception is *of*, or the percept *has*, a quality which was not present in any of the constituents involved in the process which caused the perception or percept to occur.

One of two conclusions seems inevitable: either the physicist's and physiologist's accounts of the process of perception are mistaken, or a description of the physical and physiological processes which occur when we perceive something, and the occurrence of which is an indispensable condition of our perceiving, is not strictly relevant to the question, 'What is it that we perceive?' In other words, the epistemological question cannot be satisfactorily discussed in terms of physics. The second conclusion is assuredly the right one.

The general conclusion of the three lines of criticism followed above is that Mr. Russell's view refutes itself. Physics, as I have already pointed out in (2)(*a*), has developed out of common-sense knowledge by a gradual transition which can be historically traced. It is in essence an extension and refinement of common-sense knowledge. This being so, it cannot, it is obvious, be used to impugn the validity of the knowledge upon which it is based and from which it springs without thereby impugning itself. In other words, unless perceptual knowledge be in the main veridical in the sense of giving us true information about an independent and external world, physics cannot itself be true; therefore physics cannot be used to show that perceptual knowledge is not veridical. Yet it is precisely this conclusion which physics is in fact invoked to support, for, if Mr. Russell is right, there is no common perceived world and the only events we know are those in our own heads, the properties of which are strictly mathematical.

The import of this general criticism which appears to me to be valid against many theories of perception which base themselves upon modern physics may, perhaps, best be illustrated in the following way. There are, it seems to me, quite a number of statements which I am in a position to make about the familiar world which I normally believe myself to perceive, statements of the kind which we all frequently make, of which I can affirm two things: first, I know them to be true; secondly, if they are not true, then physics cannot be true. Examples of such statements are: I am now seeing a brown, oblong shiny patch; I am now knowing a table; that to which I am pointing out there in space *is* the brown shiny patch; other people can see very similar oblong shiny patches; other people can know the same table. Admittedly my knowledge of the table is of a different order from my seeing of the shiny patch, and my knowledge that other people can know the same table is different from both. Admittedly also there is considerable controversy as to the precise meaning of these statements, and the task of determining their meaning is accordingly difficult. But whatever their precise meaning may be, it is nevertheless a fact that I do know that these statements are true, and the circumstance that I may be unable to give a satisfactory analysis of their meaning does not in the least diminish the certainty of my knowledge.

And the bearing of my comparatively certain knowledge of the truth of these statements upon the theory of perception which Mr. Russell founds on modern physics seems to me to be this. In the first place the certainty of my knowledge that these statements are true is much greater than the certainty of my knowledge of the conclusions of modern physics, which I know to be the result of a series of difficult and possibly mistaken inferences. The statements, therefore, seem to me to be more likely to be true than the conclusions. If, therefore, any theory of perception which is based upon the conclusions is such as to imply either that I do not know what the statements assert, or that the statements are not true, I am compelled to reject it. Secondly, the statements, if they are true, presuppose that there is in some sense a public world of common facts, which other people besides myself know. This view is also a presupposition of physics. If, therefore, the statements are not true, it will follow that physics does not, as it appears to do, furnish us with an account of an objective world, and the conclusions of physics will be reduced to the status of an adjective of the mental contents, or a modification of the cerebral tissues of physicists. Hence the truth of physics stands or falls with the truth of these statements, and no conclusions based on physics can be true unless the statements are.

(3) I do not propose to undertake a lengthy criticism of Mr. Russell's neutral monism, as the position has been extensively discussed in recent philosophical literature. It involves the elimination of the act of experiencing as a separate occurrence, and identifies it with that of which it is an experiencing. Now I am completely unable to understand how this elimination can possibly be effected. That an experiencing, which I call mine, goes on and that this experiencing is an active and dynamic process is a fact of

which I am convinced. I know it even more certainly than I do the truth of the statements enumerated in (2) above.

I am also unable to understand how this act can be identified with its object; how, to use Mr. Russell's language, sensation and sense datum can both be neutral percepts. Such a view seems to me to confuse the distinction between subject and object—I can see absolutely no reason to suppose that when I see a blue sense datum of oblong shape and know that I am looking at Mr. Russell's *An Outline of Philosophy*, I am, or am identical with, in any sense whatever the blue sense datum or Mr. Russell's book—and it has the effect of destroying the uniqueness of mind. But if mind is not unique in the sense of being a free dynamic activity, one may well be tempted to ask how Mr. Russell can know that it is not. Mr. Russell's philosophy is a system of thought, a system which he has presumably arrived at because, as the result of an impartial and comprehensive survey of the evidence, it seems to him to give a better and more accurate account of what happens and what is than any other. It presupposes, therefore, a free thinking mind and it is offered for our acceptance because it purports to correspond with fact.

But if Mr. Russell's account of thinking be true, his mind thinks what it does, not because it has been constrained by the evidence—it is doubtful, indeed, whether taking cognizance of evidence is an activity which, on Mr. Russell's view, can legitimately be attributed to a mind—but because his brain is in a peculiar condition. His thoughts are, indeed, his brain states taken in a particular context. Moreover, to ask whether his thoughts are true in the sense of asking whether they correspond with or have a particular relation to the facts about which they are thoughts is to ask a meaningless question. Material or neutral events cannot be true; they can only happen. Hence to ask whether a thought which is, if Mr. Russell is right, a brain state or a neutral event is true is as meaningless as to ask whether a blood pressure is true. But, if Mr. Russell has not been led to his conclusions as the result of the operations of a free mind impartially surveying the evidence, if they have been forced upon him by the state of his body which they reflect, and if it is meaningless to ask whether they are true, since in the last event they *are* his body, there is no reason why we should give them the compliment of our attention, especially as in any event our own attitude to them will be determined, not by the merits or demerits of the conclusions themselves, but by the condition of *our* bodies and brains. In other words, if Mr. Russell's account of the nature of mental events were correct, it would be meaningless to ask if it is true.

A further important criticism which may be mentioned is put forward by Dr. Broad in *The Mind and its Place in Nature.* Mr. Russell's rejection of dualistic views of perception and the theory of neutral monism in which it issues imply that to say of the visual datum X that it is perceived, and to say that it belongs to a certain visual perspective is to say the same thing. In other words the properties of "being an object of an act of perception" and "belonging to a particular visual perspective" are logically equivalent. Thus the visual perspective to which the datum which is experienced belongs fulfils the function which is normally attributed in visual perception to an experiencing mind; it is, therefore, substituted for the experiencing mind.

Dr. Broad's criticism of this view is as follows: A sense datum which is part of a visual perspective which is not experienced cannot itself be experienced. Hence to "be experienced by a mind" and "to belong to a visual perspective" mean the same thing *only* if it is *logically* impossible for there to be a visual perspective which is not experienced. Now a visual datum can exist which is not experienced, and Mr. Russell agrees that it can; there is, therefore, no logical reason why a visual perspective should not exist which is not experienced. Hence, "to belong to a visual perspective" and to "be experienced by a mind" cannot mean the same thing.

Other objections are also advanced by Dr. Broad, but the one quoted seems to me to be conclusive against the theory. If I am right in so regarding it, it follows that whatever may be the proper analysis of "being experienced by a mind," in the case in which a datum is experienced, it is not equivalent to "belonging to a visual perspective." Thus this important argument of Mr. Russell's for the rejection of a unique activity of experiencing in which a mind expresses itself must be rejected.

CHAPTER IV

A CRITICISM OF METHOD

In this chapter I wish to draw together the threads of the criticisms I have ventured to offer of the various metaphysical views which are advanced by contemporary scientists on the basis of developments in modern physics. The chapter is thus in the nature of a summary and will be short.

The theories which I have considered, those of Professor Eddington, Sir James Jeans and Mr. Russell, have one feature in common; they all affirm for various reasons that the world as it appears, the familiar world of tables and chairs and people, is not the real world; it is an appearance of a reality which is of an entirely different character. Thus they introduce the familiar distinction between appearance and reality. For Professor Eddington and Sir James Jeans this reality is mind, possibly, even probably, God's mind; for Mr. Russell it consists of neutral particulars. Sir James Jeans and Professor Eddington assert that the scientist's world is also not the real world, thus introducing a further distinction between appearance and reality. "The ethers and their undulations, the waves which form the universe, are, in all probability, fictitious," says Sir James Jeans. "They exist in our minds . . . and something must exist outside our minds to put this or any other concept into our minds."[1]

For these writers, therefore, there are two worlds that appear, the world of science and the familiar world of sense, both of which are in some degree illusory. These conclusions are reached by means of deductions and inferences based upon investigations by scientists into the nature of the familiar world. The observations which I propose to offei

[1] Sir James Jeans, *The Mysterious Universe*, p. 79.

on this procedure relate more particularly to the conclusions of Sir James Jeans and Professor Eddington.

These conclusions bear, it is obvious, a strong family likeness to the philosophies of objective Idealism which occupied the centre of the stage at the end of the last century. Like them they draw a distinction between appearance and reality; like them they affirm that reality is one and a unity, while appearance is a chaotic plurality; like them, too, they affirm that mind is at the heart of things and that matter is its phenomenal appearance. The metaphysical views which find favour with Professor Eddington and Sir James Jeans are thus in several important respects similar to those of the English Hegelians, and some of the arguments, for example, those derived from the symbolic character of scientific objects, with which they are supported are strongly reminiscent of those used by Bradley in *Appearance and Reality*. But while, as I say, these cosmic speculations by modern scientists belong to the metaphysical family of philosophical Monism, two important differences have to be noted.

In the first place, Professor Eddington and Sir James Jeans postulate two worlds of appearance, and not one. They describe and discuss not only the familiar world of sense experience, but also a world of scientific objects which is totally unlike that of sense experience. Professor Eddington, as we have seen, even affirms that the world of atoms and electrons is objectively real ("modern physics has . . . assured me that my second, scientific table is the only one which is really there—wherever 'there' may be"),[1] whereas the familiar world is not. Nevertheless, the world of scientific objects is in the last resort denied full title to reality, so that the two worlds apparently represent degrees of appearance. In the second place it is claimed that the distinction between appearance and reality which formerly belonged to the category of metaphysical speculation is now supported by

[1] Eddington, *The Nature of the Physical World*, p. xiv.

the demonstrable conclusions of sober science, a fact which is thought to place it on a different and more stable footing. "It places a somewhat different complexion on the matter when this is not merely a philosophic doctrine to which intellectual assent might be given, but has become part of the scientific attitude of the day, illustrated in detail in the current scheme of physics."[1]

In spite of this alleged support, however, I cannot feel that the metaphysical doctrine is more convincing than it was thirty years ago, or that the force of the objections which were brought against it then has been in any way diminished. The objections are in the main those with which realist theories of knowledge have made us familiar. As I pointed out in the Introduction, the speculations of modern scientists pay little or no attention to modern Realism, and proceed as if what may not unreasonably be regarded as the most important movement in twentieth-century philosophy had never taken place. To restate these objections now would be to cover familiar ground, and I do not propose to do more than briefly to mention two of them. As for the alleged support for what was previously merely a "philosophic doctrine" derived from the researches of scientists, this need not, I think, seriously concern us, since the same scientists repeatedly point out that science gives us no information about the nature or reality of things; it is difficult, therefore, to see how it can on this supposition offer any contribution to metaphysics. It only appears to do so because scientists supplement their accounts of the physical world with metaphysical chapters, in which they seek to infer from the information which science has collected what the nature of the universe must be. But these chapters, conveying as they avowedly do the speculations and not the discoveries of their authors, come under the category of "merely philosophic doctrines," and cannot, therefore, be counted as evidence of a new order derived

[1] Eddington, *The Nature of the Physical World*, p. 332.

from science and not available to metaphysicians as such. There does not, therefore, appear to be any ground for supposing that the fact that these metaphysical doctrines are put forward by scientists entitles them to some *special* claim upon our attention, to which their philosophical merits might not by themselves entitle them.

The two objections which I wish to bring forward apply not only to the conclusions which Professor Eddington and Sir James Jeans have reached, but also to the metaphysical methods by means of which they reach them. They should be regarded merely in the light of special applications of objections which have been generally thought to have weight against idealistic Monism.

(1) If the worlds both of science and of sense are appearances only of a reality which underlies them, how is the fact that there are such appearances to be accounted for? The appearances, it must be remembered, are continually stigmatized as unreal in some sense in which the underlying reality, whether Creator's thoughts or generalized mind stuff, is real. They are, then, quasi-real appearances of a reality which must somehow be credited with the power of generating what is less real, or becoming what is less real than itself. Assuming such a feat to be possible, it follows that we must qualify the unity of the real with the capacity for generating, or expressing itself in, or appearing as—the difficulty remains unaffected whatever terminology we use—the world or worlds of appearance. And not merely with the capacity for generating *any* world or worlds of appearance, but just those particular worlds with all their richness of qualitative differentiation which do in fact appear. Reality must, to use an expression of Professor Whitehead's, be patient of the fact that water is H_2O, that a substance with the specific gravity of gold should be yellow, and that white ant queens lay eggs at the rate of about one every three seconds. But if the potentiality for all the distinctions and characters that do in fact appear must be conceived

to be latent in reality in order to account for the fact that the world or worlds of appearance appear to be just as it is or just as they are, it is difficult to see in what sense it or they can be *merely* appearance.

One way of meeting this difficulty is to locate the origin of the worlds of appearance not in reality but in the mind to which they appear. This way, as we have seen, is the way which some modern physicists seem disposed to take, Professor Eddington and Sir James Jeans attributing the properties of the worlds both of science and of sense to the constructive or abstractive activities of the human mind. But this suggestion does not really meet the difficulty. For according to the views of both the writers we are considering, our minds are themselves a part or an aspect of reality, since they are continuations of mind stuff or expressions of the Creator's mind. Our minds, then, must be credited with the power of projecting or externalizing quasi-real worlds, and the question remains, how can we conceive of reality (in this case our minds) generating what is less real than itself?

If we waive this difficulty, a further one arises in connection with error. There is no doubt that most of us think that the familiar world of sense is real, whatever we may think of the world of science. If we hold, with Professor Eddington, that this attribution of reality to an unreal or quasi-real world is illusory, an error born of the partial character of our understandings, the error, as I have already pointed out, must itself be a real error. If the error itself belonged to the world of quasi-reality, then it would not be the case that in thinking, as we do, of the world of sense as a world which is real and really there, we were *really* making a mistake. Error, then, if it be the case that the world of sense is not truly real, is of the essence of reality. I see no logical objection to this view, if it be conceded that reality must therefore be error through and through; but, so far as I am aware, none of those who maintain the character of the real world as a unity do in fact hold that it is a unity of error.

To the view, moreover, that the worlds of sense and science are quasi-real creations of our minds, there is a further objection, an objection which is raised by the question, 'Why should we create them as we do?'

Modern scientists often write as if the mind had *carte blanche* to manufacture whatever sort of familiar world it pleased. We are asked, for example, to think of the physical universe as a world of point-events characterized by a minimum amount of structure. The point-events themselves are evanescent, but they are distinguished by certain characteristics, characteristics apparently of pattern and structure, which have the quality of quasi-permanence. For appreciable periods, it seems, the point-events fall into more or less stable groupings. Or, on some views, the mind imposes these groupings upon a chaotic flux of point-events. But whether the mind selects, as being of special interest, features of permanence which it finds, or whether it imposes them; whether, in other words, the initial function of the mind is selective or creative, its subsequent operations are on both views the same. And its subsequent operations consist of working up the patterns of point-events into the familiar perceptual world.

The inference is obvious; the familiar world is what it is because our minds are what they are. Creatures with different minds, Martians for example, would select or impose different patterns as features of special interest, and would work up differently the patterns imposed or selected. Thus Martians faced with an identical objective world of point-events would perceive and inhabit a different everyday one.

But if the features of the familiar world are those that our minds have put there, why, I repeat the question, do they put there the features that they do? If the mind has *carte blanche* to carve out from a featureless world of point-events whatever kind of familiar world it pleases, is it conceivable that it would carve out motor smashes, wars, missed trains and dentists' drills? Are we no driven to the view that reality must contain, and contain in its own right, certain marks or features which the mind discovers and which constitute the framework within which the 'working-up' process takes place; that, in other words, the reason why my mind carves out 'tiger' in circumstances in which I cannot escape from tiger, and not 'kitten,' is that something corresponding to a tiger really is there?

But on this view reality is not a mere flux of point-events; it contains in germ all the features and articulations of the familiar world. The articulations conceivably are different from the world of objects we know; but the world of objects we know is really there, in the sense that reality must be credited with all the differentiating features we discern in it. Reality contains, if not all the objects and differences we know, at least the ground for all the objects and differences we know. We cannot, then, regard the familiar world as a structure fashioned by the mind from a featureless world of mathematical point-events, unless we are prepared to answer the question, Why do we not fashion it better than we do? That we could, if we had a free hand, create a better world, in the sense of a world nearer to our hearts' desire, the necessity which most of us are palpably under of constructing an imaginary world to make up for the defects of the real one we perceive, is sufficient evidence. And the imagined worlds are really created worlds, just because the perceived world is not.

This difficulty seems to me to present itself in one form or another as a stumbling-block to any metaphysic which seeks to attribute the features of the familiar world to the creative or constructive powers of the human mind. It presents itself, however, with considerably increased force if we complicate the familiar perceptual world by the addition of the unfamiliar scientific one. For this, too, if we are, to believe modern physicists, is not an objectively real world. It is a world of symbols and abstractions, and, like the perceptual world, it is mind-created.

What determines the creation of this second world of appearance we are not told. The position we are asked to accept is, then, that mind, faced with a world which is mental through and through, whether because it is a thought in God's mind, or because it is a continuation of our own consciousness, carves out of it what is sometimes a world of electrons and protons, quanta and point-events, sometimes a world of chairs and tables. Personally, I do not believe that it can or does do anything of the kind. Granted, however, that it could, the question still remains, why on any given occasion does it carve out one rather than the other? Or, if we credit it with two different powers or capacities of construction, why does it sometimes employ the one faculty and not the other? To these questions there is, so far as I can see, no answer in the works of modern scientists. The mind admittedly is a very peculiar thing, but I find it difficult to believe that its peculiarity takes just this particular form. And these difficulties, I suggest, inevitably beset the attempt to account for the world of appearance, or worlds of appearance, on the assumption that reality is something fundamentally other than what appears. If these worlds are generated or evolved by reality itself, we must presume that reality is originally qualified by the capacity to generate them, and contains them within the matrix of itself *ab initio*. But, in this event, they are really *there*, and are not properly described as appearance. If they are created by the mind of the percipient, the question arises why they are not created such as to please the percipient.

(2) The second objection is directed against the dialectical process presupposed by philosophies of the appearance-reality type, and applies, I think, with particular force to the particular views under discussion. Briefly the objection is that, in so far as the conclusions at which I have glanced

are correct, they require us to suppose that the steps by which they have been reached are invalid.

This result comes about in the following way. Science is based upon observation of the physical world, and reaches its conclusions by reasoning about what it has observed. What it observes is the familiar world of sense; what it affirms is the world of modern physics. Nevertheless, the metaphysical views of Professor Eddington and Sir James Jeans require us to suppose that this observation is mistaken, since there is, in fact, no objective world of sense, and the reasoning faulty, since there is in fact no objective world of physics. But, if scientific observation does not reveal to us reality, and scientific reasoning does not give us truth about the reality we observe, then the metaphysical conclusions, which are based upon the scientific observation and presuppose the scientific reasoning, cannot themselves be ultimately valid. You cannot reach the truth about the real world by observation of the phenomenal one, especially if the alleged truth about the real world is reached as the result of a train of reasoning which, starting with observation of the phenomenal, follows out the implications of what has been observed. Data which are phenomenal, and which are used as the basis for phenomenal reasoning, can lead to conclusions which are only phenomenally true.

The point I am here making is, in fact, two points, one of which relates to observation, the other to reasoning.

(1) The world which the scientist observes is the familiar world known in sense experience. If this is not objectively real, then his observations which purport to reveal to him a world other than himself are misleading. Conclusions about the universe based upon these observations are, therefore, untrustworthy. The philosophies of Professor Eddington and Sir James Jeans consist of conclusions so based.

(2) The scientific world is reached by inference and deduction from experiments performed on objects belonging to the familiar world. The conclusion that the material

world contains such entities as atoms and quanta is, therefore, one which is reached by reasoning. The metaphysical views of Sir James Jeans and Professor Eddington are reached by a further process of reasoning, which takes as one of its starting-points the existence of such entities as atoms and quanta considered as real facts. This further process of reasoning leads to the metaphysical conclusion that the universe is not such as to contain atoms and quanta as real and independent facts; they are abstractions and symbols; what is real is mind. Hence, if the further process of reasoning is valid, the first process of reasoning was mistaken. But the further process of reasoning takes as one of its starting-points conclusions reached by the first. Hence, if the further process concludes that the results of the first process are mistaken, the further process is vitiated by the mistaken results upon which it is based. But, if the further process is vitiated, there is no reason to accept its conclusion to the effect that the first process is mistaken. Hence the world may in fact contain such entities as quanta and atoms as objectively real constituents.

If these considerations are valid, their moral seems to be, first, that metaphysical reasoning which is based on the conclusions of science cannot legitimately be used to discredit observation of the familiar world, or to suggest that such observation does not truly acquaint us with the nature of what objectively is. If it is so used, it undermines its own foundations. Secondly, metaphysical reasoning based on scientific results cannot be legitimately employed to show that scientific reasoning which appears to be valid, in the sense that it is conducted according to the accepted laws of reasoning, is in fact invalid in the sense that it reaches misleading results. If it is so used, the suspicion that it casts upon the human, reasoning faculty inevitably reflects upon itself. In other words, the metaphysical reasoning of modern scientists, in suggesting, as it does, that their reasoning as scientists did not reach true conclusions about the world, suggests also that it does not itself reach true conclusions about their reasoning as scientists.

The following results emerge. The philosophies of the universe put forward by Professor Eddington and Sir James Jeans which I have considered are based upon the interpretation of modern physics. As such they are open to objection in the following respects:

(1) Because they regard the familiar world of sense experience as not objectively real, but in some sense a product of the observer's mind.

(2) Because they regard the world of modern physics as not objectively real, but in some sense a product of the scientist's reasoning.

(3) Because they despise brute collocations of given fact and seek to analyse them away into mind or law.

(4) Because, starting from certain premises, namely, what the plain man perceives and what science has discovered, they reach conclusions which suggest that the premises are misleading in the sense that the plain man does not perceive what he thinks that he perceives, and the discoveries which science has made do not truly represent the nature of what is. Mr. Russell's philosophy, while not open to objections (1), (2) and (3), is peculiarly exposed, as I have tried to show, to that urged in (4).

Now these mistakes, if mistakes they are, arise, I suggest, not from false science, but from false theory of knowledge. What, I cannot help feeling, eminent scientists misconceive is the nature of the act of knowing and the nature of its relation to the object known. I say misconceive, yet what, perhaps, is chiefly noticeable is less that the problem of knowledge is incorrectly conceived, than that it is simply not tackled. It is this failure to tackle the problems of epistemology that leads to many of the confusions which I have been unable to avoid in summarizing the thought of Professor Eddington and Sir James Jeans. It leads Professor Eddington, for example, to exhibit the world which the scientist knows sometimes as a creation of the scientist's mind and sometimes as an aspect of reality which is independent of mind; to make statements which are intelligible only on the basis of an extreme subjective Idealism, and to make others which presuppose that something exists which is unaffected by our knowledge of it; to describe the relation of sense experience to the object experienced in half a dozen different ways, and of the thinking mind to the object thought about in almost as many. It leads Sir James Jeans to argue as if to be constructed by a mind and to be a thought in a mind were the same thing, and as if the relation of the mind to what it knows is the same as the relation of the mind to what it creates. It leads Mr. Russell to write as if to be a member of a sense field which is a visual perspective were the same thing as to be the object of a visual apprehension. . . . Examples could be multiplied indefinitely. The conclusion which emerges is that before a satisfactory metaphysic can be constructed on the basis of modern physics, certain preliminary investigations must be undertaken into theory of knowledge.

What, one wants to know, is the proper analysis of such a proposition as "I am now seeing a fire"? The question is a difficult one, and to answer it we must come to some measure of agreement as to what we mean by 'a fire,' and what by the mental act of 'seeing.' Are two entities involved in the process of 'seeing things' or three, and what part in the process does the mind play? The various problems involved have been complicated by modern physics. Physics tells us that the fire is a collection of atoms and electrons. Are these, then, known, and if so, are they known in the same way as that in which the fire is known? Does the proposition, "I am now seeing a fire," assert a fact of the same type as the proposition, "I am now knowing a collection of atoms and electrons," and are the atoms and electrons constituents of the external world in the same way as that in which the fire is a constituent? What, finally, is the relation between the fire, which I certainly *think* I see, the red patches of various shapes which I actually apprehend, and the atoms and electrons which, according to the scientist, are what the fire really is?

It is a consistent failure to realize the importance of these questions that renders the metaphysical theories put forward by modern scientists so peculiarly exposed to criticism. It accounts for their slipping so easily into a somewhat naïve Idealism, and for a certain vagueness which characterizes their statements when they leave the realm of exact science. To a consideration of these questions I now turn.

CHAPTER V

SENSE DATA AND PHYSICAL OBJECTS

INTRODUCTORY

To ask a number of physicists what they conceive the external, material world to be like is an instructive experiment. The replies are very various, but it cannot be said that the picture they indicate is as clear or as consistent as could be wished. If he has some slight acquaintance with philosophy, the physicist will insist upon the Kantian tendencies of modern science. Science, he will point out, does not tell us what things are; it only gives information about the mode under which in certain conditions they will appear, and the way in which under certain conditions they will behave; or he will stress the fact that the scientist is concerned with the relations between entities, not with the nature of the entities related; or he will make the point that science is capable of dealing only with certain selected aspects of phenomena, those, namely, which are measurable, or which happen to interest the scientist; their reality, he will say, eludes scientific method. Another answerer will emphasize the part played by our sense organs in modifying the phenomena we know. The objects of sense experience are, he will point out, the outcome of the impact of an external reality upon our sense organs and nervous system. The external reality is and must remain an unknown X.

Whatever line is taken, the way is open to a Kantian distinction between a noumenal world of things as they are in themselves and a world of phenomenal aspects which science catalogues and common sense affirms. The world of science is, it is often said, rational only because the human mind makes it so; there is no reason to suppose that it exists independently of the mind which has imposed its categories upon it; it is in no sense the world as it would appear to a being who added nothing to what he perceived and could see things as they are in themselves. This probably is the most generally accepted of the answers which contemporary physics is disposed to offer to our question, or it would be, if the average scientist were not too little conversant with philosophy to be acquainted with it. Suggesting that the world as studied by science is not the world as it really is, it leads directly to an idealist attitude towards the scientific and also to the sensory worlds. The conclusions in which this attitude issues I have already discussed in Chapters I and II, in connection with the views of Professor Eddington and Sir James Jeans, and I shall not, therefore, further consider this particular answer here. Moreover, as I have just hinted, it requires a greater acquaintance with philosophy than many scientists have the time or patience to acquire.

Wishing, therefore, to ascertain the views of what might be termed the average non-philosophically minded physicist, I have actually put to a number of practical laboratory workers the question asked above. Their answers, stripped of technical terms, may be summarized somewhat as follows: The external world is material; matter may be analysed into its basic constituents, of which there are ninety-two; these ninety-two elements are themselves analysable into various kinds of atoms; there is some difficulty in determining what these atoms are, but it is probable that they may be correctly although not satisfactorily described as consisting of charges of positive and negative electricity. The material objects which populate the external world really consist, therefore, of immense numbers of charges of positive and negative electricity. This answer immediately provokes a question as to the source of the obvious difference between a world so described and the world of our everyday experience. The former has spatio-temporal qualities and motion; the latter colour and temperature; it smells, moreover, and can be touched and tasted. Whence, one asks, do these differences, differences which thrust themselves upon the attention in the shape of these added qualities of colour, temperature, smell, touch and taste, which the one world possesses but the other does not, arise? To this question there are, I think, two rather different answers which the scientist is inclined to give; the first that they are bestowed upon the first world by the mind of the perceiver, the second that they are somehow brought into being by its impact upon his sense organs. Both answers have this in common, that they attribute to the world of protons and electrons an objective status which they deny to the world of everyday experience. Professor Eddington himself apparently subscribes to this view, and regards science as having demonstrated not only the objective reality, but the sole objective reality of the world as physics conceives it. Speaking, for example, of the two tables, the table of common sense and the electrical table of the physicist, with its atoms embedded in empty space "like currents in a cake," he says:—"Physics has by delicate test and remorseless logic assured me that my second scientific table is the only one which is really there—whatever there may be."[1] In the same vein Sir James Jeans speaks of "the small-scale phenomena" of physics as containing the clue to the nature of reality. It is in "these," he says, that "the ultimate nature of things lies hidden, and what we are finding is waves";[2] and I have already quoted his statement that the "ethers and their waves" are "the most real things of which we have any knowledge or experience."[3]

The world of everyday experience may, therefore, be said on this view to be regarded as subjective in the sense that the various qualities which it palpably exhibits only exist relatively to the subject that perceives them. If there were no perceiving subject, there would be no warmth, no colour and no smell. "It is Mind," to quote Professor Eddington

[1] Eddington, *The Nature of the Physical World*, p. xiv.

[2] Sir James Jeans, *The Mysterious Universe*, p. 44.

[3] Ibid., p. 80.

again, "who transmutes the symbols. The sparsely spread nuclei of electric force become a tangible solid; their restless agitation becomes the warmth of summer; the octave of aethereal vibrations becomes a gorgeous rainbow."[1]

This, or something like it, is, I think, the orthodox scientific view; it is, that is to say, the view which, I think, most contemporary scientists are inclined instinctively to adopt. Whether they have thought out all its implications may be doubted. For myself, I find these implications frankly incredible. That a table is really charges of positive and negative electricity suitably arranged, and that its apparent brownness and hardness are qualities imposed upon it by the circumstance of my perceiving it, is indeed just conceivable; but to hold that one's friend or one's wife is similarly constituted, and that the qualities of shape and colour and mass which constitute the bodily form of a loved human being are not really 'there' at all until I put them there, that, in other words, they cease to exist altogether when nobody is perceiving the bodily form in question, this I do not believe. What is more, I doubt if many scientists believe it either. Yet this, and nothing less, seems to me to be the plain implication of the kind of view I have been sketching. As for the indwelling spirit, that which constitutes the personality of the loved person, science has never been altogether at its ease in accounting for that. The fact of its association with the blood and bones and nerve cells of a human body and brain is in any event difficult enough to explain; but the difficulty becomes insurmountable if, analysing the body and brain in terms of the entities with which physics deals, we are compelled to envisage the association of spirit with charges of positive and negative electricity.

The fact that the implications of what I have called the orthodox, scientific view are incredible is not, perhaps, in itself sufficient to warrant its rejection. If, indeed, the view

[1] Eddington, *The Nature of the Physical World*, p. xvii.

started with a strong initial plausibility, it might be necessary to accept them at least provisionally until we were in a position to refute it.

In previous chapters I have considered more particularly that aspect of contemporary scientific thought which regards scientific objects as in some sense subjective, and, therefore, in some sense unreal. I have tried to show that there are no good arguments in its favour, and there are strong ones against it. I now turn to the somewhat different view that the entities into which physics analyses the plain man's world of external objects are objectively real in some sense in which the objects of everyday life are not. I have politely called the view different from, although it is, of course, entirely inconsistent with, the one which I have hitherto mainly been considering. It constitutes, however, the assumption from which the implications to which I have referred are chiefly derived, and it is this assumption that I wish to call in question.

To do so it is necessary to inquire a little more closely into the nature of the entities of which we are in fact aware when, as we say, we perceive the external world. And when I say 'we' I wish to embrace by the pronoun the physicist as well as the ordinary man. For there is nothing peculiar about the physicist's manner of perception; the world which the ordinary man perceives is also the world which he perceives; the only difference is that he perceives it under certain carefully selected conditions, in order that he may examine it more closely. Hence the objects of which in sensory experience he is aware, although they may in fact be, and usually are, different objects from those of which the ordinary man is aware, are nevertheless objects of the same sort and belong to the same order of reality. They must, that is to say, in so far as they are directly apprehended in sensory experience, possess in common with the objects of the everyday world such qualities as shape, size, colour and temperature. If they did not possess these qualities, it would not be possible for the physicist to have sensory experience of them.

Sense Experience as the Apprehension of Sense Data

Now it seems to me quite plain that these objects of which both the physicist and the plain man have direct sensory experience are not scientific objects, such as positive and negative charges of electricity; nor are they so-called physical objects such as chairs and tables, but they are objects such as patches of colour, raps of sound, smells, and the hard or soft entities which are experienced in sensations of touch, to which philosophers have given the name of sensa or sense data. And before I can proceed to the question of the nature and status of the world of scientific objects, it is necessary that I should say something about the status of sense data.

I propose to consider their relations first to physical objects, and, secondly, to scientific objects. I hope to show that a recognition of the fact that our sensory experience of the so-called material world always takes the form of a direct awareness of sense data will throw considerable light upon the vexed question of the status of scientific objects. That the objects of sensory apprehension are, in fact, appropriately described as sense data has, to my mind, been convincingly shown by twentieth-century realist philosophers, and I do not wish to undertake here an analysis which others have already carried out much better than I could. I shall, therefore, confine myself to briefly recapitulating some of the main considerations in favour of this view, and be content to refer the reader for a more extended treatment to Professor Moore's *Philosophical Studies* and Professor Broad's *The Mind and its Place in Nature*, from which works the following arguments are chiefly taken.

(1) If I am looking at a bell, nobody would maintain that what I see is, or is identical with, the whole of the surface of the bell. For example, the bell has an inside as

well as an outside; yet what I see is a coloured patch of indefinite boundaries, which, although it may be part of the outside, is certainly not part of the inside. Therefore what I see is not identical with the whole surface of the physical object which we call a bell.

(2) The bell, considered as a physical object, is extended not only in space but in time; it has a past and a future, and the length of its history from the time of casting to that of demolition is in theory measurable. What I see is a single, comparatively short contemporary event. It may be true that the short contemporary event which is the object of my seeing is also a contemporary slice of the history of the bell, but it certainly is not identical with the whole stretch of the history of the bell, which extends backward into the past and forward into the future.

(3) A bell is more than a coloured surface, and the surface itself has qualities other than that of colour; it is, for example, also hard and cold. What I see when I look at the bell has colour but is neither hard nor cold. Therefore what I see is not identical with the surface of the bell.

(4) What I touch when I touch the bell is both hard and cold, but is not coloured. The surface of the bell is coloured. Therefore what I touch is not identical with the surface of the bell. It is also different from what I see when, as I say, I look at the bell. The conclusion is that neither in visual nor in tactile experience is what I directly apprehend by means of my senses the *whole* surface of the bell.

(5) Let us suppose that I place a half-crown and a florin in positions in which the half-crown is considerably farther away from me than is the florin. Then the shining elliptical patch which I shall see in the place in which the half-crown is will be smaller than the shining elliptical patch which I shall see in the place in which the florin is. But the half-crown is larger than the florin; also both are circular. Therefore the patches which I see cannot be identical with the surfaces of the half-crown and the florin.

(6) I can be the victim of what are commonly called hallucinations. A hallucination is a state of mind in which I believe myself to see things which would in common parlance be said not to be 'there.' A similar state of mind attends intoxication; the drunkard sees what he calls pink rats in circumstances in which no person who is not drunk sees them, and in which consequently there would be common agreement among all sober persons that the pink rats were not 'there.'

Accepting this argument at its face value, assuming, that is to say, that the drunkard's experience is, as we say, delusive, in the sense that there really are no pink rats 'there,' then we are justified in saying that, whatever it is that the drunkard perceives—and he certainly does perceive something—is not identical with a physical object, since in this case no such object exists.

The above are some of the considerations which to my mind make it difficult to suppose that what we are aware of when we have direct experience by means of our senses of the external world is, or is identical with, a so-called physical object. So far as the sense of smell is concerned, this is recognized by the plain man; there is, that is to say, a general consensus of lay opinion to the effect that *what* I am actually aware of when I smell a flower is not identical with the flower itself, is not even part of the flower, but is an exhalation or gas given off from the flower. A similar concession might be made in respect of the sense of hearing; it might, that is to say, be conceded that *what* I hear is not a physical object, such as a trumpet or violin—although the plain man is in such an inextricable muddle with regard to the question of what precisely it is that is the object of my direct apprehension when, as I say, I listen to something, that it is difficult to say what he believes—but it is not, so far as I can see, generally conceded in respect of the objects of the senses of touch, taste and sight.

On the strength, however, of the considerations adduced

above, I do not see how it is possible to deny that the entity (which I shall henceforward call a sense datum) which I directly apprehend when, as I say, I see something, is not identical with the physical object which I should normally be said to be seeing, and that the data which I directly apprehend when, as I say, I touch or taste something, are not identical with the physical objects which I should normally be said to touch or taste. Thus the coloured, round, green patch which I directly apprehend when I look at an apple is not identical with the apple, the sharp, angular ridge which I directly apprehend when I run my hand along the edge of the table is not identical with the table, and the sweet-tasting 'something' (the language is without an appropriate word for the immediate objects of our taste experience) which I directly apprehend when I put a lump of sugar into my mouth is not identical with the lump of sugar. Nevertheless it seems clear that the sense datum does stand in some very important relation to the physical object, since otherwise I should not be led to say that I see or taste the latter when in fact I only directly apprehend the former.

What, then, is the nature of this relation? If I call the sense datum S, the physical object O, and the relation R, the question is, What is the nature of R when S is said to be related to O?

The Relation of Sense Data to Physical Objects

To this question many answers have been suggested, but I doubt whether any of them is entirely satisfactory.

The following are two of those most commonly put forward. It is said (1) that S, in a case in which S is a visual datum, is *part of the surface* of O, and it is also said (2) that O *is the cause of* S.

(1) To the view that S is part of the surface of O, I will mention two objections:

(*a*) Let us suppose a case in which the surface of an O

would normally be said not to have changed. Then if we focus our vision upon a certain part of what would normally be called the surface, the object which we do in fact directly apprehend does perceptibly change according to the position from which and the conditions under which we look at the part. If we look at the alleged part from a greater distance, that which we actually see is different from what it is if we look at the part from a smaller distance, different if we look at the part obliquely from what it is if we look at the part from a position vertically above it, different if we look at the part after santonin has been put into our eyes from what it is if we look at the part when our eyes are in a normal condition. Most noticeably of all, the object which we feel when we touch the part is quite different from the object which we see when we look at the part.

Thus the object which we directly apprehend perceptibly changes according to changes in our position and changes in the state of our visual organs. The object seen is also a perceptibly different object from the object touched. Yet we have assumed a case in which the surface of the physical object does not change. If the whole surface of the physical object does not change, no part of it can change. Therefore the object of our direct apprehension is not identical with a part of the surface of the physical object; S, in other words, is not a part of the surface of O.

(*b*) If two people with different eyesight, or two people standing at different distances, focus their vision on what would normally be called the same part of the surface of O, they will each directly apprehend a different S. Since the Ss are different, they cannot both be identical with the same part of the surface of O. It is of course just possible that one of them may be in fact identical with the part in question and the other not, but there is absolutely no reason to suppose that this is the case; there is no reason, that is to say, to suppose that of the infinite number of positions from which O can be viewed, one and one only is privileged in the sense that from it and from it alone the S which is directly apprehended is identical with a part of the surface of O. Moreover, even if it were the case, it would be quite impossible to say which of all the possible positions the privileged position was. I conclude, then, that we cannot know of any S that it is or is identical with a part of the surface of O, and that it is practically certain that no S is or is identical with a part of the surface.

(2) The view that O is the cause of S has very frequently been entertained by philosophers in different forms. Nevertheless it seems to me to be open to two conclusive objections.

(*a*) That whenever we directly apprehend something by means of our sense organs, we directly apprehend an S and not an O or part of an O, I shall, in the light of the preceding analysis, assume. If we did in fact apprehend O, there would be no point in introducing S at all, and then proceeding to discuss the relation of S to O on the assumption that they are different.

If we always know S and never know O, and if O is a constituent of the physical world, all our knowledge of O, such as it is, will be dependent upon our knowledge of a number of Ss. We shall have, in other words, no *direct* knowledge of O. Having no *direct* knowledge of O, we cannot know any of its properties (except in so far as we may be said to know them indirectly by directly apprehending S). Now the property of being able to cause S is not a property of O which we know through directly apprehending S. Therefore, since we cannot know this alleged property of O by any other method, we do not know that O has the property of being able to cause S. In other words, the knowledge that O is the cause of S would involve just that direct acquaintance with O, an acquaintance which is independent of and obtained otherwise than through S, which, if I am right, we do not possess. Hence, if O is the cause of S, we cannot know that it is.

(*b*) The suggestion that O is the cause of S is open to the further difficulty that it presupposes that S has one cause and one cause only, and that this cause is O. This is certainly not the case.

S has a number of different causes, some of which, as we saw in Chapter III, are certainly bound up with the state of my sense organs and nervous system at the moment when I perceive S. Thus, to take a simple example, if I put santonin into my eyes the colour of S is different from what it is if I see with normal vision. Others of the causes are bound up with conditions external to myself which are, nevertheless, not part of or dependent upon O. For example, S varies according to the state of the atmosphere, the quality and intensity of the light in which I look at it, and the direction from which the light strikes my retina. Now it seems to me that we have no ground for postulating of O that it is *the* cause of S in some sense in which these factors, and many others which I have not mentioned, but which indubitably determine the properties of S, are not its causes.

It is, of course, conceivable that O *may* play some part in causing S, but, if it does, it is quite impossible to assess the relative parts played by the causative influences of O and of these other factors respectively, or to say which of the properties that S perceptibly exhibits are due to O and which to the other factors. Hence the view that O is, in fact, a cause of S must remain a belief for which, in the nature of things, there cannot be any evidence, since it will never be possible to affirm of any of the properties of S, for which the causative influence of O is invoked, that they are in fact due to O and not to one or other of the other factors. In point of fact there are cases, such as those of the drunkard's perception of the pink rats, in which it would be commonly said that there is no O at all. Nevertheless, in these cases Ss are certainly apprehended. If, then, the common view is correct, we must suppose that the other factors, to some of which I have referred, are in such cases exclusively responsible for the occurrence of S.

Nor, I imagine, would anybody wish to deny that the causation of the Ss of which a man is aware when drunk must be ascribed largely to the influence of factors operating in the drunkard's own body. Yet there is no *intrinsic* difference between my perception of pink rats when drunk and my perception of a postage stamp when sober. So far as introspection is concerned they are on all fours. In each case I believe myself to be receiving information about an independently existing, physical object. It is, indeed, characteristic of the state of drunkenness that the drunkard is convinced that he is receiving such information. If, then, it is possible for the conviction to be mistaken in one case, it is at least theoretically possible that it is mistaken in all cases. Hence, for all we can tell to the contrary, there may be no physical object to constitute even a partial cause of my sense datum.

For these reasons I do not think it can be maintained that the relation R between O and S is one which can be described by saying either that O is a cause of S or that S is a part of O. There appear to me to be objections no less serious to identifying R with any other familiar relation, such as the relations implied by the words "manifested in" when it is said that O is manifested in S, or "participating in" when it is said that S participates in O, or "mode of appearing to," when it is said that S is the mode of O's appearance to a mind.

Failing a satisfactory account of the relation along any of these lines, it is difficult to resist the conclusion that so-called physical objects are not what we experience when our senses bring us into contact with the external world. The notion of a persistent physical object is logically no more than a hypothesis to explain the fact that the objects of a number of perceptual situations can be correlated. To endow this logical postulate with substantiality as an actual existent in the material world is to create a mere Ding-an-sich. There have been enough of these in the history of philosophy, and it is more prudent to avoid adding to their number. Nevertheless, although it may be very difficult to say what the relation of S to O is, the fact that there is such a relation is indubitable. And there are two things which may, I think, safely be affirmed in regard to it.

In the first place, we rarely, if ever, do directly apprehend an S without unconsciously assuming that we are in fact knowing an O or part of an O. I say unconsciously because the assumption is hardly ever explicit. We do not in ordinary life assume the presence of a table because we see an oblong, shining, brown surface; still less do we believe in or judge or infer it. It would never occur to anyone outside a philosophical lecture room to raise the sort of question with regard to the status of physical objects which I am raising here; and, unless the question were explicitly raised, it would never occur to us to suspect that there was any difference between an S and an O, or to wonder what the relation between them might be. Hence the assumption with regard to the S, namely, that it is not an S at all but an O, or part of an O, to which I have referred, is not an explicit one. Nevertheless, I think some such unconscious assumption is in fact made, and I would suggest that it is to the effect that the particular thing I am now seeing is not an isolated, self-subsistent entity, but forms part of a larger whole which is an enduring physical object. This unconscious assumption, according to Dr. Broad, expresses itself mainly in a mode of behaviour. On apprehending the brown, shining surface which leads us to say we are seeing a table, we adjust our bodies and sense organs as if, on moving a certain distance in the direction in which we see the patch, we should experience the resistance of something hard; in other words, we act as if the S were not merely an isolated existent but formed part of a spatially extended physical object. We may express this by saying that all experience of sense data carries with it an unconscious reference to physical objects.

Secondly, all our knowledge of propositions about physical objects is "based on" our experience of sense data and of the relations between them. If I did not see brown, shining patches, it would never occur to me to affirm the existence of tables. Moreover, it is obvious that my knowledge of the properties of the table, that it is of such-and-such a length, of such-and-such a colour and so on, is "based upon" the direct apprehension of sense data. I have, however, placed the words "based upon" in inverted commas with the object of drawing attention to the ambiguity of the expression. The notion of "based upon" may include that of "beginning with"; it may also include that of "springing from." Now I believe that, although all our knowledge of propositions about physical objects begins with the experience of sense data, it does not all spring from such experience, nor is it exhausted by it. I shall, however, return to this point in a later chapter.

In the light of these two conclusions, that all our knowledge of sense data carries with it an unconscious reference to physical objects, and that all our knowledge of propositions about physical objects is based on our experience of sense data, it seems clear that the proposition, I apprehend a particular sense datum, also implies another proposition, namely, that the sense datum in question has a certain relation to a physical object, and the only question is what can that relation be.

We have seen that existentially the physical object is not directly apprehended as an inhabitant of the physical world, and that logically it is a mere postulate to explain the fact that many of my data are correlated in such a way as to enable me to affirm as the result of my experience of a particular sense datum, that if certain conditions were to be realized in the future, then I should experience certain other data. Hence no conception of the relation which implies either that the physical object is an inhabitant of the physical world or that to know a physical object is the same thing as directly to apprehend a sense datum is tenable.

For the present, then, I will content myself with the suggestion that the relation must be such as to provide for the admitted fact that the direct apprehension of a sense datum causes the apprehender to think of a particular physical object.

all the other entities which physics believes to constitute the basis of the physical world and with which it deals.

The point is important because, if Xs are never directly apprehended by the senses and Ss, in so far as they are known at all, are always so apprehended, then it will follow that Xs are never the same as Ss. In view of the importance of this point to the argument, I propose to examine a little more closely the nature of the objects which actually are apprehended by the senses, in cases in which it might at first sight have been supposed that these were scientific objects.

Although there may be some difference of opinion as to the nature of the objects of which our senses make us aware, all plain men and some philosophers believing them to be Os, and some philosophers, including myself, maintaining that they are Ss, that the external world is apprehended as possessing certain *qualities*, such as heat, hardness, solidity, noisiness, is matter of general agreement. Now it is precisely these *qualities* that physics analyses into something else. Take heat, for instance. Heat, according to the physicist's description of it, is caused by or *is* (I use both expressions in a Pickwickian sense. The relationship between the entities which we directly experience and Xs being the question under discussion, I must not beg it by defining the relation in advance. I simply adopt non-committally the kind of expression which might be found in any textbook on science.) the energy both kinetic and potential of the motion of molecules. Consider, for example, the case of a gas. It consists of molecules of about a hundred-millionth of an inch across, with comparatively large spaces between them, moving about in all directions with an average speed measured in hundreds of yards a second. The molecules meet and collide, and in consequence of their collision the gas has a certain temperature. If the gas is placed in a flame or hot body, the molecules of which it is composed will gain in energy, moving more rapidly and colliding more violently. Imperceptibly the temperature of the gas goes up; heat, as we say, is generated. But the cause of this heat is the greater energy of motion of the molecules; or, to put it as a textbook on physics would put it, heat *is* nothing but the energy of motion of molecules.

Similarly sound is said to be caused by, or alternatively to *be*, waves in the atmosphere. These waves vary in length, in frequency of vibration and in mode of vibration. Variations in length determine the loudness, in frequency of vibration the pitch and in mode of vibration the quality of the sound. By the quality of sound I mean that property which distinguishes the note of a trumpet from that, say, of a violin; if the vibrating body, which is the sounding body, moves with a uniform speed from the position of rest to its two extreme positions, the note sounded is of a different quality from that which is produced by a body moving as a pendulum moves—that is, moving more slowly as it reaches the two extreme positions. Sound, then, is produced by atmospheric waves. Atmospheric waves are described as regions of pressure and rarification in the atmosphere moving forward with a certain velocity, and the movement of such a region of the atmosphere is the cause of, or simply *is*, sound. Thus the properties of the atmospheric waves which the sounding body gives out determine the character of the sounds which are heard.

Solidity, again, *is*, or is caused by, or is a characteristic of, a certain spatial relationship between atoms. A solid is composed of atoms which are so crowded together that their electrical forces interfere with those of one other, a liquid of atoms less tightly packed, a gas of atoms still less crowded; in a gas there is enough space between the atoms to enable them to radiate frequencies which can be detected and assessed without entanglement with those given off by neighbouring atoms.

Hardness (or, perhaps, I should say the sensation of hardness; the confusion of language into which one inevitably falls when trying to give an account of common-sense objects in terms of physical concepts, is sufficient witness to the confusion which besets the subject) is caused by the repulsion of electrical forces between the parts of the body by which the hardness is felt and the object felt to be hard. If a finger-tip is pressed against a 'hard' table, the electrons and protons composing the finger-tip and those composing the table do not actually make contact, but an electrical repulsion is developed between them. A soft object, a gas, for example, or a liquid, is one in which, the atoms not being closely packed, there is room for the repelled electrons and protons to get away. In a solid, however, this is not the case. The sensation of hardness when we press a solid is caused by the fact that the repelled electrons and protons are unable to move away and are jammed by other electrons and protons close behind them. The greater the pressure, the more the finger-tip is repelled, and the greater seems the 'hardness' of the table.

Smell is, or is caused by, or consists of, molecules given off in the form of vapour by the substance which in ordinary language is said to smell, if, *pace* Dr. Johnson, I may use the verb intransitively. Smell, it is interesting to note, is not even for common sense a property which is attached to the object.

Most significant of all is the case of colour. Colour is often described as a quality of light; it is, at any rate, intimately bound up with light, so that where there is no light, there is no colour. Now light itself is, or is caused by, or is a property of, certain wave-lengths in the electro-magnetic spectrum. It is now established that many different kinds of waves which produce no *visible* effects are of the same type as light waves. By saying that they are of the same type, I mean, among other things, that they produce in common with light waves the same characteristic effects of interference and diffraction, and suggest the same necessity for a subject or medium in which to undulate. Moreover, like light waves, they exercise an electro-magnetic force at right angles to the direction in which the undulatory movement of the wave is travelling. This magnetic force is, perhaps, the most important common characteristic of all these waves; it is in virtue of it that their presence is detected, and it varies as the wave-length and frequency of the undulations vary.

Modern physics deals, therefore, with immense numbers of electro-magnetic waves, which, so far as their intrinsic characteristics are concerned, differ from each other only in point of speed, wave-length and frequency. In terms of their wave-lengths and frequencies they are graded in the electro-magnetic spectrum. The rays which are called 'light rays' occupy only a small part of a spectrum, at one end of which can be found the so-called cosmic rays (designated by Sir James Jeans as cool radiation of immensely high frequency and short wave-length), and, at the other, wireless waves whose wave-length is measured in hundreds of yards. We may express this by saying that in the scale of wave-lengths and frequencies, according to which waves are arranged in the electro-magnetic spectrum, there is a certain section of waves which are, or which have effects which are, visible; these are called light waves.

Light, therefore, is, or is caused by, a certain set of wave-lengths of varying frequencies in the electro-magnetic spectrum. Within this section of wave-lengths which are or which cause light, certain subsections are earmarked for the different colours. At one end of the section, that containing waves of shortest wave-length and highest frequency, are violet rays; at the other, red rays. Beyond violet are the ultra-violet rays, which are called violet only by courtesy, since they cannot be seen; below red, at the other end of the section, are the infra-red, which equally are red by courtesy only. Between lie the other colours. Thus just as light waves constitute a section of the waves graded by the electro-magnetic spectrum, most of which are not visible, so each colour is constituted by a subsection of waves of particular frequency and wave-length falling within the light section.

These scientific descriptions of the qualities which characterize the world of our everyday experience have an important point in common; the scientific objects in terms of which the qualities are analysed are themselves devoid of the qualities in question. The jostling molecules are not hot and do not smell; the atmospheric waves are not noisy; the atoms are neither solid nor hard, and the electro-magnetic waves are not coloured. So much at least physics implies, if it does not actually assert; it implies or asserts, that is to say, that scientific objects are devoid of any qualities other than those which are strictly spatio-temporal. And if it be objected that scientific objects are not directly experienced, that we are not, therefore, in a position to say what qualities they do have, and that it is just possible that they may have the very qualities which they are invoked to explain, I can only answer that, although in theory this may be so, there is absolutely no reason to suppose that it is so, and no physicist, so far as I am aware, has ever maintained that it is so. I shall conclude, then, that Xs are without heat, noise, solidity or colour.

Now the objects which we directly apprehend in nature do sensibly possess these qualities. Visual data, for example, are all coloured, tactile data are all in some degree hard and solid, or the reverse. It follows that whatever the objects we directly apprehend may be, they are not scientific objects; Ss, that is to say, are not Xs. What, then, is the relation of Ss to Xs?

Before I proceed to suggest an answer to this question, it will be instructive to consider the sort of answers that contemporary scientists put forward. It should in the first place be pointed out that there is no agreed answer among contemporary scientists to the question when put in this form, because they do not put the question in this form.

Scientists do not, so far as I know, subscribe to the conclusion reached in the last chapter, according to which our sensory knowledge of the external world always takes the form of a direct apprehension of Ss and never of Os. It is, indeed, probable that most scientists are not aware of the analysis on which this conclusion is based. What, accordingly, I imagine the average physicist believes to be the object of his immediate experience is a physical object. Since physical objects have texture, temperature and colour, the question becomes for him, how do such objects as chairs and tables come to be hard and brown when the atoms of which physics shows them to be composed are neither? To this question there are, I think, three main answers which contemporary scientists have suggested.

(1) The external physical world has no qualities except spatio-temporal ones. Qualities other than spatio-temporal qualities, which we directly apprehend in it, are imposed upon it by the mind of the person apprehending. This view derives authority from Kant, and leads to the idealistic conception of the external world which Eddington seems to favour. The objections to it have been considered in Chapter I. In brief, it reduces the external world to the status of a *noumenon*. It is never itself known, and its only function is to act as a cause of the world which is known. There is, therefore, no good ground for retaining it at all.

(2) The external world has no qualities except spatio-temporal ones. Qualities other than spatio-temporal qualities, which we directly apprehend, come into being as the result of the impact of the world upon our sense organs, and are, therefore, the products of our own brain and nervous system. I considered this view in detail in Chapter III. Briefly, it would assert that colour, for example, is the end result of a complicated chain of physical and physiological events. The physical events are etheric vibrations which strike the retina, and produce physiological events which are totally different both from the etheric vibrations and

from the colour, the awareness of which in some unexplained way supervenes upon the physiological events.

The popularity of these two views, which may, I think, be regarded as typifying the orthodox scientific answer to my question, emphasizes the degree to which in current physics the external world is stripped of practically all its perceptible properties. Colour, for example, entails the occurrence of vibrations; it is, that is to say, a necessary, although it may not be a sufficient, condition of there being colour, that there should occur electro-magnetic waves of a certain wave-length and frequency. It follows that colour cannot characterize anything which is briefer than one frequency-unit of the vibrations. Hence colour cannot be an intrinsic characteristic of the external object apprehended, which may in theory exist during a period of minimal brevity. Therefore, if physics is correct, nothing which exists in the external world can possess colour as an *intrinsic* characteristic, and we can only conclude that colour is the product of a physiological activity in ourselves, whereby our sense organs and nervous system do for the external world what it cannot do for itself.

The objections to this view have been considered in detail in Chapter III. Briefly they are two.

(*a*) Having denied to physical objects the properties which we normally suppose them to possess, it invokes, in order to explain the appearance of these properties, physical objects such as sense organs, nerves and brain, which are conceived as possessing in their own right just the properties in question. While asserting, that is to say, that there are not chairs which are brown and hard, it implies that there are nerve cells and brains which have texture and colour.

(*b*) It suggests that our knowledge of the world is limited to and by the events occurring in our own bodies and brains. Apart from the fact that we do not directly apprehend our own brains and know very little about what is happening in them, it reduces itself to a physiological solipsism which, though not logically refutable, is, so far as I know, no more acceptable either to scientists or to philosophers than psychological solipsism.

(3) It is just possible that a scientist might suggest an answer to our question on some such lines as the following, although I do not profess to know whether any scientist has in fact suggested it.

Such qualities as colour and temperature are real properties of the external world, dependent neither upon the mind nor upon the sense organs of the perceiver. They come into existence or supervene upon particular combinations of molecules, much as new faculties are held by the theory of emergent evolution to come into existence or to supervene at certain levels of development in living organisms. This theory would apply fairly well to such properties as heat, which might be conceived as *really* characterizing molecules running at certain speeds and possessing certain energies. But I am afraid it would find itself in serious difficulties when it sought to explain qualities such as those of sound and smell, since it would have to suppose that noisiness was really an intrinsic property of atmospheric waves, and smells of molecules given off in the form of vapour.

If we suppose these difficulties to be waived, there arises the further problem of the nature of the relation between the spatio-temporal properties which all external objects are admitted to have in their own right and those qualities which emerge only upon certain combinations. Atoms of hydrogen and oxygen, for example, are not wet, but water, which is the product of their combination, undoubtedly is. Is the water wet in the same sense as the atoms of oxygen and hydrogen are spatially extended, and if it is not, in what other sense? I do not know that anyone has suggested a satisfactory answer to this question. It might further be asked what it is that the property of wetness characterizes? Presumably water. Yet water, according to the scientists, *is* oxygen and hydrogen present in certain proportions and combined in a certain way, and admittedly neither of these is wet.

This third answer, it is clear, raises problems which call in question the validity of the whole scientific analysis. Nevertheless, although I cannot accept it, it is, I feel, more nearly right than either of the other two. In particular it rightly refuses to attribute the qualities of the objects of our direct apprehension to the activity of the mind or the nervous system of the person directly apprehending. To say that each of these answers is for various reasons unsatisfactory is only to repeat in different language what I have had occasion so often to reiterate, that the question of the nature of scientific objects and of their relation to the world of everyday experience is in a state of considerable confusion.

The confusion arises in part from a failure to realize the truth of the proposition which I have endeavoured to establish in this chapter, namely, that scientific objects are not experienced. If the truth of the proposition is conceded in theory, its implications are ignored in practice. What the scientist, in common with everybody else, experiences are sense data, and it is the experience of sense data which characterizes and confirms every step of his research.

To realize how widespread the confusion is, let us consider the typical procedure of the physicist. The physicist conducts experiments whereby old hypotheses are tested and new ones are suggested. These experiments must be observed, and observation of gases in test tubes, or of bands in the spectrum, is, in common with any other kind of observation, analysable in terms of the direct apprehension of sense data. When the physicist reaches conclusions, he verifies them by more experiments, the results of which are again observed as sequences of sense data. Thus the scientist begins his reasoning from the observation of sense data; it is by observation of sense data that he checks its stages, and it is by observation of sense data that he verifies its conclusions. Yet, and here the paradox of the situation lies, the scientist believes himself to observe not sense data but physical objects, and his conclusions purport to apply neither to sense data nor to physical objects, but to scientific objects. These scientific objects are conceived after the model of physical objects stripped of most of the perceived qualities of physical objects, and the physicist believes that they are theoretically, e.g. by the aid of a sufficiently good microscope, perceivable. He further believes that on occasion he does actually perceive some of them. Moreover, some of his conclusions imply (as we have seen in Chapters I and II) that the sense data (which provide the foundation of all his conclusions) are not objectively real entities, but are the projections of his own mental or cerebral activities. He believes, therefore, or should believe, that knowledge of them does not give him information about the external world.

In this situation there are latent all the possibilities of a first-class muddle, and, as I have tried to show, the possibilities have been fully realized. Any attempt to clear up the current confusion which can hope to succeed must, it is obvious, endeavour to give some account of the relation to each other of the three types of object involved: the scientific object, which I have called X, the so-called physical object O and the sense datum S. With the relation of S to O I have already dealt in the last chapter; it remains to say something of the relation of S to X.

The first point to which, in the light of the preceding analysis, I wish to draw attention is the similarity which exists between this relation and that of S to O. S R O may not be the same as S R X, but it has at least many features in common with it. It will be helpful to indicate these features.

(1) I mentioned in the last chapter two views which are often put forward as to the nature of the relation between O and S, the view that S had to O, the relation of being a part of the surface of, and the view that O had to S, the

relation of being the cause of. Now although nobody, so far as I am aware, maintains of any S that it is a part of the surface of any X, it is frequently asserted that X is the cause of S. When summarizing the accounts given by physics of common qualities a few pages back, I deliberately used both the expressions "the scientific object *is* the quality" and "the scientific object is *the cause* of the quality," because they are, in fact, both used by the scientists. Thus certain accelerated movements of molecules in a gas both *were* and *were the cause of* heat; a certain arrangement of tightly packed atoms both *was* and *was the cause of* solidity. To say that certain movements of molecules literally *are* or *are identical with* heat is clearly to be guilty of loose reasoning, if only because, as I have already pointed out, the heat is directly apprehended and the molecules are not. And for this reason most physicists would, I think, express the relationship in the other form, the form which asserts that the scientific objects *are the cause of* the perceived qualities. And stated in this form, the view is, I think, clearly open to the same objections as the view that Os are the cause of Ss.

These objections were stated in the last chapter. Briefly, they were that the view assumed a direct apprehension of O which we do not in point of fact have, and that it presupposed that O was *the* cause of S in some sense in which a number of other factors were not. These objections are, I think, equally conclusive against the view that X is the cause of S, and I shall, therefore, assume that 'being the cause of' is not the relationship in question between X and S.

(2) In considering the relation between S and O, I pointed out that all experience of Ss involves an unconscious, external reference to Os. We assume unconsciously that Ss are, or are parts of, Os, and unconsciously adjust our bodies as it would be reasonable to do if there were in fact physical Os which we should experience if we moved in a certain direction. And the ground upon which this

assumption is made is, as I have tried to show, lacking, since Ss are not Os, nor are they parts of Os.

Now it seems to me that most contemporary, educated people make a similar unconscious assumption with regard to the relation between Ss and Xs. I say contemporary, educated people because I am taking it for granted that savages have never heard of Xs and therefore do not make any assumption in regard to them, whether conscious or unconscious. And even to educated people belonging to previous civilizations it would not, I think, occur to make the assumption. But in the case of the contemporary, educated man it is, I think, a fact that his familiarity with science and with the scientific description of the natural world is such as to engender the belief that the objects which he directly apprehends (which he believes to be physical objects) are not what they appear to be, but are susceptible of analysis into entities such as atoms and electrons, and that this analysis gives more accurate accounts of them than the description which he himself would offer at the common-sense level.

I do not, of course, mean that the educated man cannot apprehend an S without thinking of its alleged analysis in terms of Xs, but I do mean that he believes that such an analysis is possible, and that, if the question were raised, he would be inclined to assert that Ss are not independent and isolated entities, but possess a certain relation to Xs. And I do not know how to express this relation which the educated man assumes all Ss to have to Xs better than by saying that he believes Ss to be wholes of which Xs are parts or ingredients. Hence, just as Ss are unconsciously assumed to be parts of Os, so are they unconsciously assumed to be composed of Xs.

(3) In considering the relation of Ss to Os, I drew attention to the fact that all our knowledge of Os was based on, in the sense that it began with, the direct apprehension of Ss. It is, I think, a plain implication of what has been

said in this chapter, that precisely the same may be asserted of our knowledge of Xs. If no scientist had ever experienced Ss, no scientist would ever have guessed at the existence of Xs. And just as I hinted at the end of the last chapter that our knowledge of Os, although based upon the direct apprehension of Ss (in the special sense in which "to be based upon" is equivalent to "to begin with") was not limited to such apprehension, so in precisely the same way I should say that our knowledge of Xs, although it begins with the apprehension of Ss, is not limited by such apprehension, so that we can now obtain information about Xs otherwise than through the direct apprehension of Ss.

In the light of these considerations, I described the relation between S and O at the end of the last chapter non-committally, by saying that the apprehension of a particular S caused us to think of a particular O. So far as the argument of this chapter has gone, I do not feel that I am justified in doing more than making the same non-committal statement about the relation between Ss and Xs. I will content myself, then, with saying for the present that the relationship is such that the apprehension of a particular sense datum *may* cause the person apprehending it to think of a particular scientific object; but I should add that the thinking is inspired by a different interest and is exercised at a different level of mental development from the thinking of a physical object.

I will try to explain what I mean by the expressions thinking "inspired by a different interest" and "exercised at a different level of mental development" in the next chapter.

CHAPTER VII

PHYSICAL OBJECTS AND SCIENTIFIC OBJECTS

I. Introductory

I want in this chapter to try to draw together the suggestions made in the two preceding chapters, with a view to establishing some sort of intelligible relationship between the objects of sense and of science.

So far I have tried to demonstrate the radical difference which exists between three types of object, sense data (Ss), physical objects (Os) and scientific objects (Xs). I have tried to show that the objects of sense experience are always Ss, and I have suggested that the relation of these Ss to Os, whatever may be its precise character, has several important features in common with the relation of Ss to Xs. I have also indicated in a general way what sort of relation the relation is, by suggesting that Ss have the property of being able to make us think of Os and of Xs. In order to amplify this suggestion I must say something on a topic which has not yet been discussed, that, namely, of the nature of the activity of the Mind (M) when it apprehends the external world.

The question which first arises for discussion is that of the nature of the R between S and M, between O and M, and between X and M, in the cases in which M is said to know or to apprehend S, O and X, respectively; and the position which I want to establish is that the relation is in each of these cases the same relation. The subject is, of course, a familiar one in the history of philosophy, and I do not propose to retread well-worn ground, especially as I have already treated the subject at length elsewhere.[1] I propose, therefore, to follow the procedure I adopted in discussing the relation between Ss and Os, and to summarize

[1] See my *Matter, Life and Value*, Chapter III.

certain conclusions reached by others which seem to me to be convincing. I shall, therefore, make use of the analysis of the act of sensing which, I think, first appears in the writings of Professor Moore.[1] I am not sure whether Professor Moore would still subscribe to this analysis; in certain particulars, indeed, I think he would not, but as it seems to me to be convincing, I propose to use it nevertheless.

II. Knowing a Unique Activity

That when we apprehend the external world some sort of mental activity is involved is, I think, matter of common agreement among philosophers. I propose to call this mental activity an act of apprehension (A), and the object of it non-committally (O). I say non-committally because I am not at the moment concerned with the question whether the object is a physical object or, as I am proposing to assume, a sense datum. Now there are four different views, each of which has, I think, been held by some philosophers with regard to the nature of the act of apprehension A and its relation to the object O. No doubt there are many others, but for my immediate purpose these four are the most important.

(1) We may hold that A is directed not upon O but upon I, I being some intermediate entity, whether idea or visual image or representation or cerebral event which is said to be caused by O or by the impact of O upon the body (or in some views upon the mind).

(2) We may hold that A is not a bare act but an act with a content C; that A and C are inseparably bound together to constitute a whole or unity, such that, although the two elements in the whole may be distinguished in thought, nevertheless to treat them as if they were *in fact* distinct is to falsify both them and the whole; that such wholes are mental, that they logically precede the aspects

[1] See "The Refutation of Idealism," Moore, *Philosophical Studies*.

A and C which are distinguished in them, and that it is of wholes of this kind, and of the larger wholes of which they in turn form part, that the universe consists. On this view C takes the place of O.

(3) We may hold that there is an A, and also an O which it is not a fiction to regard as separate from A, and that A knows O. In knowing O, however, A modifies it, investing it with elements contributed by the mind (or the body) of the knower, so that O as known is necessarily different from O before it enters into knowledge. Since O as known embodies mental elements, O is sometimes spoken of as the content C of the act A, so that this view becomes a variant, albeit a confused one, of view (2).

(4) We may hold that A is simply a way of knowing or experiencing an object O; that the relation of knowing or experiencing is unique, and is different both from the relation of a thing to its qualities and of a substance to its attributes; that this unique relation only holds in the case in which one of the terms related is a knowing or experiencing mind; and that it is both a peculiar characteristic of mind's experience of its objects, and is also a common characteristic of all mental experiences of objects, of whatever kind the experiences may be. When, therefore, a mind apprehends the external world, there are involved on this view not three entities, A, I and O, or A, C and O, but two only, A and O.

To views (1), (2) and (3) there are, it seems to me, overwhelming objections.

Briefly, view (1) invokes an O, which *ex-hypothesi* is never known to be the cause of an I which is. But, if the O is never known, we cannot know any of its properties; we cannot know, therefore, that it has the property of being able to cause I. As this property is the only one in virtue of which we postulated its existence, we have no reason to suppose that it exists.

View (2) leads directly to Solipsism. Those who hold it are fond of emphasizing the fundamental similarity of all mental acts. If it is true that my awareness of red is an indivisible mental whole of which red is the content, the same will be true of my awareness of other people; they, too, will be merely the contents of my acts of awareness. There will be, in fact, on this view no such thing as my awareness of anything; there will be only successive acts of awareness with varying contents which only by courtesy can be regarded as mine. For even I myself am only a content of acts of awareness which admittedly I call mine, but which have no existence except in so far as I am a feature of the content of the acts.

(3) seems to me to be only a confused statement of view (2), to which it is logically reducible. It asserts that the O which I apprehend is a compound. There is a core which belongs to the external world, and this core is surrounded by an aura of characters with which it has been invested by my mind or (on some views) by my body. But, since I do not know which of the total qualities of the presented object are contributed by me and which come from outside, I have no justification for saying in respect of any one of them that it is not in fact contributed by me. Hence, for all I know to the contrary, the whole of the object apprehended may be merely an inseparable content of my act of awareness; at least, I never can be sure that it is not.

The above are only a few of the objections to which the first three views seem to me to be exposed; nevertheless, they seem to me to be convincing objections, and I should therefore strongly favour view (4). This view has, moreover, the advantage of according with the presumption of common sense, which unhesitatingly assumes that in preception the mind is in direct contact with Os, which, during the time when we are aware of them, are precisely the same as they would be if we were not aware of them. Common sense does not, that is to say, so far, at least, as most of the objects which we apprehend in sensory experience are concerned, suppose that the mind plays any part in modifying, still less in creating or supplying them. In refraining from making any such supposition, common sense, I feel convinced, is right; it falls into error only with regard to the nature of the objects of which in sensory experiences it believes itself to be directly aware. For these objects, which common sense believes to be physical objects, if I am right, are never physical objects but are always sense data.

If view (4) gives the correct analysis of the process of sensory experience, the relation of mind to object is one of direct apprehension, in which nothing is contributed to the object apprehended. What I now want to suggest is that this same relation of direct and non-contributory apprehension characterizes *all* types of mental experience; that this *awareness* of something not itself is in fact both the common element in all kinds of mental activity, and also the peculiar characteristic of mental activity, so that to say of anything that it is a mind is to say of it also that it has to things, which are other than itself, this unique relation of being directly aware of them.

I cannot here defend this assertion at length. Many of the arguments in its favour are familiar in philosophical controversy. In particular, there are a number of negative arguments which are devoted to showing the difficulty of holding any other view of the relation of mind to its object, which, so far as sensory experience is concerned, win fairly wide acceptance. It is, nevertheless, a fact that comparatively few philosophers seem prepared to push the implications of these arguments to what seems to me to be their logical conclusion, the conclusion, namely, that all mental activity, including the activity of thinking, is to be similarly interpreted as a direct awareness of non-mental objects.

There is, indeed, a fairly general agreement to the effect that the relation of experience to its objects must always be the same. Even idealist philosophers, who hold that in sensory experience the object known is the content of the awareness of it, are anxious to maintain the same view with regard to judgment or thought, holding that what is judged is the content of the judgment. And it is, I think, the case that it is extremely difficult to hold that mind's relation to the object of its apprehension varies according to the nature of the mental activity involved. Hence, if I am right in supposing that in perception the relation of M to S is one of direct apprehension of something which is precisely the same as it would be if it were not apprehended, then it will follow that in thinking or judging the relation of M to the object thought or judged will be equally one of direct apprehension of what is independent of and unaffected by the thinking or judging.

There are many philosophers who seem prepared to accept the implications of this view in its bearing upon our knowledge of what are called universals, and there are epistemological theories, of considerable reputation in the history of philosophy, which regard knowledge as being in its essential character immediate vision, which tend in the same direction by representing the act of knowledge as fundamentally revelatory in character. There is, for example, Aristotle's conception of immediate as opposed to demonstrated knowledge (*νοῦς* as opposed to *ἐπιστήμη*), which draws attention to the likeness between the immediate certainty of our apprehension of sensible fact and the immediate certainty of our apprehension of the ultimate principles of thought and demonstration. The facts belonging to the special sciences are also known, for Aristotle, in the same immediate way. In all these cases knowledge is, as I say, represented as essentially a process of *vision*, and the notion of vision suggests, indeed it requires, that what is viewed should be not only something other than the vision of it, but also independent of and unaffected by such vision.

But while there is recognition of this essentially revelatory character of some types of knowledge, with all that the notion of revelation implies in the way of independence and objectivity of the object, there is hesitation in ascribing the same character to all mental activity.

In spite of this hesitation I would, nevertheless, venture the suggestion that this is, in fact, the distinguishing character of mental activity, and that all experience of whatever kind, whether it takes the form of thinking, judging, knowing, opining or perceiving, is to be interpreted as experience of something which is strictly external to and other than the experience; and what I propose to do is to try and apply this general view of the nature of mental activity to the special case of our knowledge of physical objects and of scientific objects.

III. Physical Objects as Subsistents

Applied to the case of physical objects, this view commits us to the assertion that, when we know physical objects, the relation of the mind to what is known is a direct apprehension of entities which remain precisely what they were before they were apprehended. Yet such entities, I have affirmed, are not met with in our sensory experience of the external, material world. I have also argued in this chapter that they are not part of, or an aspect of, the content of our awareness of them, and that there is, therefore, no reason to regard them as mental. It is, of course, possible that, although they are not an inseparable aspect of the perceiver's experience, they may nevertheless be an aspect of some experience; but, unless we are prepared to take a whole-heartedly idealist view of the universe, there is absolutely no ground for thinking that they are.

If they are not to be met with in our sensory experience of the external, material world, are not mental but are nevertheless directly apprehended, what status are we to assign them? A hint of the answer may, I suggest, be found in the language which, on the view of sense experience I have adopted in a previous chapter, must be used to describe our experience of them. The plain man, I have suggested, directly apprehends a green, visual datum; nevertheless, he *thinks* that he perceives a leaf; moreover, he *thinks* that he perceives a leaf whenever he apprehends a green, visual datum of a certain sort.

And it is the introduction of the word 'thinks' which, if we take this view of sense experience, we are compelled to employ when describing the mind's knowledge of a physical object, which suggests a hint of the answer to my question. For the word 'thinks' suggests that the leaf, if it is in fact not an object of visual apprehension, may be an object of *thought*. In saying this I am anxious to guard against two possible misunderstandings, to which such a statement is particularly liable. (1) I do not mean that the leaf is a *product* of thought any more than I mean that the green datum is a product of visual apprehension; (2) I do not mean that the relation of the mind to the leaf when we think of it is in any way different from the relation of the mind to the green, visual datum which we directly apprehend by means of our sense organs. In each case the mind is directly aware of something other than itself.

Nevertheless, the experience of thinking of a leaf—and, since we never directly apprehend it by means of our sense organs, it follows that if we are to experience it at all it must be in non-perceptual thinking—is a totally different experience from that of directly apprehending a visual datum. But it is different, not because the mental acts involved are different, but because the objects upon which the two acts respectively are directed are different; that is to say, the type of object of which we are aware when we think of a leaf (whether the leaf is as we say existentially present, when we are falsely said to perceive it, or existentially absent, when we are said to remember or imagine it) belongs to a different order of reality from that of which we are aware when we directly apprehend a visual datum.

And that this is so is, I think, abundantly evident from a consideration of the machinery of perception. That the material world is perceived through and by means of our sense organs is not, I take it, denied by anybody. What account does science give of this process in the case of visual perception? A certain physical stimulus is applied to the retina of the eye, is carried along the optic chord and reaches the brain, where it produces a disturbance in the nerve cells of the brain, as a result of which we have the psychological experience, which consists in a direct apprehension of a visual datum (S). Unless the stimulus is applied, there is no act of direct apprehension; when no datum is existentially present, there can be no external stimulus, and consequently no movements along the optic chord and no resultant events in the brain of the kind which are caused by such movements and only by such movements. Thus when we think of an object which is not present, none of the physical events, the occurrence of which is the indispensable condition of the direct apprehension of the visual datum S, take place. I do not wish to suggest that the occurrences at the retina and along the optic chord are the sufficient conditions for the visual apprehension of S, when S is present; it is enough for my purpose to point out that they are necessary. Since they do not occur when we think of an object, it follows that at least one part of the total cause of the two mental experiences, which are, respectively, thinking about an O and directly apprehending a visual S, is different in each case. Different causes produce different effects, and it follows that the resulting mental experiences must themselves be different in the two cases; the difference is, indeed, open to inspection.[1]

[1] The account in the text follows the description of the machinery of perception given by physicists and physiologists, and presupposes such assumptions as most scientists would be prepared to make. In particular, it presupposes the existence of physical objects, the retina, the nerve cells and the body itself as constituents of the physical world. Reasons have been given in Chapter V for holding that physical objects do not

The above constitutes one very important reason why thinking about a fire which is absent is a different experience from seeing a fire which is present.

The fact that the word "fire" is used in the description of both experiences naturally suggests that the object of both experiences is the same, namely, the physical object which is what we call "the fire," and accordingly invests with an air of paradox the statement that the fire that we see is not the same as the fire we think about.

The belief that the object of the direct visual apprehension is the physical fire is, however, as we have seen, a delusion. What I directly apprehend is, as I have tried to show in the last chapter, a red datum of a certain shape, but what I think about is not a datum at all but a fire. Thus all that I am in fact asserting is that the object fire which I think about is different from the red datum which I directly apprehend with my visual organs, and the hotness which I directly apprehend with my tactile organs and, when this is realized, the air of paradox disappears.

And the point I am trying to make is that this admitted difference between the mental experiences of seeing and feeling red and hot sense data and thinking about a fire is due, not to any intrinsic difference in the mental acts involved, nor to any difference in the relations between the mind and the objects involved, but to differences between the objects, two of which, the red and the hot data, are

belong to the realm of physical existents, and the above account should therefore be taken strictly at the scientific level.

If the body is not a constituent of the physical world, there is no ground for differentiating between somatic and external sense data. Thus the real difference between thinking of an absent object and 'perceiving' a present one is that, while the former experience is, in fact, the apprehension of a so-called physical object, the latter is an apprehension of sense data. I have, however, allowed expressions which presuppose the *physical* existence of the physical object, which is the human body, to stand in the text, because my object was to show that, if we take the ordinary scientific account at its face value, the objects of thought and perception must be different.

constituents of the physical world, while the third, the fire, is not. And, since we never do have a sensory experience of a fire in the sense in which the fire is a physical object, but always of such entities as red and hot data, it will follow that our experience of the fire always takes the form of what I have called thinking about it, and this will be the case whether what is *called* the fire, but is in fact a mass of correlated data, is existentially present to us or not.

What status, then, on this view are we to assign to the fire in the realm of existents? The answer which I venture to suggest is that physical objects belong to a third realm or order of existents, an order neither mental not material, which was attributed by Frege to logical terms and extended by Meinong to include so-called unreal existents.

Let me briefly recall some of the arguments by which this school of thought seeks to establish the existents of this 'third realm.' (1) In the interests of logic, physics and mathematics we must, it is said, adopt a view which is like that of the School of Intentional Psychologists, in that it asserts a distinction between the objects of apprehension and the apprehension of them, and the consequent "otherness" of the objects, but which goes beyond the Intentional school in maintaining that the objects of apprehension are also *independent* of the apprehension of them. Otherwise the laws of logic, physics and mathematics will have a merely adjectival status as states of the knowing mind; they will tell us, that is to say, nothing about the universe to which they purport to apply.

(2) Unless we wish to hold that the objects of sense perception are mere states of the knowing mind, we must apply a realist theory of consciousness in general to the particular case of our consciousness of the object of sense experience. Now all forms of thinking are also forms of consciousness; thus, if the objects of acts of consciousness in sense experience are other than the mind, the objects of those acts of consciousness, which are judging, opining and imagining,

must also be 'other.' Hence, 'concepts' including universals, laws, numbers, and relations are non-mental, but are nevertheless real, being objects of thought.

(3) We should not hesitate to apply this line of argument to so-called 'unreal' existents. If I represent to myself "a golden mountain" I am undergoing a certain "intentional experience," that is, my experience stands in an "intentional relation" in the sense of the term "intentional" used by Bretano to its object. But no scrutiny of the experience will reveal the object, the "golden mountain," as contained within it. Therefore the object transcends the experience.

(4) Again the experience of thinking of "a golden mountain" is different from that of thinking of a "red-headed square." Now the content of the psychical act of apprehension must be psychical, whereas what is apprehended need not be. Neither a "golden mountain" nor a "red-headed square" is psychical; therefore, they cannot be the contents of the acts of apprehending them. Therefore, they must have pseudo-existence, or what Meinong calls 'subsistence' as the objects of the acts, if only in order to account for the difference between the two experiences of thinking of them.

Now it seems to me that, if these arguments are valid for the establishment of such objects as golden mountains, if, further, they are valid, as many consider them to be, for the establishment of the objective existence of universals such as redness, they are valid also for the establishment and inclusion in the same realm as that which contains universals of all objects which are thought about but of which we have no direct sensory experience. It may be pointed out parenthetically that very similar arguments are used by Plato in the *Parmenides*, where Parmenides points out in refutation of the view that the Ideas are thoughts in the mind, that you cannot have a thought which is a thought of nothing, and I have already referred to Aristotle's view of certain kinds of intellectual apprehension as immediately revelatory of their objects. And since we do not, when our sense organs are stimulated by contact with the material world, directly apprehend physical objects, yet do nevertheless apprehend them, I can only suggest that we should assign to them a place together with universals and Meinong's 'unreal objects,' in his so-called third realm of non-mental, non-material existents. Physical objects, then, on this view, are objects of thought; but, in saying that they are, I do not wish to imply either that they are not real existents or that the relation of the mind to them when we think of them is different from its relation to sense data when we directly apprehend them. And the advantage of this view seems to me to be that it enables us to see how the experience of thinking of a fire can be different from that of seeing or feeling one, as it perceptibly is, without at the same time requiring us to hold that the mind's relation to the objects respectively concerned is different in the two cases. To think of a fire would inevitably be a different experience from seeing or feeling one if (and I should say only if) the object upon which the mind is directed in thinking is in fact a different object from that upon which it is directed in seeing or feeling.

IV. The Development of Awareness

I can now proceed to the consideration of one of the questions which I asked at the beginning of this chapter, the question, namely, of the relation of sense data (Ss) to physical objects (Os). Since it is a fact that I scarcely, if ever, do apprehend an S without thinking that what I am aware of is an O, the relation must be such as to satisfy the condition, that to say that I apprehend an S is to say also that the S has a particular property, the property, namely, of causing me to think I am apprehending an O. And this, I think, is all that I am prepared to say about the relation; I do not, that is to say, know how better to express the relation of S to O than by saying that a S or set of Ss has the property of being able to make the mind that apprehends it think of an O. The function of the material world is, in other words, to 'turn the eye of the mind' (to use an expression of Plato's) to the world of thought, that is, to the realm of non-material objects. But, and this, I think, is an important point, it is not always the same O to which the apprehension of a particular S, or set of Ss, directs the attention of the mind. For, although the "third realm" of objects of thought is itself constant and changeless, that portion of it which is revealed to the eye of the mind changes as the mind that apprehends it develops. The world of what we call physical objects which is the world known to common sense has changed in the past and is still changing in the present, and at any given moment in the evolution of life and of mind it bears a manifest relation to the minds of the beings that are aware of it. That I do not mean by this that the mind at each level of evolutionary development constructs a different world of physical objects from the data supplied by the senses the previous analysis should have made clear. What I do mean is that the area of the universe (if I may use such an expression) discovered by mind varies, and varies as mind evolves; a mind, in other words, knows only so much of the universe as, at the particular level of evolution it has reached, it is capable of knowing. As life evolves and mind develops, its faculty of awareness is refined and the scope of the faculty is enlarged; and to the developed faculty there is revealed a different world of physical objects from that known by the rudimentary one. Thus at each level of evolutionary development sense data may be regarded in the light of signposts pointing the mind to the physical objects, which, at the particular stage of development reached, it is capable of knowing.

Certain definite stages in the process may be distinguished. It may be doubted whether physical objects are known at all to organisms low down in the evolutionary scale. Difficult as it is to conceive what a tapeworm's world may be like, it seems plausible to suppose that it consists only of those objects of direct apprehension, roughnesses and smoothnesses, hotnesses and coldnesses, which I have called sense data. It is, I think, at least doubtful whether these sense data which the tapeworm apprehends ever direct its awareness upon anything approximately resembling what we call physical objects. As we go higher up the evolutionary scale we reach a stage at which it seems probable that some sort of physical objects begin to emerge from the welter of sense data. But they do not seem to be the same physical objects as those apprehended by the mind of man. The world of objects apprehended by dogs, for example, is in certain ascertainable particulars different from our own.[1] But the mere statement that it is different does not sufficiently convey *all* that I wish to imply. To say that a dog's world is different may mean either or both of two things: (1) That because a dog has different sense organs, the sense data that he apprehends are different. The character of a sense datum is partly determined by physiological conditions in the perceiver; it is fairly clear in the case of a dog that the physiological conditions are different from those prevailing in ourselves, and will, therefore, determine a difference in his sense data; the smell data of a dog, for instance, will be richer and more varied, the visual data fewer and less varied. (2) That the physical objects of which the dog is aware, consequent upon his apprehension of sense data, are different from those apprehended by man, and, since a dog's mind is at a lower level of evolutionary development, probably much more restricted. That a dog cannot think as a man can think is a matter of common agreement. Hence, if thinking is the process of the mind's awareness of non-material objects, among which physical objects are to be included, it will follow that the physical objects of a

[1] Those who feel doubt on the point may be referred to the extraordinarily interesting title essay in J. B. S. Haldane's *Possible Worlds*, in which some of the characteristics of a dog's world are indicated.

dog's world will be fewer and less varied than those of a man. And in saying that a dog's world is different from a man's I wish to assert that the differences are of both kinds,[1] that is to say that they include both the differences of sense data (1) and the differences of physical objects (2).

Coming to human beings we may note that even in our own experience the world of physical objects comes only gradually into cognizance. A baby's world, it is fairly generally agreed, is composed of sweet objects which it sucks, bright objects which it tries to grasp, noises which startle it and hard corners and edges against which it knocks itself; it is only later that it becomes aware of chocolates, the moon, barking dogs, and the legs of chairs and tables. And most of us can remember times in childhood when things "looked different" from what they do now, although we may not be able to say or even to remember precisely what the difference was. Savages, again, if some anthropologists are to be believed, "perceive" the world differently from ourselves[2]; that is to say they "perceive" a world containing objects which are in some respects different from our own, even although the similarity of their sense organs makes it probable that they apprehend the same sense data. That a tree on a dark night is "perceived" by the savage to have the form of a demon, and by a child that of an elf, is credible

[1] This statement is subject to the qualification indicated in the footnote on page 163. The first proposition, that a dog apprehends different data *because* he has different sense organs, must, that is to say, be interpreted only in a Pickwickian sense. Sense organs are physical objects which, I have suggested, belong to the world of subsistence. Thus, strictly speaking, the differences between a dog's world and my own reduce themselves to differences which are due to the fact that we have different minds. This means that *both* the differences in the sense data apprehended and the differences in the physical objects to which they direct our respective attentions are due to the different types of awareness which are exercised at our different levels of mental activity.

[2] The ambiguity of this expression must be pardoned. The point is that although savages apprehend sense data which are similar to those of civilized men, they are *nevertheless* aware of different types of objects.

enough, especially if, as I am suggesting, trees, demons and elves are all of them objects which, not being constituents of the material world of sense data, must be apprehended not by the senses but by the mind.

Now it seems to me unlikely that the advance in mental power which has accompanied the development of civilized man should not be attended by any modification in his view of the world. In the realm of material law the world of capricious spirits and moody gods of the savage has given way to the ordered passage of nature studied by the scientist. The most apparently diverse phenomena are brought within the framework of common formulae; their causes are traced and their occurrence predicted. The lightning is no longer God's angry eye but the discharge of electrified drops of vapour from one cloud into another. Similarly in the sphere of conduct, the subconscious cravings and blind urges of the animal world are transformed into the intelligent foresight and rational motivation of the human being. These things are admitted—nay more, they are taken for granted as natural accompaniments of the advancing intelligence of our species. Is it, then, too venturesome to suggest the possibility that to an intelligence enlarged in point of scope and depth of awareness the world which no longer works the same may no longer look the same? Here, again, I would guard myself against misinterpretation by emphasizing the point that I am not suggesting that the civilized man does not apprehend similar sense data to those of the savage. What I am suggesting is that the stimulus of similar sense data may on occasion turn the eye of his more developed mind to a different department of the universe, so that his awareness comes to be directed upon a new kind of object, and that this new kind of object may belong to the class of objects which we call scientific.

The knowledge of scientific objects did not come suddenly any more than the knowledge of physical objects came suddenly. The world of science, like the world cf physical objects, has been only gradually revealed to the mind of man, and, as it has been revealed, more and more varied kinds of objects have come to his notice. The gradual emergence of these scientific objects can be traced in the history of science, and, as science progresses, they grow significantly more and more unlike physical objects.

It is interesting in this connection to notice in what respect scientific objects chiefly differ from physical ones. The chief difference between modern physical objects and modern scientific objects is that the former are thought to possess the qualities of sense data, while the latter are not. Physical objects, it is obvious, are conceived on the model of sense data. They are like sense data in that they are round or square, sweet or sour, hard or soft, and coloured; they are unlike them in that while no single sense datum which is round is also sweet, and no single sense datum which is sweet is also coloured, and no single sense datum which is mine is also yours, physical objects are corporate entities which combine all these qualities in themselves and are common to many persons. In order that they may serve these purposes, they are credited with the additional quality of materiality or substance. Thus their function is to serve as centres of correlation for sense data; they are, in other words, shorthand expressions for masses of correlated data, so that, when we say something about the qualities of a physical object, what we say can be analysed into a statement about the sort of sense data which we should experience if certain conditions which are not fulfilled were to be fulfilled, if certain movements which are not made were to be made, and so forth, a highly elaborate and complicated statement. Physical objects are convenient devices for avoiding these complications; but the knowledge of them involves a high degree of what is called abstraction. That is why it is only minds which have evolved at a certain level that become aware of them.

It is this function which physical objects perform of

simplifying the communications which we wish to make about sense data by enabling us to put our statements in shorthand form, that I had in mind when I said some pages back that the common-sense world bears a manifest relation to the minds of the beings that are aware of it. Perception has, it is obvious, grown up in connection with action, and the belief in a world of material physical objects has been largely determined by practical needs. These needs it is admirably fitted to meet. By correlating immense masses of data and then proceeding to regard the correlated data as a single object possessing material existence and forming part of the physical world, the mind of primitive man effected an immense saving of time and energy. As a result he was enabled to assume the existence of what was tantamount to a common physical world, an advance not dissimilar in kind and in its effects from the creation of a common currency to replace primitive barter. But the advance was only rendered possible when mind had reached a level of development at which it was capable of the awareness of objects of thought; that is to say, of those objects into the direct apprehension of which our knowledge of physical objects should, as I have tried to show, be analysed. And since, although the common physical world was fictitious, the common thought world was not, the fictitious common physical world was enabled to serve all the practical purposes of a real one.

Nevertheless, as soon as we pass beyond the practical considerations which led primitive man to assume its existence, the belief in a common-sense world of physical objects has manifest limitations. Two in particular may be noted. In the first place it is not logically defensible. It ignores, for example, comparatively rare cases of perception such as those of mirror images, cases in which there would normally be said to be no physical object in the place in which the mirror image appears; it ignores the fact that the objects actually apprehended by different observers, who would normally be said to be observing the same object (or by the same observer, who is perceiving what is called the same object through different senses), exhibit to careful inspection important differences, and it ignores the part played by the physiological machinery of the perceiver in determining the character of the objects apprehended. In this respect it is exactly the kind of belief which primitive races whose pre-occupations were exclusively practical might be expected to hold, and the physical world whose existence it asserts is exactly the kind of world which would be most appropriate to their purely practical purposes. Ignorant of the machinery of perception, and having no incentive to inspect minor differences in the directly apprehended objects of different observers, primitive men would naturally not be troubled by the defects to which I have referred. Nevertheless, it is precisely these defects which render the view of the material world as consisting of physical objects logically untenable, and necessitate an interpretation of sensory experience in terms of the direct apprehension of sense data such as that here advanced.

In the second place, the belief, in so far as it purports to render an exhaustive account of the constituents of the universe—and for a time with certain exceptions in favour of gods and demons it did purport to do this—is manifestly inadequate. As civilization advances, the mind of the race released from the pressure of the immediate urgencies of the struggle for existence becomes curious and speculative. It wants to know, for example, what the external world is made of; in particular, it is disposed to wonder whether it cannot be analysed into simpler constituents, than the mass of varied objects which immediately appear. And in the endeavour to find out whether it can be so analysed, it comes upon the world of science.

V. The Discovery of Scientific Objects

I have now reached a point at which the implications of the preceding argument in their bearing upon the status of scientific objects can be examined. Before, however, I proceed to consider them, I must once again guard myself against misapprehension. By the "mass of varied objects which immediately appear," I mean the world of physical objects; yet these are not, I have argued, included in the realm of material existents. And by the world of science I mean the world of scientific objects, and these also are not to be found in the realm of physical existents. Let me here recall the positions I have tried to establish.

Both the plain man and the scientist directly apprehend through their senses a world of sense data. This world of sense data turns the eye of the mind in the direction of the non-material world of thought. Constituents of this world are physical objects, which the plain man apprehends but which he falsely believes to be inhabitants of the physical world. Constituents of this world also are scientific objects, and when I speak of the early scientist as a man who, becoming curious about the physical world, sought to analyse its immediately presented variety into a smaller number of common constituents, what, putting the point precisely, I am actually asserting is that, as the race develops, the mind of the scientist is directed by his apprehension of sense data less and less to an awareness of physical objects, and more and more to an awareness of scientific objects. I propose to illustrate this gradual diversion of attention by citing a few illustrations from the course actually followed by scientific thought. In doing so I can take up again the question I raised some time ago of the difference between physical and scientific objects.

I have already pointed out one obvious difference, which is that, while physical objects are modelled on the basis of sense data and derive all their properties from sense data, the resemblance to sense data in the case of scientific objects is less marked. As science advances, the resemblance diminishes, until, when the modern wave-mechanics are reached, it vanishes altogether. The substitution of scientific objects for physical objects is, however, a very gradual affair. Just as the world of sense data only gradually gave way to the world of physical objects, so the world of physical objects only gradually gave way to the world of scientific objects. In their early stages scientific objects are remarkably like physical objects; the gold and the lead of the alchemist are in fact physical objects thinly disguised, while such entities as the elixir of life and the philosopher's stone are physical objects endowed with a few additional and highly desirable qualities. It is not until the beginnings of modern science proper that the emergence of the true scientific object from the matrix of the physical object begins. And the emergence is marked by the gradual dropping of the more obviously perceptible of the qualities which the physical object derives from sense data. By the more obviously perceptible qualities I mean those qualities of taste, sound, colour, temperature and texture, by means of which we chiefly distinguish one sense datum from another.

It is by virtue of their lack of these qualities that the first scientific objects are chiefly distinguished from physical objects. For a considerable time, however, they retained the less obviously perceptible differentiating qualities, such as spatial extension and impenetrability. It was the contemporary conception of the scientific object as possessing these latter qualities only, combined with the presumption that the scientific object is objectively real in some sense in which the physical object is not, that led to the distinction in seventeenth- and eighteenth-century philosophy between primary qualities and secondary ones. Primary qualities are objectively real; they inhere, that is to say, in nature because scientific objects possess them. Secondary qualities, are not, because scientific objects do not possess them. Hence, it was held, secondary qualities are the products of the mind, and physical objects were regarded as scientific objects dressed up by the mind in the garments of secondary qualities.

The distinction, never logically defensible, has been superseded by the continued stripping away from the scientific object of the qualities derived from the sense data. Elements of substances had weight, shape and mass; so in theory had molecules, although nobody had ever seen a molecule; so too, until recently, had protons and electrons, although the size of and mass of the electron, reduced practically to vanishing point, could be spoken of only in a Pickwickian sense. Even its motion was queer, since, when it moved from place to place, instead of traversing the space between the two places like a familiar object, it turned up first in the one and then in the other without apparently having taken the trouble to 'get' from the one to the other.

Such concepts as those of electricity, magnetic force and quanta of energy strain our imaginative capacity to its utmost limit in the attempt to conceive of them in terms of the objects we know. Conceived, indeed, as physical objects they are the merest ghosts, retaining only spectral vestiges of a very few of those qualities in virtue of which a so-called physical object lives and has its being.

With the coming of modern wave-mechanics the attempt had definitely to be abandoned. First, there was the difficulty of picturing the atom as a centre of electrical force which was at the same time without materiality. The proton, it is true, could be thought of as a positively charged piece of matter,[1] but the electron was not a tiny piece of a material

[1] Positive charge, unlike negative charge, cannot be obtained free of matter; we can have negative electricity in an isolated state, but positive electricity only in the form of a positively charged atom or assembly of such atoms.

something carrying a negative electric charge; it simply was an electric charge. Matter, in fact, when the electron stage was reached, had lost the primary quality of materiality.

It may be pointed out in passing that the recognition of the fact that scientific objects are now devoid of materiality should throw light on the time-honoured, philosophical problem of substance. The idea of substance is a notion derived from sensations of touch, that is to say, it is based upon our apprehension of sense data. On the view I am putting forward our knowledge of physical objects is relative to and determined by our practical needs. In order that they may serve these needs they are conceived upon the model of sense data, and substance, therefore, like colour or temperature, is legitimately regarded as a quality of physical objects. The significance of our knowledge of scientific objects is, however, as I have tried to show, different; it is natural, therefore, that they should lose more and more of those qualities of physical objects which derive from our apprehension of sense data, among them the quality of substantiality. Thus substance, legitimately an attribute of physical objects, is illegitimately intruded into the world of science.

More difficult still was the attempt to conceive of light rays, as we were presently asked to do, as possessing not only wave properties but also particle properties. Concentrate on the periodic characteristics of light rays, characteristics which they share in common with sound waves, and you are led to infer that they are in essence wave-like; turn your attention to the phenomena of radiation from a black body and you are forced to conclude that radiation of all kinds, including light radiation, consists of discrete particles of energy. But the statement that light rays are both waves and particles implies that atoms, too, have this twofold property. It is precisely this which is asserted by the wave-mechanics of de Broglie and Schrödinger which seek to attribute wave motion to particles, and particle motion to waves. The ultimate particle, presumably the electron, is, on this theory, associated with two separate velocities, and each velocity has its special wave-length of corresponding waves. When we remember that the particle is itself a charge of negative electricity, which is, nevertheless, a charge in nothing, we have, it is clear, reached the limits of pictorial imagination. Nor should this occasion surprise; the faculty of imagination is determined by the qualities of the objects which the mind immediately apprehends in thinking and in sensory experience; hence modern scientific objects cannot be conceived pictorially just because they have become divested one by one of all the qualities of what is immediately apprehended.

What is true of the faculty of imagination is true also of the capacity of language; language, too, has grown up in relation to the familiar world to serve the needs and uses of practical life. Thus it is no surprise to find that scientific objects cannot even be described in words without falsification; they demand an appropriate language of their own, and find it in the formulae of mathematical physics. Thus, scientific objects, which originated in and emerged from the world of physical objects, have by process of gradual development been transformed out of all likeness to their progenitors. And in being divested of their resemblance to physical objects, they have been divested also of resemblance to sense data, in the likeness of which the world of physical objects is formed.[1]

Nevertheless, both physical and scientific objects are constituents of the real world (although not of the physical world), and are cognized by acts of direct apprehension

[1] C. P. Eddington. "Until recently there was a much closer linkage" (i.e. between the world of science and that of common sense); "the physicist used to borrow the raw material of his world from the familiar world, but he does so no longer. His raw materials are ether, electrons, quanta, potentials, Hamiltonian functions, etc., and he is nowadays scrupulously careful to guard these from contamination by conceptions borrowed from the other world" (*The Nature of the Physical World*, p. xv).

exercised at different levels of mental awareness. If this analysis is on the right lines, the physicist must be conceived as a person whose mental activities take place on a number of different planes. Four planes or levels of mental activity may, I think, be distinguished: (1) The scientist, in his capacity of plain man, experiences sense data and thinks he perceives physical objects. The analysis of this process that I have suggested is that the sense data which the plain man directly apprehends direct his attention to those physical objects which for practical purposes it is useful for him to know.

(2) The scientist, in his capacity of experimenter, still experiences sense data and still thinks he perceives physical objects. He thinks, that is to say, that he perceives scales, balances, test-tubes, retorts, gases and interferometers, when in fact he is perceiving sense data which, as before, direct his attention to physical objects.

(3) He experiences sense data, thinks, as before, that he perceives physical objects and is, in fact, aware of scientific objects. This is the stage at which, to use ordinary language, the scientist infers from the phenomena he observes facts about other phenomena, molecules, for example, which he does not observe. For example, if a gas is heated in a sealed space, the increased pressure against the sides of the containing body, which is what the scientist measures and the effect of which he observes, is said to be due to the greater energy of the molecules of gas. What the scientist experiences are sense data; what he *thinks* he perceives are such physical objects as heated containing bodies, thermometers, and the pointer readings of an apparatus for measuring pressure; what he is actually thinking about is the movements of molecules, that is, he is thinking about scientific objects.

(4) A fourth stage is now being reached in which, instead of the round-about route from sense data to scientific objects via physical objects, there is a direct reference from sense data to scientific objects. The interpolation of the physical

object is, in fact, dispensed with. Consider, for instance, the procedure of the scientist observing light bands on the spectroscope or interference phenomena. The scientist so engaged can scarcely be said to be perceiving physical objects. He is noting certain sequences of visual data, and from these sequences he proceeds direct to inferences about atoms.

The following example may serve to illustrate this important point in greater detail. When an atom of helium (an alpha particle) is discharged by radium C, it knocks electrons out of the various atoms it meets in its path, leaving a line of positively charged atoms (ions) in its wake. If the air through which the alpha rays pass is moist and is then cooled, the positively charged atoms become centres of condensation; that is to say, they act as occasions for the gathering of droplets of moisture. Thus the path of the alpha particle is marked by a fine white line of foggy condensation, and it is from observation of this line that the path of the particle is deduced. The point of this illustration lies in the difficulty of supposing that it was observation of the behaviour of any physical object which led the physicist to his conclusions about the behaviour of the particles. Certain occurrences are observed in the form of visual data (in this case a white foggy streak) and these visual data direct the physicist's mind to conclusions not about physical objects but about scientific objects.

The case is typical of a short-circuiting which is characteristic of modern scientific thought. There is, that is to say, a growing tendency to think in terms of scientific objects and to dispense, so far as possible, with the intermediate physical object. A race of men is arising who think of electrical quantities as fundamental, and explain the behaviour of mechanical objects, which are familiar and obvious to most of us, in terms of them. Electrical self-induction is to these men a familiar thing, although the occurrences which self-induction implies can neither be visualized nor imagined. What is interesting is that the physical phenomenon, e.g. the behaviour of the mechanical model, has come to be thought of as something derivative, less easily understood than the electrical induction in terms of which it is explained. Thus knowledge of the behaviour of scientific objects is used to explain the behaviour of physical objects, instead of, as has hitherto been the case, knowledge of the behaviour of physical objects being used to explain that of scientific objects. Translating in terms of our formula, we may say that the experience of sense data first directed the awareness of the human mind solely upon physical objects. Later it was directed first upon physical objects and then through physical objects upon scientific objects. To-day the experience of sense data is turning the attention of scientists immediately to scientific objects, the intermediate apprehension of physical objects being dispensed with. Thus a new level of awareness is being developed at which sense data direct the mind's apprehension, not to physical objects, but to scientific objects.[1]

Those of us, however, who are not accustomed to scientific thought are incapable of the degree of abstraction from everyday experience involved. To think of a scientific object is still for us to think of a ghostly physical object; that is to say, to think of something to which scientific thought is increasingly inapplicable. Hence the difficulty for the layman of modern physics.

Summary

The positions which I have tried to establish in the last three chapters may be summarized as follows:

[1] C. P. Eddington again: "I can well understand that the younger minds are finding these pictures" (e.g. of an electron as a hard, red, tiny ball) "too concrete, and are striving to construct the world out of Hamiltonian functions and symbols so far removed from human preconception that they do not even obey the laws of orthodox arithmetic. For myself I find some difficulty in rising to that plane of thought; but I am convinced that it has got to come" (*The Nature of the Physical World*, p. xviii).

(1) Our experience of the physical world is never an experience either of physical objects or of scientific objects, but is always an experience of sense data.

(2) This experience takes the form of a direct apprehension which adds nothing to what it perceives. Sense data which are apprehended are, therefore, precisely the same as they were before they were apprehended.

(3) Since physical objects are not directly apprehended as existents in the physical world, there is no reason to suppose that they belong to that world. The reasons for endowing them with physical existence as causes of, or as sources of, sense data are inadequate. This conclusion applies also to the body. The fact that the body, brain and nervous system are not themselves physical objects constitutes the only logical answer to the physiological Solipsism considered in Chapter III. Unless this is recognized, the facts which science has discovered in connection with the machinery of perception leave us no alternative but to conclude that the only physical events we know are events happening in our own bodies.

(4) Scientific objects are not directly apprehended as existents in the physical world. The reasons for regarding them as causes or constituents of sense data are also inadequate. Therefore, there is no reason to suppose that they belong to that world.

(5) Nevertheless, all our knowledge both of physical and of scientific objects is based on a direct apprehension of sense data, in the sense that it begins with such apprehension. It does not, however, necessarily all spring from such apprehension, nor is it limited by it.

(6) The relation of sense data both to physical and to scientific objects is the same.

It is a relation which can best be described by saying that the apprehension of sense data causes us to think or become aware of physical and scientific objects. In other words, the material world of sense directs the mind to the non-material world of thought.

(7) This does not mean that either physical or scientific objects are mental constructions or aspects of thought. They are objects of thought known to mind in precisely the same way as sense data are known by acts of direct apprehension. These acts contribute nothing to what is known, and the world that is "thought of," therefore, exists in independence of knowledge.

Since to experience a physical object is to experience something which does not belong to the physical world, the mind's awareness of it may be termed thinking, it being understood that thinking means merely the direct apprehension of non-material objects. The "thinking of" physical objects has become so habitual that we normally do not recognize that it is thinking at all, and falsely believe that we directly apprehend physical objects in sensory experience as constituents of the physical world.

(8) Whether the awareness which is occasioned by the apprehension of sense data is directed upon physical objects or upon scientific objects depends upon the level of evolutionary development which has been reached and upon the purpose in view. Most animals are aware only of the physical world of sense data. As evolution proceeds and mind develops the scope and range of its insight into the universe are increased and it becomes aware of the non-material world of physical objects. The knowledge of this world serves a practical purpose, that, namely, of substituting a common world of objects for individual worlds of private sense data.

(9) Physical objects can thus be regarded as devices for correlating masses of slightly varying data. They are shorthand descriptions of numbers of experiences, the likenesses between which are more important than their differences. In order that they may fulfil this function, they are conceived in the likeness of sense data and their qualities are those of sense data.

(10) Scientific objects are apprehended by minds at a

higher level of evolutionary development inspired by a different purpose. As mind develops and the pressure of practical needs relaxes, it has leisure for a more disinterested view of the universe; and with the leisure it develops the capacity. Thus the various worlds of thought, the worlds of history, of philosophy and of literature come to be discovered, and among them the world of science.

(11) Scientific objects make their first appearance as physical objects which are known under certain standard conditions; then as physical objects stripped of secondary qualities; finally as physical objects stripped of all the qualities apprehended as belonging to the sense data of the physical world: that is to say, as no longer physical objects at all. The awareness of the scientist still needs to be prompted by the apprehension of sense data, but it is no sense limited by that apprehension. We are beginning to think, and, as the process of abstraction from the qualities of the apprehended sensible world continues, we think increasingly of scientific objects in non-sensible terms.

Thus, whether a combination of red warm data makes us think we are perceiving a fire or a number of molecules of such and such substances, moving at such and such speeds, depends on the purpose which prompts our mental activity and the need which it is designed to serve. Both the fire and the molecules are equally real, and the mind which is aware of them is aware in each case of constituents of the real world, but they are constituents revealed to different levels or orders of thinking. Moreover, whatever the objects of which we think, mind's relation to them is the same relation of direct apprehension.

(12) Ultimately it is conceivable that a race of beings will evolve whose mind will be automatically and consistently directed by sense data to the awareness not of physical but of scientific objects.

CHAPTER VIII

CONCEPTIONS OF REALITY SPONSORED BY MODERN SCIENCE

It is the problem of value that, as I said in the Introduction, has chiefly prompted the writing of this book. I want in general to know what the external world is like—it is, indeed, for this reason that I have tried to assess the significance of what modern science has to tell us about it—but I want, in particular, to understand the nature of that constituent of it which is commonly denoted by the word 'value.' By 'value' I mean that which the mind apprehends in ethical, in aesthetic and in religious experience, which is at once a common element in the objects of these experiences and confers upon them their peculiar importance. There is also, I think, another type of value which is loosely denoted by the word 'truth.' And the question in which I am interested is whether value so defined is a unique factor or series of separate unique factors in the universe, apprehended as such by the human mind, or whether it is a subjective figment projected upon the empty canvas of a valueless universe by minds anxious to find a guarantee for the truth of their private convictions and a sanction for their spiritual aspirations; to find this guarantee and this sanction *out there* in the universe, if they can, and to put them there if they cannot find them.

The recent developments in physics have, as we have seen, turned the attention of scientists themselves to just this question. The relevance of these developments to the problem of value I pointed out in the Introduction. The account of the universe given by nineteenth-century science made provision for one kind of reality and recognized only one kind of law. The reality was material and substantial; it was, that is to say, of the same type as that which we can touch and see; the law was such as is appropriate to the workings of a machine. This account of the universe purported to be exhaustive. Value was not something which you could see or touch, and it did not work like a machine; it followed that value together with the mind which apprehended it must be dismissed from the catalogue of things that really and independently were; they were not real, objective factors in the world, they were phenomenal aspects of pieces of matter.

Science, in abandoning the mechanistic and materialist scheme, again permits the possibility of an objective interpretation of value. For if to be real is not necessarily to be like what we can touch and see, there is no longer any reason for writing off value as *merely* subjective. It may be so, of course, but it is not necessarily so, and science gives no ground for thinking it to be so. The question of whether it is so or not may, therefore, again be canvassed on merits.

That scientists themselves recognize the implications of this change, the account of their views given in the early chapters of this book provides ample testimony. The recognition of these implications has, indeed, chiefly been accorded in their bearing upon the religious consciousness. What science has admittedly done is so to revise its account of the universe as at least to provide for the possibility of religion being true. Science, in fact, has cleared the boards of the universe for religion. But the circumstance that the implications of the changed conception of the physical world have been chiefly stressed in regard to religion should not be allowed to obscure the fact that their significance is equally important in regard to all types of value. Professor Eddington clearly states the position as follows: "Physical science has limited its scope so as to leave a background which we are at liberty to, or even invited to, fill with a reality of spiritual import."[1]

Contemporary scientists, as we have seen, show an eager-

[1] Eddington, *The Nature of the Physical World*, p. 339.

ness to accept the invitation. Introducing a distinction between the world of appearance and that of reality, they locate value in the latter, thus giving it an objective status superior both to that of the familiar world of everyday experience and to that of the world of science. Such, at least, seems to be their view of the value revealed to the religious consciousness. They also affirm that the real world in which value resides is in some sense mental and continuous with our own consciousness, and, further, that in the apprehension of it the subject-object distinction is transcended, and the knower becomes one with the subject known. These further conclusions are, however, by no means necessitated and, as I shall try to show, are not on general grounds such as can be accepted. The discoveries of science, I should strongly urge, have no relevance to the sphere of religion, and can have none. This is not to say that religion may not be true; merely that science cannot afford any reasons for thinking it to be so. Science, as I said above, may have cleared the boards of the universe for religion, but it has no contribution to offer to the writing of the play.

In this chapter I shall try to summarize some of the reasons which are adduced in support of the further conclusions with regard to the nature of the universe as a whole and of value in particular which science is held to suggest; in the next, those which to my mind should determine their rejection. I shall also endeavour in the final chapter to indicate an alternative conception of value to which the line of thought pursued in the last three chapters appears to me to point.

First, let us see what, in the light of modern physics, can be fairly considered matter of common agreement. The implications of modern physics in their bearing upon our general conception of the universe are, as I have already suggested, negative rather than positive. The general abandonment of that view of the universe based on nineteenth-century science which required us to write off ethics, art and religion as merely subjective, constitutes, I think, an agreed foundation upon which we may safely build. While the true conception of value may remain in doubt, the falsity of that particular view, or rather of the belief that science requires it, is no longer doubtful. What certainly emerges is what I may venture to call an "all-fours" attitude to the different forms which experience assumes and to the different types of reality which they reveal to us. I chiefly wish to convey by this expression that scientific knowledge no longer possesses a primacy among forms of experience, and the world which it affirms no longer possesses an exclusive title to be called real. And it is the necessity for this "all fours" attitude to different types of human experience which may, I think, be regarded as a minimum basis of agreement among those who have reflected upon the philosophical implications of modern physics. I do not wish to imply that there are not many thinkers who, still presupposing the old mechanist background, proclaim science as the sole avenue of approach to reality; but their numbers and influence diminish yearly, and they own few adherents among the leading modern physicists. So far as English and American scientists are concerned, the leaders seem almost unanimously to disown any exclusive claim on the part of science to give us information about the nature of reality.

Professor Eddington puts this point admirably, and, as it is pleasant to record agreement with one with whom I have ventured on a number of issues to disagree, I propose to quote one or two passages from his writings to illustrate it.

Speaking of what he calls the Inner Light as the sanction of the creative capacity of the human mind in art and of the spirit's yearning towards God, he points out that science is not entitled to throw doubt upon its validity, since science itself springs from an impulse of the spirit not dissimilar. "Science can scarcely question this sanction, for the pursuit of science springs from a striving which the mind is impelled to follow, a questioning that will not be suppressed. Whether in the intellectual pursuits of science or in the mystical pursuits of the spirit, the light beckons ahead and the purpose surging in our nature responds."[1] Nor, Professor Eddington would seem to suggest, are we entitled to discriminate between the authority and the objective significance of the different forms of experience; at least, we may not use the familiarity of our experience of the everyday world as a standard by which to condemn the experiences of the saint or the mystic. "The conviction which we postulate is that certain states of awareness in consciousness have at least equal significance with those which are called sensations."[2] If it be objected that the world of sense experience, which forms the basis of our scientific knowledge, and presumably, therefore, the world of science also, are certain, obvious and public in a sense in which the world revealed to the mystical consciousness is doubtful, obscure and private, the answer is that, so far at least as the world of science is concerned, this is no longer the case: "The physicist now regards his own external world in a way which I can only describe as more mystical . . . than that which prevailed some years ago, when it was taken for granted that nothing could be true unless an engineer could make a model of it."[3] In particular the alleged certainty and universality of law has disappeared from the scientist's world. This alleged certainty and universality of law meant in practice the certainty and universality of the law of cause and effect; but "we . . . have concluded that there is no strict causal behaviour anywhere."[4] If it be objected that this is to abolish the distinction between the natural and the supernatural, between a world of order and prediction and a world of caprice, Professor Eddington admits the charge. "We can scarcely deny the charge that in abolishing the criterion

[1] Eddington, *The Nature of the Physical World*, pp. 327–328.
[2] Ibid., p. 334. [3] Ibid., p. 344. [4] Ibid., p. 309.

of causality we are opening the door to the savage's demons."[1]

He concludes modestly that "the change gives rise to thoughts which ought to be developed."[2] It is difficult to withhold agreement, and of these 'thoughts' one of the most significant and that which is likely to command the widest measure of assent is what I have called the "all-fours" attitude to the various forms of human experience and to the different worlds which they reveal. The position required by this "all-fours" attitude may be summarized as follows: Conscious experience takes many forms. Of these one is the consciousness of the scientist; this used to occupy but occupies no longer a privileged position. If this is in essence revelatory and introduces us to an external reality of objective things, a similar claim must be conceded in respect of the religious and the aesthetic consciousnesses; science, at least, may not say them nay. "We treat it" (i.e. consciousness) "in what seems to be its obvious position as the avenue of approach to the reality and significance of the world, as it is the avenue of approach to all scientific knowledge of the world."[3] If the worlds of art and religion are subjective, mere externalizations of our minds and projections of our wishes, so, too, may be the world of science. The claims of each to reveal to us an objective world must in fact be treated on merits; such, at least, I take to be the teaching of modern science.

Accepting it as our common base of agreement, what metaphysical deductions are we entitled to make? Two, I think, are permissible. They may be stated most conveniently in connection with the use of the term 'worlds.' I have been using this term loosely, speaking of the 'world' of sense, the 'world' of science and of the 'world' revealed to the mystical consciousness as if no ambiguity were involved. In fact, however, as will be seen, the ambiguity is considerable,

[1] Eddington, *The Nature of the Physical World*, p. 309.
[2] Ibid., p. 344.
[3] Ibid., p. 348.

and the attempt to clarify it involves a statement of the two possible metaphysical alternatives.

Concentrating, for the purposes of exposition, upon the three 'worlds' mentioned, and ignoring for the time being the possibility of there being other 'worlds,' we may hold either (A) that sense experience, scientific knowledge and mystical consciousness are three different ways of knowing a reality which is fundamentally the same; or we may hold (B) that there is one way of knowing what are in effect three different orders or realms of reality. On the first hypothesis reality is a unity, and sense experience, scientific knowledge and mystical consciousness reveal it to us under different aspects; on the second, reality is plural and different reals are revealed to what in all types of experience is essentially the same faculty of knowing or apprehending. The first alternative locates the origin of differences between experiences in the knowing subject; there are different modes of apprehending the same reality; the second in the objects; there is one mode of apprehending several different things.

It is to the first hypothesis that the views summarized in the early chapters of this book undoubtedly point, and it may, I think, not improperly be regarded as constituting the background of the more philosophical parts of the writings of Professor Eddington and Sir James Jeans. Their conclusions support it, and many of their arguments presuppose it. It is these conclusions, in so far as they support the hypothesis, and the arguments which are advanced in their favour that I now propose to consider.

The initial steps have already been described in earlier chapters. Arguments are brought forward to show that the worlds both of sense and of science are phenomenal, appearances, that is to say, of something else.[1] The world of science consists of symbols and of shadows; the world of sense is the result of the constructive activities of the mind operating upon the world of symbols and shadows. I have tried to

[1] C. P. Eddington, *The Nature of the Physical World*, p. xiv.

show that several different accounts are given of these activities of mind which result in the familiar world, and I am here concerned only to indicate their general drift. This, I think, is sufficiently clear, and it issues, as I have suggested, in a conception of the worlds both of sense and of science as the phenomenal appearances of a reality that underlies them. To this extent the philosophical affinity of modern physics is distinctly Kantian. The activity of the mind faced with a homogeneous world of spatio-temporal events is, if physicists are to be believed, truly constructive.

I have already referred to the mathematical physicist's attribution of the familiar world to the mind's constructional operations performed upon a comparatively featureless flux of mathematical point events.[1] The mind, on this view, imposes or selects patterns of events possessing the quality of quasi-permanence, and uses them as the basis from which to build up the world. The features of the familiar world are, in other words, those we have put there; so, too, are the laws which govern its working. Read "substratum of mathematical point events" for Kant's noumenal world, and the two conceptions are strictly analogous. There is much in Professor Eddington's metaphysics which suggests the same view. The table which is "really there" is the scientist's table of atoms and electrons; the familiar table is the fruit of "external nature, mental imagery and inherited prejudice."[2] Hence colour, shape, texture, in fact all the qualities of the familiar world, have been put there by ourselves. The more thoroughly we explore it, the more obviously do we come upon our own handiwork or 'mindwork.' "Where science has progressed farthest, the mind has but regained from nature that which the mind has put into nature." "The footstep on the sands of time turns out to be our own." In these and a number of similar observations Professor Eddington gives expression to the Kantian tendency

[1] See Chapter IV, p. 117.

[2] Eddington, *The Nature of the Physical World*, p. xiv.

of his outlook. Sir James Jeans takes what is essentially the same view. It is in the "small-scale phenomena" of physics, he says, that "the ultimate nature of things lies hidden," and the small-scale phenomena of physics are increasingly found to be "waves." Hence familiar objects which are not "waves" do not belong to "the ultimate nature of things."[1]

But what of the spatio-temporal flux itself? May it be accepted as given; or is there not reason to enquire whether this conception of the underlying physical reality may not itself be a witness to the incurable 'spatializing' tendencies of our minds? There seems to be a widespread tendency to agree that it is. In the interview in the *Observer* to which reference has already been made,[2] Professor Planck is reported to have attributed some at least of the difficulties that beset modern physics to the erroneous assumption that "everything that exists in nature, exists in space and time." "Men," he continued, "must learn to regard space and time not as objective realities to which everything must conform, but as concepts, which in this region of phenomena, must now be transcended. They are not objective realities independent of consciousness, and perhaps none such exist." And it is, I think, the suspicion that to represent reality as a spatio-temporal flux is unwittingly to impose upon it the categories of mind that leads Professor Eddington and Sir James Jeans to go further and, divesting it of the last trace of materiality, to represent it as consciousness or thought. Whether it is science which leads them so to conceive 'reality,' whether, indeed, it is the business of science to concern itself with 'reality' at all, is not altogether clear. Professor Eddington seems to think that it is not. "We feel it necessary to concede some background to the measures," (the measures which physics studies) "—an external world; but the attributes of this world, except in so far as they are

[1] Jeans, *The Mysterious Universe*, p. 44.
[2] See Introduction, p. 16.

represented in the measures are *outside* scientific scrutiny"[1] (my italics). Reality, in fact, is strictly noumenal, so far, at least, as science is concerned. Sir James Jeans, on the other hand, while attributing a similar status and function to the real world as that which "must exist outside our minds to put this," that is, the concept of "the ethers and their undulations, the waves, which form the universe . . . or any other concept into our minds," proceeds to assert that it is "this reality which it is the object of science to study."[2]

But whether it is by scientific experiment, or the operations of reason, or direct intuitional insight, that the character of this reality is known, neither Professor Eddington nor Sir James Jeans has much hesitation in affirming it to be of the nature of consciousness or thought. Thus, if the distinction between the phenomenal worlds which appear and the real world which underlies them is Kantian, there is a disposition to conceive of the real world on Hegelian lines.

Three important characteristics of reality so conceived may be noted in this connection. (I) It is real in some sense in which the phenomenal worlds of sense and science are not; (II) it is mental; and (III) it is such that in knowing it the subject-object distinction is transcended and the knower becomes one with what is known. The first two features have already been dealt with at length in earlier chapters, and I need do no more here than recapitulate the summaries already given.

I. The view that the reality which underlies the worlds of science and of sense is real in some sense in which those worlds are phenomenal is a natural inference from the conceptions of the former as symbolic, and the latter as a construction of the human mind. If the scientist's world is abstracted by the mind from an underlying content of which it is only an aspect, then we are entitled to deny its claim to be an independent and objective constituent

[1] Eddington, *The Nature of the Physical World*, p. xiii.

[2] Jeans, *The Mysterious Universe*, p. 79.

of reality. Even if we were to hold that all the features it contains are owned by reality and are discerned in it by the mind of the scientist—and the writers I am considering do not, in fact, hold this—it would, nevertheless, exist as a *separate* world only because the scientist's mind had abstracted or selected it. To say that it was in reality separate merely because a limited mind inspired by a special interest had chosen so to regard it would be like saying that the print of a book was the book merely because it is what interests the compositor. But, in fact, the mind is unable to rest in this conception of a separate scientific world; we are forced, so much Professor Eddington and Sir James Jeans readily concede, by its very inability to do justice to all the facts of experience to adopt the conception of a richer background of which it forms part and which underlies it. It is for this reason that such words as shadows and symbols are so frequently used to denote the status of the entities with which the scientist deals. Shadows presuppose an original which they shadow; symbols, a reality which they symbolize. It follows that, if the mind which selects the shadows and abstracts the symbols were eliminated, their existence as apparently separate factors of the real world would terminate. The more extreme view of the world of physics as a closed circle of pointer readings which the mind has constructed out of relations and relata declares even more plainly its dependence upon the mind which constructs it.

As for the world of sense, the common view of it, a view which is stated in many different and often contradictory ways, seems to be that it comes into being in consequence of the impact of the scientific world upon our sense organs. It is, therefore, removed at two degrees from reality, whereas the scientist's world is removed at only one. Professor Eddington plainly avows this view of it, when he tells us in the passage already referred to that the "scientific table is the only one which is really there." If the familiar world is a function of the human sense organs and mind, it is obvious that to eliminate them would be to destroy it. Subjective in status and mind—created in origin, it must be denied full title to be called real. This is a title which only the underlying world of reality deserves.

II. The view that the reality is mental is reached by many different paths, some of which I have traced. There is the argument from the fact that our knowledge of mind, that is to say our own minds, is the most direct and intimate kind of knowledge we possess. It is not, as scientific knowledge is, a knowledge of symbols, and it is exempt from the remote and precarious inferences which are involved in our knowledge of the external world. The inference is that a similarly direct and intimate knowledge of anything else would reveal it as similarly mental. Such an intimate and direct knowledge of itself is possessed only by the entity itself. In this connection it is significant that our own minds are, as it were, the only objects which we know from the inside; seen from within, that which to the outside observer is only a precarious inference from the behaviour of a material body, is known as mental through and through. Anything else seen from within might, it is argued, equally appear mental. Hence, it is inferred, reality consists of spiritual units known by themselves as such, and appearing as material only to the *indirect* apprehension of other spiritual units. And is it not in any event inevitable that when we try to conceive the nature of the underlying reality we should picture it after the model of the only thing we directly know, our own consciousness? So Professor Eddington, who, as we have seen, proceeds to postulate continuity between the underlying reality conceived as mind stuff and our own individual consciousnesses which are isolated peaks or islands of mind stuff.

There is also the argument from the fact of the closed circle which is the physicist's world, a circle in which the measurable aspects of things are defined in terms of each other. To break the circle we must introduce mind. Matter is, in fact, that which mind knows. Hence the account of a thing as it *really* is necessarily involves its relation to a mind, so that its reality consists, at least in part, in its being known. Also it is mind, which, as we have seen,[1] confers actuality, and gives to the world which *is* that quality of being, which distinguishes it from the innumerable other worlds which are mathematically possible.

Sir James Jeans's arguments take the form rather of an insistence upon the adequacy of mathematical concepts to give a complete account of the physical world, complete in the sense that it leaves no residuum of brute fact unaccounted for. Mathematical concepts are mental; they demand and presuppose that there should be a mind which conceives them. If, then, the world is completely resolvable in terms of them, if, in fact, it *is* them, it must itself be a thought in the mind that conceives it. The reality of the universe is, therefore, to be a mind, and the worlds of science and of sense are simply the modes of reality's appearing to the limited view of our partial intelligences.

I do not propose to dwell longer upon these intimations of the nature of the underlying reality, because I wish to consider in some detail the third line of approach to the quasi-Hegelian real. This has not hitherto been touched upon in the preceding pages.

III. It begins with the contention, which frequently appears in the works of modern scientists, that there is a way of knowing which is other than sense experience, and other than intellectual apprehension, a way which is intuitional, immediate and direct, and penetrates through to the inner nature of what is known, while sense experience and intellectual apprehension exhibit to us only its external aspects. If there is such a way of knowing, it is, presumably, by means of it that we know reality.

This view, so far at least as it is put forward by modern scientists, springs from a criticism of the methods of science

[1] See Chapter I, p. 31.

which is prevalent in the contemporary literature of science. It is a criticism which, appearing first in the works of philosophical writers such as Bergson and Driesch, has more recently been employed by scientists themselves. They point out, however, that it is not a criticism of scientific method if its limitations are understood, but only of the claims of scientific method to give us information about the reality of things. Thus, rightly considered, it is less a criticism than a recognition of a necessary limitation.

The method of science, it is pointed out, is to analyse and take to bits; therefore it deals with and gives information not about wholes but about parts. Moreover, it is mechanistic, and mechanism is bound to regard a whole as merely an aggregate of its parts. In so far, then, as a whole is more than this, science is unable to give an account of it.

Again, there is a well-known philosophical view which insists that the reality of a thing consists in its wholeness; from this 'wholeness' the parts are isolated and considered as parts only by an act of abstraction, which, when taken as giving a true and complete account of what is abstracted, is seen to be vicious. Now the method of analysis and abstraction is, and is inevitably, the method of science; science, then, it is urged, cannot give us information about the reality of things. Hence, if reality is to be known by us, it must be by other methods. And the positive part of the case is to insist that there is in fact another faculty which is immediate, certain and direct, where scientific knowledge is precarious and roundabout, and that it is by this faculty, known sometimes as intuition, sometimes as inner conviction, sometimes as mystical consciousness, that reality is known. I will consider these two sides of the case in turn.

(1) The method of science is, it is generally agreed, to analyse and to take to pieces. In the process it is asserted (*a*) that reality escapes, and (*b*) that individuality is destroyed.

(*a*) The view that analysis falsifies the real is bound up with the familiar doctrine that the real is a concrete whole. Professor Eddington's contention that physics can deal only with the aspects of phenomena is an exemplification of this point of view. Presented with the concrete fact, science, he holds, abstracts from it certain aspects or factors which are amenable to its particular form of treatment, and concentrates on these to the exclusion of the rest. It is, however, in the sciences which deal with the living organism, in biology and psychology, that this point of view is most prominent.

In a phrase of Professor J. S. Haldane's, scientific thought takes much of the "juice out of reality." Analysis, which is its predominant method of approach, involves treating the object not as a whole but as a collection of parts. Such procedure results, and necessarily results, in a conception of the living organism as a physico-chemical machine; for considered as an aggregation of parts this is precisely what the living organism is. But one of Haldane's main contentions is that so to consider the living organism is to set aside its biological and psychological natures and so to consider a mere abstraction. For, he holds, the distinguishing feature of the living organism is its co-ordination as a working whole. The day has long since gone by when we could regard the body as being in Addison's phrase merely "a collection of pipes and tubes." It is "a collection of pipes and tubes" no doubt, and each pipe and tube performs its separate function and exercises its separate activity. But the behaviour of the body exhibits another function and bears witness to another activity which is not that of any part. This function is the co-ordination of the various separate functions to maintain the normal behaviour of the organism. The body is a whole of living, and, in some respects, of independently living structures. Yet these separate structures, bones, skin, lungs, nerve cells, and so forth, are maintained in a more or less constant state by co-ordinated activity which is nevertheless not the activity of any part.

"We find in the living body," says Professor Haldane, "definite mechanical structures so arranged as to conduce to the maintenance of normal vital activities, or to protect normal living structure; but on close examination these structures, such as bones, skin, lungs, etc., are found to be themselves alive either partly or wholly—that is to say, they are constantly being actively maintained by co-ordinated activity; and in individual history they have all been originally formed by co-ordinated activity for which there is no mechanical explanation."[1] This co-ordinated activity is a function not of any part but of the whole; no interpretation of the organism as an aggregate of its parts can, therefore, make provision for it. Thus the procedure of the mechanical sciences, of physiology, for example, or mechanistic biology, which analyses into parts, falsifies the organism just in so far as it fails to take account of the co-ordinating activity of the organism as a whole. Its treatment of the living organism affords a good illustration of what is said to be the failure of the abstractive method of science to do justice to the concrete fact. This failure constitutes a formidable objection to the mechanistic interpretation of life. For it is the co-ordinating of parts by a unifying drive or activity which is not that of any one of the parts which distinguishes the organism from a machine.

Now scientific method, we repeat, is and must needs be mechanistic. It follows that if to take the organism to pieces, as we must of necessity do when we consider it scientifically, is to leave out precisely that which makes it a living organism, we are driven to recognize a necessary limitation of scientific method. In other words, it is just in so far as the organism is not merely an aggregate of parts that the scientific treatment of it breaks down. You can give a complete account of a motor-car by taking it to pieces, studying one part,

[1] J. S. Haldane, *The Sciences and Philosophy*, p. 69.

for example, the carburettor, apart from the rest, then turning to the cylinder and so on until every part has been separately studied. To collate all the separate accounts of the separate parts would be to compile a complete account of a car. But a living organism cannot be adequately treated in this way, and the explanation of why it cannot brings me to a new point.

Let us suppose that the various accounts which can be given of the human organism were in fact to be collated. We should begin, say, with the physiological account in terms of tubes and pipes, nerves and bones and blood vessels. These, presumably, can be analysed into their chemical compounds, and there is therefore a chemical account in terms of molecules and elements. These, again, can be analysed in terms of their atomic constituents, and there is, therefore, the physicist's account in terms of protons and electrons. Beginning at the other end of the scale, we should have to include the psychologist's account in terms of mental events, images, sensations and so forth, with special departmental accounts such as the behaviourist's in terms of language habits and conditioned reflexes, and the psycho-analyst's in terms of unconscious desire and promptings of the libido. From other points of view there is the economic man and the median man of the statistician; there is man from the standpoint of the biologist and man as he appears to the anthropologist. There is also the account of particular individual men to be found in the works of a great novelist. Each of these accounts could in theory be made accurate and complete—complete, that is to say, so far as it goes; yet each would be couched in different terms. To say that no one of these accounts conveys the whole truth about a man, but describes only some particular aspect of him which has been selected for special attention, would be to state a commonplace.

But more than this is implied in the current criticism of scientific method as concerned with abstractions. It is implied that if all the different accounts, the physiological, the chemical, the physical, the psychological, the behaviouristic, the psycho-analytic, the economic, the statistical, the biological, the anthropological and the novelist's, were collated, supplemented with other accurate and complete but partial accounts and worked up into a comprehensive survey, they would still fail to constitute *the* truth about a man. And they would fail to do this, not because some particular piece of information had been left out, or some particular point of view forgotten—for, it would be urged, no matter how complete the collection of scientific accounts might be, *the* truth would still elude them—but because they would remain only a set of separate accounts of different parts or aspects, and a man is more than the different parts or aspects which are ingredients in him. True knowledge of a man is not, in other words, the sum-total of the complete and accurate accounts of all his different aspects, even if those accounts could be made exhaustive. True knowledge is, or at least includes, knowledge of the man as a whole. To know a man as a whole is to know him as a personality, for a personality is the whole which, while it integrates all the parts and so includes them within itself, is nevertheless something over and above their sum.

Now to know a man as a personality is to know him in a manner of which science takes no cognizance. And this knowledge falls outside the methods of science not only because a personality cannot be taken to pieces and analysed into parts (psychologists, in fact, make the attempt, but the personality itself slips through their fingers), but because it is not, properly speaking, knowledge at all. The way to know a personality is to become intimate with the person; it is, in other words, the way of familiarity and affection. But in affection the subject-object distinction is, it is said, transcended; for if to understand a personality requires sympathy and insight by means of which one enters into that which one understands, to love is to become one with that which one loves. We may pause to notice this important step on the road to the monistic conception of the real, nd the implied assertion of the mystical character of our knowledge of it. What is real in the sense of what is important and worth while is, it is suggested, the whole and not the parts, and knowledge of the whole is conceived not after the scientific model, but in the likeness of the affection which one has for a friend. It is more than mere knowledge; it is self-transcendence; it is even an identification of the self with what is other than the self.

I have given this illustration at some length, not because it appears in quite this form in the works of any scientist with which I am acquainted, but because it typifies and expresses an attitude towards knowledge in general and scientific knowledge in particular, which may frequently be distinguished in the metaphysical writings of modern scientists. True knowledge, it is implied, is always of the whole; and the whole is real, at least it owns a higher degree of reality than the parts. Science, incapable of dealing with the whole, analyses into parts. Therefore the scientific method of approach does not introduce us to reality.

The attitude in question is admirably illustrated by the following example from the works of Professor Eddington. What, Professor Eddington asks, is the mental activity involved in the seeing of a joke? He points out that a joke, like a chemical compound, can be subjected to analysis, dissected into its component parts, and, after careful examination of them, pronounced to be truly a member of the species 'joke.' Having made sure of the fact, having convinced oneself that this is an authentic specimen of humour, the next step logically should be to laugh. But this, he points out, is just what in the circumstances in question we would not do. For in the process of scrutiny and classification, the quality that really makes it a joke, its laughableness, has been destroyed. It evaporated when we analysed the joke into its component parts; nor can it be recreated by putting the parts together again.[1]

Two conclusions emerge: first, the important thing about a joke, its laughableness, is a quality of a whole; secondly, the method by which this quality is known is not the method of science. The method of science is to classify and to analyse, but the way to know a joke is to have a sense of humour. A joke, then, is like a personality in three respects. It is the important thing, the *one* thing that matters in the complex in which it appears; it is a quality of whole complex, and it is known not scientifically, nor even rationally, but intuitively.

The point which has been made in regard to living organisms and illustrated by reference to humour, seems to take on an added force when we come to the case of value. For value is pre-eminently a quality which declares itself unamenable to scientific treatment, and slips through the meshes of classification and analysis. Consider, for example, the appreciation of a Bach fugue. Regarded from the point of view of science the processes demonstrably involved in such appreciation are strangely irrelevant to the aesthetic effect. Bach presumably conceived a musical idea (the ambiguity of this expression must be pardoned; I am not here concerned with the true interpretation of the aesthetic process) as a result of which a message travelled along the neural fibres running down his arm to his finger-tips, as a result of which certain forces of electrical attraction and repulsion were set in motion between the atoms constituting the extreme ends of his finger-tips and those constituting the keys of, let us say, a harpsichord. Strings were plucked and waves travelled out into the atmosphere and impinged upon Bach's ear-drums. The ear-drums were caused to vibrate, and the vibrations travelling through the middle ears reached the cochleas of the inner ears. Here they caused certain wave-like disturbances in the

[1] Eddington, *Our Knowledge of the Physical World*, p. 322.

fluids contained in the cochleas, as a result of which the cilia, long hairs ranged along the inner bones of the cochleas, were swayed to and fro; the motion of the swaying cilia transmitted certain neural impulses to Bach's brain, as a result of which, or partly as a result of which, he experienced the psychological sensation of hearing the music. Presuming that he approved of what he heard, we may suppose him to have made a series of black marks upon white paper, the score. This procedure would again involve a whole set of complicated physical processes some of which physiologists, neurologists and physicists would be able to analyse. The score is copied and recopied until some two hundred years afterwards somebody reads it—a complicated set of visual, neural processes being thereby involved—plays it, thereby setting in motion electrical, atomic processes similar to those referred to above, and causes a succession of sound waves to travel through the atmosphere. These, impinging upon my ear-drums, stimulate the machinery of cochlea, cilia and so forth, with the result that I in my turn experience the sensation of hearing the music.

The various processes to which I have referred could be described in much greater detail, and I have mentioned only a few of those that are involved. To give a complete account of all the events which take place between the moment at which Bach conceived the musical idea and that at which I hear a Bach fugue would probably fill a volume. But of the one thing that matters, the beauty of the music, no word would have been said, nor would any account have been given of the pleasure which I experience in the hearing of it, or of why I experience that pleasure. If I say that the fugue is beautiful and that the appreciation of beauty gives pleasure, the scientist will reply, "Very likely, but I know nothing of that." And the reason why the beauty of and my pleasure in the fugue are left out of the scientific description is the same as the reason why the humour of the joke is left out; it is that beauty is a character of the whole.

Hence, the scientific analysis, which is an analysis of the conditions which must be satisfied before the whole comes into being, can give no account of the characters which emerge only in and with the whole, and of the feeling which the whole alone can evoke.

What is true of the scientific account of the physical and physiological processes which must occur before the fugue can be heard, and of the conditions which must be satisfied before the aesthetic whole can be apprehended, is true also of the factors which are ingredients of the whole itself. The statement of the theme of a Bach fugue consists normally of no more than a dozen notes. To strike them at random upon the piano is to start a chain of physical processes, of the nature and apprehension of which the physicist and the physiologist between them might give a completely satisfactory account. It would be satisfactory in the sense that it would include everything of importance that there was to say about them. Arrange the same notes in such a way as to form the statement of the fugue theme, and hearing them you may be thrilled to ecstasy. The actual physical and physiological events that occur, the sound waves that travel through the atmosphere, the vibrations of the ear-drums are the same in both cases; it is only their sequence which is different. The order and sequence of the physical events is, in other words, an essential ingredient in the occurrence and appreciation of value; yet order and sequence are not themselves physical things, and no account can, therefore, be given of them in scientific terms. That in the case of the Bach fugue it is the beauty which matters would be generally agreed; and beauty is aesthetic value. Hence we arrive at the conclusion that aesthetic value is a function of a whole and cannot be grasped by the methods of science.

And what is true of personality, true of humour and true of aesthetic value, is true also of meaning and significance, whatever form they may assume. The point is emphasized that neither the parts which combine to make aesthetic wholes nor the physical and physiological machinery which conditions their occurrence have significance; yet, as we have seen, it is with parts and machinery that science is concerned. In so far, therefore, as significance is known, it is known by a faculty which is not that employed by the scientist. Moreover, in all the cases cited that which is known otherwise than by scientific method is more important than that which science is fitted and able to describe. In fact, it is *the* important property of the whole which it characterizes so that we are justified in attributing to a whole, which is significant, a degree of reality which the non-significant lacks. But, it may be objected, significance is an ambiguous word; it may be used objectively to indicate a certain kind, even a high degree of reality, or subjectively to mean interesting to the observer. To use it only in the former sense and to imply that this use is legitimate is to beg important and controversial questions. To this I can only answer that if to use the word 'significance' to describe an objective quality is to beg questions, then the mode of thought which I am trying to summarize does, in fact, beg them. And if, when I use the word 'significant,' I do so only in the former sense, the sense in which to be significant is to be objectively real, my excuse is that many modern critics of scientific method do in fact use it in this sense and in this sense only, and imply not only that to be significant is to be real, but also that the possession of superior significance confers upon that which possesses it a *superior* title to reality. In illustration of this attitude and to take the argument one stage further, I will cite a famous simile of Professor Eddington, in which he conceives a visitor from another planet visiting England on the morning of November 11th and observing the phenomena associated with the two minutes' silence. "He is," Professor Eddington supposes, "especially interested in the phenomena of sound, and at the moment he is occupied in observing the rise and fall of the roar of traffic in a great city. Suddenly the noise ceases, and for the space of two minutes there is the utmost stillness; then the roar begins again. Our visitor, seeking a scientific explanation of this, may perhaps recall that on another occasion he witnessed an apparently analogous phenomenon in the kindred study of light. It was full daylight, but there came a quick falling of darkness which lasted about two minutes, after which the light came back again. The latter occurrence (a total eclipse of the sun) has a well-known scientific explanation and can, indeed, be predicted many years in advance. I am assuming that the visitor is a competent scientist; and though he might at first be misled by the resemblance, he would soon find that the cessation of sound was a much more complicated phenomenon than the cessation of light. But there is nothing to suggest that it was outside the operation of the same kind of natural forces. There was no supernatural hushing of sound. The noise ceases because the traffic stopped; each car stopped because a brake applied the necessary friction; the brake was worked mechanically by a pedal; the pedal by a foot; the foot by a muscle; the muscle by mechanical or electrical impulses travelling along a nerve. The stranger may well believe that each motion has its physical antecedent cause, which can be carried back as far as we please; and, if the prediction of the two minutes' silence on Armistice Day is not predictable like an eclipse of the sun, it is only because of the difficulty of dealing with the configurations of millions of particles instead of with a configuration of three astronomical bodies."[1]

This vivid simile leads the author to the conclusion that if we are seeking to *understand* the silence, the material phenomena associated with it are not really relevant to our comprehension. To say that the silence "is a natural and calculable result of the motion of a number of atoms and electrons following Maxwell's equations and the law of

[1] Eddington, *Science and the Unseen World*, pp. 39–40.

conservation" is, no doubt, true. Hence the visitor, if he knows the atoms and electrons and is acquainted with Maxwell's equations, has apprehended "the reality underlying the silence, *so far as reality is a matter of atoms and electrons. But he is unaware that the silence has also a significance*"[1] (my italics).

The inference is that the visitor, who may be regarded as a personification of scientific method looking at things from the outside, will be unable to give an account of the significance, the meaning of what he sees. Now significance is for Professor Eddington a spiritual thing; also significance is real, since we must, in the light of our previous examination of Professor Eddington's views, interpret the phrase "so far as reality is a matter of atoms and electrons," in a Pickwickian sense only. For Professor Eddington does not think that reality consists of atoms and electrons, and he does think that it is mental or spiritual in character. Hence the point of the simile is to suggest that just as a complete analysis of the external phenomena associated with the silence would not yield the observer so much as a hint of its meaning or significance, so a complete account of the universe in scientific terms would fail to reveal the spiritual reality which underlies it. And just as the significance or meaning of the silence is that which makes it real and actual, seeing that without it the silence would not be, so does the spiritual unity which underlies the material universe constitute *its* reality, since without the spiritual unity the universe itself would not be. That spiritual unity, Professor Eddington suggests, is a personal God. "When we assert that God is real, we are not restricted to a comparison with the reality of atoms and electrons." It is enough that He should be "as real as the shadow of the Great War on Armistice Day."[2] The fact that science can give no account of Him is irrelevant; for the way in which we know meaning and significance is, as we have seen, other than the way of science.

[1] Eddington, *Science and the Unseen World*, p. 41. [2] Ibid., pp. 41–42.

(*b*) I have been compelled to devote considerable space to a summary of the reasons which are advanced to show that scientific method does not grasp the reality of things, since, in the process of analysis, reality escapes. The length of the summary was due to the fact that the arguments take a number of different forms varying according to the particular conception of the nature of reality, whether as personality, as value, or as significance, which in any particular case it was desired to represent as slipping through the meshes of scientific treatment. Many of these arguments may also be used in support of the doctrine that science destroys or is not fitted to grasp the individuality of things.

All the arguments which are based on the abstractive method of science are, indeed, equally applicable to the case of individuality. These are reinforced by an additional argument, the argument from classification. The most outstanding feature of scientific method is its demand for classification. All science, it is said, begins with classification; it is essential to its method that the objects with which it deals should be sorted out into different boxes or pigeon-holes, and that it should thus be able to treat the objects falling within each pigeon-hole as if they were the same. To quote an instance given by a recent writer on scientific method. "If the scientific mind is faced with five hundred balls of all shades of grey from pure black to pure white, it will separate them into groups of greys, but these are discontinuous, whereas from the common-sense point of view one could not have less than five hundred groups, for all the balls are by definition different. . . . Even in the case of two black balls, the scientific mind will sweep them into the same box, unconscious of the fact that one of them is slightly less of a sphere than the other, if it happens at the moment to be interested in blackness and not globularity."[1]

Hence to treat the objects classified together as if they were the same means to treat them as if certain differences which

[1] Joseph Needham, *The Sceptical Biologist*, p. 248.

they actually exhibit are from the point of view of the particular purpose in view irrelevant. Scientific procedure is, therefore, conditioned by an "as if." The scientist says in effect, "Let us suppose that we shall get on best by concentrating all our attention upon a particular aspect of an object, and ignoring all the other aspects as being irrelevant to our immediate purpose. Let us, then, classify the object with other objects which possess in common with it the aspect in question, even although they may possess other aspects which are different, and see what conclusion we can reach about the objects so classified." The suggestion is that the results achieved are not in fact results about the concrete objects which the scientist began by classifying; what they really give information about is their hypostatized common aspect. Provided the initial "as if" is remembered no harm is done, but, because of the 'as if,' scientific method, in so far as it purports to give an account of what things 'really are,' is, it is held, vitiated from the start. It is vitiated by the fact that in order to proceed it must classify, and in order to classify it must treat individual things not as individual things but as examples falling within a class. But, it is urged by the critics of science, everything is itself and not something else; it is, that is to say, individual and unique, so that what is regarded as an arbitrary falsification of the object's nature is a necessary condition of its being classified at all. In extreme cases this falsification for the purpose of classification is obvious. Mr. Needham quotes the case of French railway trucks labelled with the inscription, "*Hommes* 40. *Chevaux* 16."[1]

The aspect of a man under which he can be classified as a unit which, with thirty-nine other units of the same kind, occupies a space equivalent to that occupied by sixteen horses, such space being identical with the holding capacity of a certain class of railway truck, is, no doubt, truly an aspect of him, but it is not, it is obvious, that in which his indi-

[1] Needham, *The Sceptical Biologist*, p. 97.

viduality resides. To treat him, therefore, under that aspect alone, or as if he were that aspect alone, is to destroy his individuality; so much, at least, in the extreme case is clear. What is not so generally recognized is that all scientific method, involving as it necessarily does a process of classification according to aspects selected as being immediately relevant, involves a similar obliteration of individuality. If, then, the reality of a thing resides in its individuality, science is once again seen to be unfitted to grasp reality.

The point so frequently urged by modern physicists that scientific laws are not accounts of the behaviour of particular things, but are statistical statements purporting to give the probable behaviour of large numbers of things, is regarded as an admission by scientists themselves of the implications of this fact.

(2) If the method of science is such as has been described, if it is incapable of grasping wholes and lets individuality slip through its fingers; if, moreover, reality is in some sense a whole, and in some sense individual, by means of what faculty do we know it? For that we do have such knowledge is not doubted. We must have it, indeed, since, if we did not, we should have no standard by reference to which we should be justified in stigmatizing scientific knowledge as abstract and symbolic; if we did not somehow *know* what was real, we should not, it is implied, be able to recognize the world to which science introduces us as a world of symbols and shadows. The position is thus reminiscent of a stage in Plato's celebrated argument for the existence of Forms. The world of sense, Plato points out, is not entirely real; it is a world of becoming; of it, therefore, we have not knowledge but opinion merely. Nevertheless, we do have knowledge; it follows that knowledge is not of the world of sense. The Platonic argument is from the fact of knowing to the necessity for an object; the modern scientific argument from the fact of reality to the necessity for a faculty by means of which it mav be known.

To press for a detailed account of the faculty is to receive very indefinite information. The language which is used to describe the nature of our knowledge of the real world, though vague and allusive, is, however, in general, strongly reminiscent of Bergson's treatment of the faculty of intuition. It expresses, that is to say, a belief in the possibility of a way of knowing which is directly revelatory of its object, as contrasted with sense, reason and analysis, which are regarded as blind guides leading to illusory views, or to a knowledge merely of our own mental creations. Bergson's 'intellect' again has considerable affinity with the observational methods and reasoning processes employed in modern science. Like them it analyses and takes to pieces; like them it destroys wholes and concentrates on parts; like them it interposes stops and gaps in what is regarded as a fundamentally homogeneous stuff, articulates the real, and concentrates upon the aspects thus unreally segregated in which it happens to be interested.[1] It is inevitable, therefore, that the faculty by means of which the real is known should, for modern physicists as for Bergson, be defined chiefly by reference to and in opposition to the intellect. Intuition, then, as Bergson calls it, 'inner conviction' as Eddington terms it, is the antithesis of the intellectual reason. Four characteristics of the faculty thus variously named may be distinguished.

(*a*) It is direct and immediate in its operations, and the language which may appropriately be used to denote it is the language of immediate vision. We either 'see' a joke or we do not; if we do, we see it immediately. Our feeling

[1] C. P. Bergson, *Introduction to Metaphysics*, p. 1. There are "two profoundly different ways of knowing a thing. The first implies that we move round the object; the second that we enter into it. The first depends on the point of view at which we are placed and on the symbols by which we express ourselves. The second neither depends on a point of view nor relies on any symbol. The first kind of knowledge may be said to stop at the *relative*; the second, in those cases where it is possible, to attain the *absolute*."

for Nature or our aesthetic appreciation of a piece of music is similarly direct. There are no preceding stages of conscious mental activity, such as the stages of reasoning which precede a logical conclusion. The conviction of humour or beauty comes as it were fully formed into the mind; if there is a leading-up process we are not aware of it.

(*b*) It is its own authority and carries with it the guarantee of its own authenticity. For those truths which we know intuitively no reasons can be adduced, simply because they are not reached by a process of reasoning. Reason, no doubt, may be enlisted later to produce arguments in their favour; for, if "metaphysics" is, as Bradley suggested, "the finding of bad reasons for what we believe upon instinct"; "to find these reasons is no less an instinct." But the process by means of which an intuitional conviction is reached is independent of this process of later rationalization, which is irrelevant to the truth of the conviction. Reached by non-rational processes, although it may be subsequently defended by rational ones, an intuitive conviction must carry its guarantee of authenticity within itself. The basis of all reasoning process is, it is generally agreed, similarly intuitional,[1] but we do not distrust mathematics because its premises are undemonstrated.

Similarly with religious convictions. "The attribution of the religious colour to the domain," i.e. that of the underlying reality, "must rest on inner conviction; and I think we should not deny validity to certain inner convictions, which seem parallel with the unreasoning trust in reason which is at the basis of mathematics, with an innate sense of the fitness of things which is at the basis of the science of the physical world, and with an irresistible sense of incongruity which is at the basis of the justification of humour."[2]

(*c*) Instead of standing outside, it enters into its object and by sympathy becomes temporarily one with it. Bergson

[1] See above, Chapter VII, p. 160.

[2] Eddington, *The Nature of the Physical World*, pp. 349–350.

describes intuition as "the kind of intellectual sympathy by which one places oneself within an object in order to coincide with what is unique in it and therefore inexpressible."[1] Attention may be drawn in this connection to the appreciation of a piece of music. The scientific treatment of it, as we have seen, is to analyse it into its component notes, and the notes into their constituent vibrations; science breaks up the whole and concentrates upon its parts. But the faculty with which we appreciate the beauty of the symphony represents it to us as an aesthetic whole. It is as a whole or unity which is such that the subtraction of any one of the parts would destroy the aesthetic effect that we find it valuable. And just as it is by intuition that we enter into and appreciate the meaning of the symphony as an indivisible whole, so it is by intuition that we enter into and grasp the nature of reality as an indivisible whole.

But, if intuition is involved in the appreciation of a picture or a symphony, it is involved still more directly in their creation. The great artist creates by penetrating through the superficial appearances presented by his subject to the reality beneath: it is, in fact, his vision of this reality that constitutes his greatness as an artist. This vision he places upon the canvas, and it is in the reality of the vision and not in the paint, the colours, the form, the technique, or the faithful portrayal of the subject that the essence of the picture lies. And just as it is only by entering through sympathy into the meaning of his subject that the artist succeeds in grasping it, so it is through the sympathy, which is intuition, that we are enabled to enter into the nature of the reality which underlies the phenomenal appearances of science and of sense.

If appreciation of great art implies an entering of the spirit into the reality of that which is appreciated, the affectionate knowledge of a personality involves, it is said,

[1] Bergson, *Introduction to Metaphysics*, p. 6.

a yet higher and more intimate degree of communion. The fact is testified by the metaphors of common language. We speak of "entering into the mind and heart of one's friend," and of "the community of heart and soul" which is said to be one of the distinguishing marks of true lovers. To love nature is "to be at one with her," and God is worshipped in "oneness of spirit." We may go further and think of two persons intimately acquainted and deeply loving each the other, as creating a new spiritual unity, a common soul, as it were, in which the separate personality of each is fused and by which it is transcended. There is much in the writings of the mystical poets to lend countenance to this conception.

Even if we do not wish to identify ourselves with this somewhat mystical point of view, there is real plausibility in the suggestion that, whereas to have experience of a thing through the senses or to accumulate facts about it as in science is to know from outside, in moments of aesthetic appreciation we enter into, in moments of intimate personal communion we feel with, because we for the time being *are* that which is known. This view frequently finds expression in the writings of Professor Eddington. "The harmony and beauty of the face of Nature is at root one with the gladness which transfigures the face of man,"[1] he writes; and again, "In the mystical feeling the truth is apprehended from within and is, as it should be, a part of ourselves."[2]

And this conception of the intuitional faculty as uniting and synthesizing knower and known is, I suggest, a natural inference from the conception of the scientific intellect as analysing, abstracting and dividing. It may, therefore, legitimately be included among the many metaphysical hypotheses which modern physics has sponsored.

(*d*) Fourthly, the intuitional faculty is said to be a natural human attribute, as natural and universal as the sense of sight or hearing, so that lacking it a person may be justifiably

[1] Eddington, *The Nature of the Physical World*, p. 321. [2] Ibid., p. 321.

regarded as being in virtue of his lack not fully and completely a human being.

It is, moreover, pre-eminently the faculty which assures us of the meaning and significance of things, so that without its assurance we should be justified in concluding that the universe is as it appears to mechanistic science, without a point or purpose. Nor is it only of meaning and significance that it assures us, but of a divine meaning and a personal significance. I will take two quotations from Professor Eddington in illustration of these two points. "There are some to whom the sense of a divine presence irradiating the soul is one of the most obvious things of experience. *In their view a man without this sense is to be regarded as we regard a man without a sense of humour. The absence is a kind of mental deficiency*"[1] (my italics).

"If we have no such sense then it would seem that not only religion, but the physical world and all faith in reasoning totter in insecurity."[2]

I have now summarized to the best of my ability some of the reasons which are adduced in favour of the view, first, that scientific knowledge does not give us knowledge of reality, and, secondly, that reality is revealed to some other faculty which is intuitional and immediate in character. This reality is asserted to be of a different order from the familiar and the scientific worlds; the world known to science and the world of sensory experience are in fact merely phenomenal aspects of it. The position is, then, that behind the changing show of fact upon which the intellect feeds and the stimuli which release the play of our sensations there is a world of a different order. It is a world which is a unity; it includes value, and the worlds of which we normally have experience are merely its phenomenal aspects.

How is this world to be conceived? As mind stuff, according to Professor Eddington; as a mathematician's mind, according to Sir James Jeans; as an immaterial

[1] Eddington, *The Nature of the Physical World*, p. 322. [2] Ibid., p. 336.

ether according to Sir Oliver Lodge; as an *élan vital* or spiritual impulsion, according to Bergson, whose general criticism of the intellect and insistence upon the metaphysical importance of the intuitive faculty entitle him to be regarded as a member of this school of thought.

Can we not be a little more specific? Not very easily; precision on this subject is not lightly to be attempted nor readily achieved. Nor should it be insisted upon. As I shall later try to show,[1] if there is in fact knowledge of what I shall non-committally call the "real world," it is not to be communicated in language appropriate to the uses of the phenomenal one; or not without grave risk of misapprehension. If mysticism could give an account of itself, it would cease to be mysticism, while even the attempt to express the quality of our emotions on hearing a Bach fugue is usually pitiably inadequate and had better not have been made. Moreover, if we accept the account of the intuitional faculty given above, any attempt to describe its deliverances, involving as it must of necessity do the operations of the intellect, will falsify what is described, abstracting from the concrete experience and offering us merely a symbolic representation of that which can only be fully realized by being lived through. I shall return to these points in a later chapter. For the present it is sufficient to notice that if they are valid, they may be held to excuse those who conceive of reality as a unity underlying the phenomenal worlds of familiar experience from giving any very specific account of the reality they conceive.

Nevertheless, when all allowance is made for this necessary limitation, the account actually given by Professor Eddington —and I choose Professor Eddington from among the writers summarized in the earlier part of this book because he concerns himself in greater detail with the nature of the reality of which the world of science is an aspect or symbol —cannot be regarded as satisfactory. It is less an account

[1] See Chapter X, pp. 307, 308.

than a series of hints. Of these hints some are inconsistent with others; while considerable ambiguity infects not only the conception of the real world itself, where, perhaps, it is pardonable, but also the account of the relation of that world to the knowing mind.

The view of this relation most generally expressed is affirmed by means of an analogy with our knowledge of the familiar world. The reality of the table is, says Professor Eddington, a scientific reality; this impinging upon our sense organs causes us "to weave images and illusions about it."[1] Hence the familiar table is neither illusion nor reality; it consists of a core of reality enwrapped with attributes imposed by the sense organs and the mind. Similarly a real world comes into contact with our higher faculties, and it, too, causes them "to weave images and illusions about it." Hence the conception of the spiritual world, like that of the familiar world, contains a core of reality enwrapped with attributes projected upon it by our spiritual natures; "it is an everyday world to be compared with the material world of familiar experience. I claim it as no more real and no less real than that."[2]

The point is elaborated on a number of occasions. The reality of colour is wave-length, but "we do not pluck out our eyes because they persist in deluding us with fanciful colourings."[3] There is, indeed, a sense in which to represent the glorious colours of our surroundings as real is not, after all, misrepresentation as we have been led to suppose. For "it is a very one-sided view which takes the environment to be all-important and the conscious spirit to be inessential."[4] It is in just the same way that "the bare external qualities of the spiritual world"[5] have been "transmuted by a religious colour"[6] through our spiritual faculty. But to hold that this "religious colour" misrepresented the spiritual world would be again a one-sided view, for the faculty which so transmutes

[1] Eddington, *The Nature of the Physical World*, p. 324. [2] Ibid., p. 324.
[3] Ibid., p. 335. [4] Ibid., p. 335. [5] Ibid., p. 335. [6] Ibid., p. 335.

the bare qualities may be the "divine element in man's nature."[1] In other words, there is just as good ground for regarding the world known to the spiritual sense as real as there is for regarding the familiar sense world as real. Each is constructed by the mind from a datum which is independent and objective. In the former case the datum is "the real world"; in the latter, the world of the physicist.

For the guarantee of this objective core we are bidden to look to the "feeling of purpose in ourselves"[2] which makes us seek a solution of the problem of experience—experience, that is, of all types. This feeling of purpose cannot, unless the universe is quite meaningless, be without significance. It is a faculty with which we are endowed "which must find a status and an outlet in the solution"[3] of the problem. There must, therefore, be a solution in the sense in which the discovery of an objective real or end to which the purpose impels us would be a solution. This is not to mould truth to our own nature; it is rather to insist "that the problem of truth can only spring from a desire for truth which is in our nature."[4]

In other words, the feeling of inner conviction which assures us that there is a purpose and a reality beyond carries its own sanction with it. This sanction extends even to the assurance of personality as the form of the reality of which we are convinced. It warrants, in fact, the validity of our sense of and longing for God. "In a yearning towards God the soul grows upward and finds the fulfilment of something implanted in its nature. The sanction for this development is within us, a striving born with our consciousness or an Inner Light proceeding from a greater power than ours."[5]

A number of quotations could be cited in support of this view of the real world, whether conceived as value or personality, as an independent objective real known to

[1] Eddington, *The Nature of the Physical World*, p. 335. [2] Ibid., p. 328.
[3] Ibid., p. 328. [4] Ibid., p. 328. [5] Ibid., p. 327.

consciousness but not owing its being to the consciousness that knows it; for example, our "deeper feelings are not of ourselves alone, but are glimpses of a reality transcending the narrow limits of our particular consciousness,"[1] or the comparison already quoted between our sense of reality and the experience of 'seeing a joke,' an experience which is said to be "a not unfair analogy for our mystical feeling for nature; and I would venture even to apply it to our mystical experience of God."[2] Now nobody supposes that one is or is even continuous with the joke which one sees.

But this view of the independent and objective character of reality is by no means always maintained. Frequently Professor Eddington adopts a more subjective attitude, according to which the underlying world of spirit is part of and continuous with our own spirit, and lapses at times into a complete subjectivism which represents it as a projection of our own minds. Consciousness, that is to say our own consciousness, we have already seen in Professor Eddington's view to be continuous with the background in which the world of science is embedded. This background is specifically stated to be the abiding place of value; hence it is with value that our consciousness is continuous. "If values . . . are absolute, they must belong to the background, unrecognized in physics . . . but recognized by consciousness which has its roots in the background."[3] And by saying that it "has its roots in the background," Professor Eddington means that our consciousness belongs to it—belongs to it, moreover, in just the same sense as the universal mind or spirit, the existence of which Professor Eddington believes in the light of modern physics to be at least a plausible hypothesis, belongs to it. "In this background we must find first, our own personality, and then perhaps a greater personality." For "The idea of a universal Mind or Logos would be, I think, a fairly plausible inference from the present state of

[1] Eddington, *The Nature of the Physical World*, p. 321.

[2] Ibid., p. 322.

[3] Ibid., p. 330.

scientific theory."[1] And this "World Spirit we must be able to approach in the midst of our cares and duties in that simpler relation of spirit to spirit in which all true religion finds expression."[2]

Thus, instead of being something which, although known by us, is completely other than we who know it, the 'real' is now represented as something fundamentally continuous with our spiritual natures. It is both "a greater personality" and a universal spirit, from which both our own personalities and the greater personality take their rise and to which they still belong.

But traces of yet a third attitude may be detected; for Professor Eddington sometimes speaks as if value, which is an integral part of the underlying background, were a creation or projection of our own minds. "So far as broader characteristics are concerned," he says, "we see in Nature what we look for or are equipped to look for,"[3] from which the further assertions, "we have to build the spiritual world out of symbols taken from our own personality,"[4] and "in the mystical feeling the truth is apprehended from within and is, as it should be, a part of ourselves,"[5] follow naturally.

And this suggestion that mystical truth, which assuredly must be reckoned part of the background, is not a reality external to ourselves with which our minds may establish contact, but resides within us, is reinforced by a remarkable passage wherein that which we seek to denote by such words as 'value' and 'significance' is spoken of as if, devoid of independent and objective reality, it were projected into a valueless and non-significant world by the minds that conceive it. In this passage Professor Eddington is considering what is meant by such common expressions as those which attribute gaiety and gladness to nature on a spring morning. Such attributes, he points out, are obviously not 'there' in

[1] Eddington, *The Nature of the Physical World*, p. 338. [2] Ibid., p. 338.
[3] Ibid., p. 330. [4] Ibid., p. 337. [5] Ibid., p. 321.

nature, but are in our minds. "When we think of the sparkling waves as moved with laughter, we are," he says, "evidently attributing a significance to the scene which was not there."[1] He then proceeds to point out in respect of the physical characteristics of the scene, that they, too, are not 'there'; they are put 'there' by the mind. The same conclusion is then applied to the so-called mystical attributes, that is, to significance and the aesthetic value we seem to find in nature. These do not really belong to nature; like the emotional and physical properties of the scene, they are imputed to it by our own minds. "The physical no less than the mystical significance of the scene is not there; it is *here* in the mind."[2] If we ask, 'What, then, really is *there*?' the answer seems to be, "the physical elements of the water—the scurrying electric charges"[3] that is the world of the physicist, and these are assuredly "guiltless of any intention to convey the impression that they were happy."[4] But if "mystical truth" and "mystical significance" are in ourselves, if we see in nature the beauty that "we are equipped to look for,"[5] it seems difficult to resist the conclusion that all those other aspects, under which we are asked by Professor Eddington to conceive the underlying reality, "mind stuff" and "personality" and "value," are really mind created, and that the conception of the underlying reality itself has been put by the mind into a universe that "is guiltless of any intention to convey the impression" that it is either significant or personal.

Recurring traces of each of these three attitudes to the underlying world, the attitudes which represent it respectively as separate and objectively real, as continuous with our own consciousness, and as a product or creation of our minds which somehow project it into a non-significant world, may be found in Professor Eddington's final chapters.

[1] Eddington, *The Nature of the Physical World*, p. 329.
[2] Ibid., p. 329.
[3] Ibid., p. 329.
[4] Ibid., p. 329.
[5] Ibid., p. 330.

The last implies a frank subjectivism which I do not suppose that he would for a moment be prepared to accept; nor do I think that he would have stated his view in this way, if he had realized what its implications were. The reason why, as I think, he does continually slip into this subjectivist attitude to reality is to be found in the very real difficulty of maintaining any intermediate position between a thorough-going realism and an extreme subjectivism. Either mind explores or it creates; and, once you concede to it the creative faculty, it is exceedingly difficult to assign limits to its exercise.

I have now to the best of my ability summarized the various lines of thought which may be detected in the works of modern scientists, pointing in the direction of the first of the two metaphysical alternatives cited at the beginning of this chapter, that, namely, which represents the worlds of sense and of science as phenomenal aspects of an underlying reality, which is a mental unity. In the next chapter I shall offer some criticisms of this conception, and of the arguments by which it is supported. I shall then consider the second metaphysical alternative, which I shall endeavour to advocate.

CHAPTER IX

CRITICISM OF THE CONCEPTIONS OF REALITY SPONSORED BY MODERN SCIENCE

In the last chapter I indicated what appeared to me to be the minimum conclusion with regard to metaphysical questions which the developments in modern science might be held to justify. This minimum conclusion I ventured to call the "all-fours" attitude to various types of experience, an attitude which refused to claim for scientific research an exclusive or even privileged position as a means of obtaining knowledge about the universe. There was, I suggested, a fairly large measure of common agreement with regard to this minimum conclusion, and scientists themselves are increasingly willing to concede that other forms of experience, in particular those of the artist and the mystic, are legitimate avenues of approach to a knowledge of reality. Many, I pointed out, go further, and are inclined to suggest that the nature of reality is more truly revealed in artistic and religious experience than by the slow, groping methods of the scientist, which acquaint us merely with phenomenal aspects of it. This view led to the formulation of the hypothesis that I designated A, namely, that reality is a unity, in all probability a mental unity, different aspects of which are known in different types of experience.

I endeavoured in the last chapter to elaborate this view in the form in which it has been put forward by modern scientists, and considered some of the reasons advanced in its favour. I pointed out, however, that it was by no means the only metaphysical possibility, but that there was an alternative view of the nature of reality, which I called hypothesis B, which would be equally compatible with the conclusions reached by modern science.

I do not wish to suggest that these alternatives exhaust

the possibilities. I cited them because they were in the nature of extreme views constituting limits within which other hypotheses, which are for the most part variations of A and B, would naturally fall. The alternative view was to the effect that reality was or contained a number of different orders or realms, and that the difference between various types of experience, between the experiences, for example, of the scientist, the ordinary man, the artist and the saint, was to be interpreted in terms of the different orders or realms of which in each type of experience the knower was aware.

These two alternative hypotheses constitute, it is obvious, one way of stating the two metaphysical views according to which the universe is either a unity or a manifold, and the difference between the hypotheses is ultimately the difference between monism and pluralism. The second or pluralistic hypothesis is the one which seems to me on the whole to offer the fewest difficulties, and I shall in the next chapter endeavour to relate it to the particular questions discussed in this book. In the present chapter I shall try to point out the difficulties to which the former alternative, in so far as it is suggested or thought to be suggested by the conclusions of modern science, is exposed and the reasons why I find it unacceptable. I propose, then, to examine the contentions summarized in the last chapter, purporting to show that reality is a unity, that this unity is or contains value, that it is probably mental, that the worlds of science and of sense are phenomenal aspects of it, and that, when we know it, the subject-object relation is transcended.

The objections which I wish to raise to these contentions fall under two main heads. (I) From the side of the object they involve an inadmissible conception of degrees of reality. (II) From the side of the subject they involve an inadmissible conception of different faculties or ways of knowing, and in particular of a special intuitive faculty.

I. Criticism of the Concept of Degrees of Reality

That the conception of degrees of reality is involved by the hypothesis outlined in the last chapter is, I think, fairly clear. Reality is said to be a unity; it is also variously spoken of as thought, as mind stuff, as deity, or as value. Now it is clear that the world of science and the world of sense, whatever may be the true analysis of them, do not appear to be any of these things. Why, then, is it that they appear as they do? Three different answers may be given to this question. We may say (*a*) that they are created by the mind of the observer; (*b*) that they are equally real with and exist, as it were, side by side with the reality which is thought, mind stuff, deity, or value; or (*c*) that they are phenomenal aspects of reality, or ways in which reality appears to the knowing mind.

Now it is, I think, clear that Professor Eddington and Sir James Jeans do not adopt either of the two former alternatives, although the language used by both writers in unguarded moments frequently suggests the first of them. What they really believe is the third. The worlds of sense and of science are not, on this view, quite real in the sense of being features of the universe as it is independently of the knowing mind; nor are they unreal in the sense of being merely subjective creations of the knowing mind. Hence they are accorded a position as quasi-reals, a position which proclaims their status as neither subjective nor objective, but as emergents upon or functions of a complex in which both reality and the knowing mind are ingredients. They are more real than subjective illusions; less real than the mental unity which underlies them. There can, I think, be no reasonable doubt that the language so frequently used about both worlds, and about the world of science in particular, by both Professor Eddington and Sir James Jeans, which represents them as selections or abstractions from reality, does suggest this somewhat equivocal status.

Now I am unable myself to attach any meaning to the conception of degrees of reality. That there should be different orders or realms of reality, in the sense of a number of different departments of the universe the constituents of which though irreducibly different are nevertheless all real and equally real, I can comprehend. But that of two things which exist one should be more real than the other is to me a meaningless conception. Either, I should say, a thing exists, or it does not. If it does, it is real, and nothing can be more or less real than it is. Nor, I think, is there much difficulty in showing that the arguments which are brought forward to show that the worlds of science and of sense own a lower degree of reality than something else are in fact fallacious. To the consideration of these arguments I now turn.

1. *The Limitations of Scientific Method.*—I do not propose to discuss in detail all the different arguments to which reference was made in the last chapters, which, basing themselves upon the alleged nature of scientific method, purport to show that science does not give us information about the reality of things. The objection which I wish to raise to these different arguments is in essence the same objection, but it requires to be stated somewhat differently according to the way in which the criticism of scientific method is itself stated.

A number of different contentions with regard to the nature and limits of scientific knowledge were summarized in the last chapter. There was the contention (*a*) that science cannot give an account of wholes; (*b*) that it cannot give an account of individuality; (*c*) that it cannot give an account of conscious process, and in particular of the conscious processes of human minds; (*d*) that it cannot give an account of significance or value, and the objection assumes a slightly different form in its application to each contention.

(*a*) and (*b*) The statement that science cannot give an account of wholes or of individuality is, I am prepared to assume, correct. I do not wish positively either to assert or to deny that it is correct, but it seems to me quite possible that it is. It is, in other words, possible that the suggestion that, when the biologist sets out to give an account of, say, a living organism, there is something which evades his treatment, and that his account is therefore deficient in respect of this something, is true. It may also be true that this something is both individual and a whole, although the senses in which these words are used are so many and so ambiguous that I am not by any means sure that I know what is meant by them. But from this fact, if it is a fact, I am unable to see that it follows that that of which science does give an account is not real, or that the account which science gives of it is not true, and, so far as I can see, not the faintest reason is adduced for supposing that it does follow. That there is a sense in which some wholes are more than the sum of their parts is, I am inclined to think, true. But this does not constitute a reason for thinking that the parts of such wholes are not real or are not truly their parts. If the whole is really a whole and not a blank unity, it must have parts which it is not a fiction to treat as parts, and, therefore, as possessing reality independently of their position in the whole.

A man is admittedly more than a collection of 'pipes and tubes'; but he undoubtedly is a collection of 'pipes and tubes,' and I cannot see why the account which physiologists give of his body in terms of them should be suspect merely because it is not complete. I am aware that arguments have been brought forward by philosophers to show that the parts of what is called an organic whole are different entities in respect of their position as parts of the whole from what they are when taken in isolation. It is beside my present purpose to discuss these arguments; it is sufficient to point out that, whether they are valid or not, the parts taken in isolation are admittedly something—nobody, so far as I know, holds that an eye or a lung cannot be abstracted from the body and considered by itself—and that it is, therefore, presumably permissible to describe them in isolation and possible to describe them truly. The resulting description will, then, apply to something which undoubtedly is, and there is no reason why the information which it gives about this 'something' should not be true. Also it may be important.

In this connection it is pertinent to point out that the category of 'importance' is a subjective category. There is, so far as I can see, no reason to suppose that what we happen to think important should for that reason be conceded a fuller title to reality than that to which we are indifferent, or that knowledge of unimportant things is less properly described as knowledge or is less true than knowledge of important ones. The fact that a book which is universally regarded as of great literary value happens to run to three hundred and seventy-nine pages is as much a fact about the book as the fact that the contents are a landmark in the history of literature. Admittedly the fact is only one among many; admittedly, too, it may justifiably be regarded as an abstraction from the total number of facts which are facts about the book. Moreover, the mind which attends to this fact to the exclusion of the rest is admittedly selective and arbitrarily selective. But no one of these considerations, each of which is undoubtedly true, affords any reason for supposing that the fact is not a fact or that the mind cannot truly know it. It is, indeed, difficult in the light of the facts which biology has accumulated indicative of our recent emergence and brief history in the life of the planet to hold that what appears important to the mind of a twentieth-century adult is therefore more real than what appeared important to his Paleolithic predecessor or will appear important to his remote descendant. To equate 'importance,' in the sense in which 'importance' means important to us, with reality is a feat of parochialism which the most cursory acquaintance with the facts of evolution should by now have rendered impossible.

I turn from the question of 'importance' to the related question of individuality. The connection between these two questions is close. Arguments were summarized in the last chapter to the effect that the classifying method of science precludes it from penetrating through to the individuality of things. One of the implications of this argument was that, since the individuality of a thing is what really matters or is really important, the information which science gives us is not the most important kind of information. The further implication was then slipped in that, since what matters or 'is important' was *ipso facto* more real than what does not, science, in virtue of its inability to give an account of the individuality of things, was unable also to give an account of their reality. Even, however, if we admit the two premises that science cannot deal with or give an account of individuality, and that the individuality of things is their most important attribute, the conclusion does not seem to follow. I have already pointed out that there is no ground for supposing that because we happen to think a thing important, it is therefore 'more real' than what we do not think important. To insist that it is, is to adopt a view which is indistinguishable from Pragmatism, and, unless we are prepared to defend the pragmatic point of view throughout —and, so far as I can see, writers like Sir James Jeans and Professor Eddington show no disposition to do this—we are not entitled to base any conclusion touching the reality or non-reality of the world studied by science upon the fact that the individuality of things is lacking from it.

But is there, in any event, any substance in the suggestion that the individuality of things is necessarily more important than their common aspects? Importance, as I have pointed out, is a purely 'subjective' concept, and is not therefore appropriately to be invoked as a criterion of reality. But even by the purely subjective standard of what is important to us, there is, so far as I can see, no ground for stigmatizing the scientist's world as not fully real, because it is in some sense not 'important.' It should not be forgotten that it is by emphasizing common elements for purposes of classification and ignoring individual differences that science has achieved its results. It is a commonplace that these results have changed and in countless ways improved human lives. By means of the discoveries of science our lives have been made brighter and healthier; they are less exposed to pain, less subject to fear. It is, therefore, at least arguable that the common characteristics of things to which science pays attention are at least as "important" as that in what their individuality consists. It may even be urged that the features which a guinea-pig's brain possesses in common with a human brain, by studying which we have been able to locate the origin of cerebral lesions in human brains, are *more* 'important' than the guinea-pig's individuality.

I know of no reason why this sense in which I have just used the word 'important,' according to which whatever improves the conditions of human life is 'important,' should not be regarded as equally valid with any other. If, therefore, the arguments summarized in the last chapter suggest, as at times they seem to do, that the property of being "important" or "mattering" confers a title to reality upon that which has it, it is pertinent to point out that those common characteristics of things with which science is concerned are in certain instances just as "important" as the wholes and individualities with which, according to the arguments in question, it is not competent to deal.

I do not propose to dwell further on the arguments which are based upon the scientific treatment or lack of treatment of "wholes" and "individualities," because they presuppose and illustrate a position which is familiar in the history of philosophy. This is the position that reality is in some sense a whole and in some sense individual; that wholes are, therefore, more real than their parts, and that the reality of a thing consists in its individuality. It follows that knowledge of parts is not knowledge of reality, since the parts when abstracted from the wholes to which they belong, are not truly real. Individuality, moreover, is regarded as a characteristic of wholes and only of wholes, and the conclusion is, therefore, drawn that no knowledge which is not knowledge of a whole can give us information about reality. What, among other things, this position entails is the axiom of internal relations. The considerations which I have just urged, that parts are real independently of the wholes to which they belong, that it is not, therefore, misleading to consider them as parts, that the common characters of things really are their characters, and that knowledge of parts and of common characters may, therefore, be true knowledge of reality, presuppose that this axiom is invalid; they presuppose, that is to say, that relations are external to their terms, and that the nature of the terms is not, therefore, affected by their relations to other terms. This is not the place in which to argue this issue afresh, even if I had any new considerations to bring to bear upon it. I content myself, therefore, with pointing out that it is only if Hegel's philosophy, or some philosophy like Hegel's, is true, that these particular criticisms of scientific method have weight. If, however, reality is not of the character which Hegel supposed, then there is no reason, so far at least as these particular arguments are concerned, why we should not hold that scientific knowledge may give us information about the real nature of things.

(*c*) The view that science is unable to give an account of conscious process was not among those actually described in the last chapter. I there summarized some of the reasons which are given for supposing that 'personality' must elude scientific treatment, and that science is unable to grasp the nature of the living organism. Both these contentions appear to me to raise the same point, and it is one which can be most conveniently discussed in relation to the nature of consciousness. What I have to say on the subject of scientific method in its relation to conscious process may, therefore, be applied *mutatis mutandis* to 'personality,' and to the living organism. The consideration I wish to advance is not essentially different from the arguments of (*a*) and (*b*). So far as the actual process of consciousness is concerned, I am prepared to concede that it cannot be known and described by scientific method, and this for the reason that it cannot be known at all. Conscious process consists, in my view, of a continuously exercized awareness, this awareness being, as I suggested in Chapter VII, the unique and peculiar form of mind's relation to what it knows. The only way in which this process of conscious awareness can be comprehended is, to use a phrase of Bergson's, by being "lived through."

Now you cannot, I should say, present the activity of the experiencing subject to the subject that experiences, just because it is the nature of the subject to experience and not to be experienced. It follows that the experiencing of the subject, that is to say, whatever the subject experiences as thinking subject, must be different from anything that the subject can experience as object. As James Ward says somewhere, you cannot see your own seeing, although you can realize what you see.

It is, of course, perfectly true that we can know our own thoughts, know them, that is to say, in the sense in which to know is to contemplate. But our thoughts as contemplated are different from our thinkings, that is from those acts of awareness which form the actual stuff of our experience. The acts of awareness cannot themselves be thought about, for the reason that they possess a unique characteristic as experiencing subjects, which is lost so soon as they are converted into the objects of fresh acts of experience. Thus we can never know what thinking is like, in the sense of being able to describe it, although all of us know in our own experience what thinking is.

The act of thinking is from this point of view only a

special case of the act of living, i.e. it is the awareness of a special type of object. What is true of it is true of living, which is the being aware of any type of object. Life, in other words, is realized in experience, and experience can only be lived through; it cannot be known. We can only speak of it in so far as we know it, and in knowing it, in making of it, that is to say, an object of experience, we falsify its character as experience itself.

But in saying that experience can be lived through by a subject, but not known as an object, I have mentioned only one of the reasons which preclude us from giving an account of it. A second and not less important reason is that experience is continually changing. The considerations emphasized by Bergson in his celebrated account of the nature of change are primarily derived from an examination of the nature of living process. Bergson affirms that "we change without ceasing, and the state itself is nothing but change."[1] "There is no feeling, no idea, no volition which is not undergoing change at every moment; if a mental state ceased to vary, its duration would cease to flow."[2]

This conclusion, that living process is only change, carries with it the corollary that there is nothing which changes, or, in other words, that there is nothing to change, since, in postulating such a something, we should be admitting the existence of something other than change. What is true of any internal state which the 'ego' may be supposed to possess is true also of the 'ego' itself. The human mind is not an entity to which things occur; it is a stream of dynamic activity, of which the only thing we can with certainty affirm is that at every moment the stream is different. If this is in fact the nature of living and also of thinking process, it follows that no account can be given of what living or thinking is like. In order that a thing may be described, it is necessary, as Plato pointed out, that it should for a definite period *be*, that it should in fact *be* itself. Now a thing is not

[1] Bergson, *Creative Evolution*, p. 2. [2] Ibid.

itself if it is continually in process of becoming something else, for the reason that it is not at any given moment anything at all. Hence a process of "becoming," which is a true "becoming," evades description. Now living, that is, the actual experience of being alive, if Bergson is right, and I think that he is, is essentially a process of becoming. For this reason all attempts to describe the experience which we have of living must of necessity falsify it, freezing what is a process of flow into a temporary immobility, and holding it fixed for the purpose of examination and description. For these reasons psychology, in so far as it seeks to give an account of the actual process of consciousness as lived through, is unlikely to be successful.

But it does not, therefore, follow that the object of psychology is non-existent, or that the information which psychology obtains is not information about something. All that has been shown is that the object of psychological investigation, when psychologists explore and describe the nature of living process, and—I should be prepared to add—the object of philosophical thought when philosophers reflect upon the nature of self-consciousness and its implications, is in each case different from the actual experience which is lived through. Life as thought about, in fact, is different from life as lived. But it does not follow that what is studied is not therefore real, or that a true description may not be given of it; it does not follow, in other words, that psychology is necessarily fiction. Psychology is clearly about something, and there seems to be no reason to deny to that something existence merely because it turns out on analysis to be other than the living experience which purports to be the object.

It is beyond my immediate purpose to discuss the nature of the object of the psychological sciences; it is sufficient to emphasize that it exists, yet is other than that experience of living which, in some of its aspects, we call the process of consciousness, so that arguments of the type summarized in the last chapter, which purport to show that science can give no account of conscious process or living experience, afford no reason for supposing that it does not therefore tell us, and may not on occasion tell us truly, about the nature of what independently *is*. It may not, however, be out of place to add, in order to bring this discussion into line with that of Chapter VII, that the objects with which psychology is concerned are, in my view, to be appropriately regarded as members of that realm of subsistence in which, I have suggested, scientific objects should be placed. If this view is right, the relation of conscious living process as lived through to the objects of psychological research as subsequently studied would be similar to, if not the same as that which, I suggested, holds between sense data and physical objects. It would, that is to say, be one of the functions of conscious experience as lived through to direct the mind's awareness upon the stream of images, desires, sensations which the psychologist studies, just as it is the function of sense data to turn 'the eye of the mind' to physical objects. I do not want here to pursue or to defend the view. I mention it only as an illustration of one of the ways in which it seems to me to be possible, while conceding that science is unable to give an account of conscious process as lived through, to affirm, nevertheless, that it does give us information about something to which there seems to be no reason to deny a full title to reality.

(*d*) (i) The arguments which are brought forward to show that science is unable to give any account of value or significance raise a similar point. That these arguments are correct in what they assert nobody would, I think, wish to deny; what is open to question is the deduction which appears to be based on their assertion. What is, I think, clear is that the accounts which physicists and physiologists give of the various physical and physiological processes which take place whenever there is aesthetic appreciation of, say, a piece of music, give no information about the significance of the piece of music or of that consciousness of, its significance, to which we give the name of 'aesthetic appreciation.' As Dean Inge has epigrammatically remarked, nobody would be prepared to accept the statement, "Mr. So-and-So is only dragging the tail of a dead horse across the entrails of a dead cat," as an adequate account of the performance of a violinist rendering an unaccompanied violin sonata of Bach. We may therefore accept it as a matter of common agreement that a description of the conditions which must be satisfied, and of the processes which must take place before aesthetic appreciation occurs, is not a description of aesthetic appreciation or of that for which it is felt.

Does it therefore follow that the processes in question do not occur, or that the description does not truly describe them? I cannot see that it does, or even that any reason is given for supposing that it does. Science, it is agreed, catalogues only those qualities and processes which, admittedly necessary to the occurrence of aesthetic appreciation, possess properties in common with processes which result in no such appreciation, and the properties in question are admittedly not those which interest us. But, as I pointed out above, the fact that they do not interest us, at any rate as persons desirous of understanding the nature of aesthetic satisfaction, does not afford any presumption for supposing that they are not real. I should conclude, therefore, that from the fact that science gives no account of aesthetic significance or value, it does not follow that when it describes the physical processes which condition its occurrence and the physiological processes which condition our consciousness of it, science may not truly acquaint us with the nature of what is.

(*d*) (ii) Moreover, the arguments summarized in the last chapter overlook what appears to me to be an important consideration. The position these arguments are designed to support is that reality is a unity, that aesthetic value is one important aspect of it, but that the familiar world and the world of science are mental abstractions or constructions. Value, it is implied, is therefore independently real in some sense in which the familiar world is not. The argument presupposes the validity of contemporary physicists' attitude to the familiar world as an abstraction from the real world made by mind and dependent upon mind, and it undoubtedly implies that the being of the familiar world, as also of the scientific world, is of a lower order than that of the world of value.

The conception of degrees of reality is one to which I personally am unable to attach any meaning. I do not wish to suggest that philosophers who employ it do not mean something by it; merely that I have never been able to understand what it is that they mean. Although, however, the conception undoubtedly implies that different objects may exist at different levels or own different degrees of reality, it does not, I think, include the view that the *same* object may have properties which are at such different levels or own such different degrees. The degree of reality which attaches to any particular object must, that is to say, so far as I can see, attach to all its properties.

In the case of aesthetic appreciation, that which possesses the property of significance or has value is a work of art. A work of art, for example a picture, is, from the point of view of physical science, a collection of material particles. If these, for reasons which are by now familiar, are denied full title to reality, then their properties or qualities must equally be regarded as to that extent and in that degree not wholly real. It would follow, therefore, that the property in virtue of which they have 'value' or 'significance' cannot itself be fully real. It does not seem, therefore, that those who avail themselves of arguments to show that the objects of the familiar world are phenomenal appearances or abstractions, are entitled to exempt those qualities of an object, in which its value or significance resides, from the scope of their arguments. Pictures are objects belonging to the familiar world; they may also be regarded as collections of particles, in which capacity they belong to the world of science, and, although that property of them in virtue of which we say that they possess value or significance may be related to a different *order* of reality from their colour or their materiality, it cannot *belong* to a different *level*. In particular, it cannot belong to a *higher* level of reality than the picture which possesses it.

I should affirm, then, that the admitted fact that science is unable to give an account of significance or value affords no reason for supposing that the scientist's world is not real. The scientist's account of the processes which condition aesthetic experience brings us, I should suggest, just as truly and just as directly into contact with reality as the experience itself; it happens, however, that the reality in regard to which it gives us information is not that which excites or in general even interests us.

Nevertheless, the fact that the apprehension of the object *as a whole* is an essential ingredient in aesthetic experience is not without its significance. The objects with which science brings us into touch are, I have argued, members not of the physical world, but of the world of subsistence. Scientific objects have therefore, in my view, characteristics in common with physical objects rather than with the sense data which are immediately apprehended in sensory experience. I have suggested that the apprehension of sense data directs the attention of the mind in some cases to the physical, in others to the scientific object. Hence to apprehend a picture as a whole and not merely as a collection of sense data, means to apprehend it as a physical object. The point is significant, for it may, I think, be plausibly argued that, just as it is the function of sensory experience to direct the mind's awareness upon subsistent objects, so it is or may be a function of the experience of subsistent objects to direct the mind's awareness upon objects of value. I shall endeavour to elaborate this suggestion in the next chapter.[1] For the present it is sufficient to point out that there is no reason to infer from the fact that the objects of aesthetic appreciation elude scientific treatment, that the objects with which science does concern itself are abstractions or constructions, and that science does not therefore bring us into touch with reality.

2. *Criticism of Scientists' Accounts of Value.*—I turn now to the metaphysical conception of value which is implied by the treatment of the subject outlined in the last chapter, a question which raises considerations of a rather different order. I wish to apply to this treatment the general criticism of the philosophical methods followed by modern physicists which I suggested in Chapter V. For the conception of value in the wide sense of the word which I defined at the beginning of Chapter VIII (see p. 186), which modern physics has sponsored, seems to me to be exposed to the same objections as the conception of reality as a unity criticized in Chapter IV. Let me briefly recall this criticism.

Many modern scientists suggest that the worlds both of science and of sense are in an important sense dependent upon consciousness. They are dependent upon consciousness whether they are more properly to be regarded as abstracted by consciousness from reality, as worked up by consciousness from a comparatively featureless flux, or as constructed by consciousness as a condition of their being known. Whichever view we take, they possess no title to be called real except such as is bestowed upon them by the categories of the abstracting or constructing mind. They are not, in other words, separate and independent factors of reality. Assuming this account of the origin of the scientist's world and the familiar world to be correct, what view, I asked, were we to take of the activity of the knowing mind. Two alternatives, I pointed out, seemed to be possible. Either reality is a featureless flux of events, and the mind's activity in constructing or abstracting from it the worlds of science and of

[1] Chapter X, pp. 278–279, 295, 299–300.

sense is free and unconstrained by any limiting feature in the given, or reality contains within itself the seeds of all the qualitative distinctions which subsequently appear, and the mind's activity is limited to working up the features which it finds. On the first hypothesis it seemed difficult to understand why mind, free to create the familiar world as it pleased, created it as it did; on the second, there seemed to be no reason why we should deny the worlds of science and of sense full title to reality, since reality is qualitatively differentiated from the outset by all the features which these worlds are found to contain.

It is precisely this same criticism that I wish to apply to the particular conception of value, whether conceived as personality, as deity, as beauty, or as a mental unity which may or may not be identified with personality or deity, which is suggested explicitly or implicitly in the writings of modern physicists. And the criticism takes the form of asking on what principle we are to distinguish between the nature of the mind's activity when it knows the familiar world and the world of science, and the nature of its activity when it enjoys aesthetic satisfaction or is conscious of moral obligation. If the former activity is construction or abstraction, what right have we to assign 'limits' to the exercise of the mind's constructive and abstractive capacities and regard the latter as merely exploratory? If the latter activity merely discovers a world to which it does not contribute, why should we suppose that the former creates its objects out of a featureless medium?

The view that mind is throughout constructive seems to me to be untenable. It requires us to suppose that the element which in religious and aesthetic experience we value, and which endows these experiences, the one with its peculiar significance, the other with its peculiar charm, is merely a projection of our own consciousness. It presupposes, that is to say, that our feelings and aspirations are limited by necessarily human values, values bound up with the life and development of the human race. The mind, on this view, has no power to transcend these limitations. Upon the triviality of the implications of this view and upon its prejudicial effect upon that character of value which, for most of us, endows our lives with significance, I shall comment in the next chapter. For the present I am concerned merely to point out that this purely human conception of value really *is* one of its implications, and to note the difficulties to which, in virtue of this implication, it is exposed. Three in particular may be mentioned.

(i) If value is in fact a mental construction or projection, if mind creates it, as it were, without let or hindrance from a featureless reality, why do we not create more of it than we do? Aesthetic satisfaction is, perhaps, the most delightful experience that life has to offer. Why then, if the objects which cause us to feel it are such as we ourselves have made, do we not choose to have more of them and it?

Again, religious experience is one of the most precious, albeit one of the rarest, privileges of the human spirit. Is it really conceivable that the mystics who endured the agonies of "the dark night of the soul" because they believed God to have withdrawn Himself from them, would not have summoned Him back if, being a projection of their own consciousnesses, He had in fact been summonable at will? Nobody, so far as I am aware, has ever suggested what, if value be something which is born of our own consciousness, are the conditions which determine its birth, or why we should sometimes deliver ourselves of it and at other times so unaccountably fail.

(ii) A similar difficulty arises in connection with the objects in which value is presumed to reside. When all allowance is made for variations of aesthetic taste, variations from age to age, from place to place, from civilization to civilization and from individual to individual, it would, I think, be generally conceded that some objects may justifiably afford an appropriate occasion for the passing of aesthetic judgments, in a sense in which others do not. What particular objects these objects may be is a matter of doubt and controversy. But that a sonnet may be truly made the object of aesthetic judgment in a sense in which a government blue book cannot, and that the noise of a symphony may be beautiful in a sense in which the noise of a committee meeting can never be beautiful, would, I think, be generally admitted. The point I am making is not that some professedly aesthetic objects succeed in being beautiful while others fail, but that it is only in regard to some objects that we are impelled to pass the judgment, which purports to determine whether they be beautiful or not. And, when all allowance is made for idiosyncrasies of taste, it is, I think, the case that we do regard certain classes of objects as potentially aesthetic, as constituting, that is to say, an occasion for the passing of aesthetic judgments, whether favourable or the reverse, while others are regarded as aesthetically neutral. If this be agreed, the question I wish to ask is, Why, if aesthetic value is a creation or projection of our minds, do we project it into some things rather than into others? Is it possible to resist the conclusion that there must be certain distinguishing marks or features in reality, in virtue of which we regard certain elements in it, and certain elements only, as being in the aesthetic sense potentially significant; that there must, in other words, be pegs upon which judgments of value may, as it were, be appropriately hung? If reality is a featureless flux, or an indistinguishable mind stuff, to be carved into shapes of value by the mind as it pleases, it seems impossible to explain why the mind should project beauty into some shapes and not into others, so that aesthetic value, which presents itself to us in paint and stone and metal and sound, does not appear clothed in the guise of pen and ink and paper. It is difficult, I say, not to infer that the difference between what is valuable and what is not is a fundamental distinction in reality itself, that value, therefore, is a factor of what is, a true inhabitant of an objective world, that some things accordingly possess it in a sense in which others do not, and that aesthetic experience is to be regarded as the process by means of which mind, in its exploration of the universe, discovers these things and proceeds to that enjoyment of them which we call aesthetic appreciation.

(iii) The view that value is created by the mind of the perceiver obscures the admitted distinction between imagination and perception. That there is a difference between the experience of conceiving a beautiful picture and that of seeing one, between imagining a lovely landscape and walking through it, is obvious. This difference is usually expressed by saying that in conception and imagination the mind creates its own objects; seeing pictures and contemplating a view we are in contact with objects other than ourselves. If, however, we assert that in the second class of case the objects which we view are projected by our own consciousness, it is difficult to see what the grounds for this admitted distinction can be. If we are to maintain that there is a distinction, we are, I think, driven to postulate that the value we enjoy in aesthetic experience is not the product of our own thinking. Personally I should go further and assert that the value of the picture we imagine is equally non-mental. The distinction between the value we imagine and the value we enjoy can, I think, be explained in terms of the differences between the objects upon which, in imagination and perception, the mind's awareness is respectively directed. I shall return to this point in the next chapter.

The objections to the view of value as purely subjective, which I have enumerated under (i), (ii) and (iii), would probably obtain fairly general agreement. Few are, I think, anxious to maintain the view that value is *merely* a projection of human consciousness. In particular I doubt whether the scientists whose theories I have summarized would be prepared to subscribe to it. The point of my criticism is that if the constructive activity with which they endow the mind in scientific knowledge and sense perception is really a function of the mind, they have no ground for resisting this view. If the mind imposes the features of the objects which we know, both in the sensory experience of the familiar world and in the investigation of the objects of the scientist's laboratory, by what right do we deny to it the exercise of this power of 'imposition,' when it enjoys the aesthetic experience which we assert to be the characteristic of our apprehension of beautiful things? The religious experiences of the saint and the mystic, as the prevalence of naturalistic and psychological accounts of the mystical experience plainly shows,[1] can be only too easily interpreted on subjectivist lines.

Nor is this subjectivist mode of interpretation lacking from the works of modern scientists. Although he contrasts the objectivity of the deliverances of the religious and aesthetic consciousness with the merely symbolic character of the physicist's world, and claims that a reality is somehow revealed to us in religious experience which is withheld from sensory experience and scientific knowledge, Professor Eddington is unable to prevent the subjectivity, which lurks in his attitude to knowledge as a whole, from infecting his interpretation of aesthetic enjoyment and mystical experience. I drew attention in the last chapter to the different conceptions which in various places he suggests of the relation of the mind to the underlying reality, and pointed out that in spite of his manifest desire to maintain that the latter is both objective and independent, he frequently lets drop unguarded expressions which suggest that its features are mind created and therefore mind dependent.[2]

I should like in particular to recall the passage from *The Nature of the Physical World* which enumerates the various elements in our enjoyment of sparkling waves on a sunny

[1] See especially *The Psychology of Religious Mysticism*, by James H. Leuba.

[2] See Chapter VIII, pp. 220–224.

day, and represents the different features of the scene as owing their origin to the mind of the perceiver. The account concludes with the following sentence: "The physical no less than the mystical significance of the scene is not there; it is *here* in the mind."[1] And this conception of "mystical significance" as "in the mind" follows, I think, inevitably from the general view of mind as contributing the features which it discerns in the world it knows. I can myself see no ground for postulating the occurrence of different types of knowing activity which vary with the different characters of the objects which are known. As I have already pointed out,[2] there seems to be agreement among many philosophers that the function of the mind in knowing is the same throughout. If, then, it is admitted that the mind, whether its activity be regarded as one of creation, of construction, or of the elaboration of rudimentary distinctions in the given, contributes the features of the worlds of science and of sense, it must, I feel, also be held responsible for those features in virtue of which we attribute to the world significance and value.

If, however, it is urged, in answer to the objections suggested above, that the reason why we do not enjoy more value and enjoy it more readily is *that we do not in fact create it for ourselves*, that the reason why some things have value while others have not is not that our minds arbitrarily project it here and not there, that the quality value, in a word, is discovered and not in any sense made, then there is no reason for refusing to make a similar assertion in regard to the qualities of scientific objects and the features of the familiar world.

I should myself accept this view. Value, I should say, is a real factor in the universe, and in aesthetic, in ethical and in religious experience we in various ways and degrees apprehend it. This view implies that the features of signifi-

[1] Eddington, *The Nature of the Physical World*, p. 329.
[2] See Chapter VII, p. 159.

cance which we discern in things are in fact really their features, and are in no sense dependent upon the mind that discerns them. But if this view be taken, there seems to be no ground for holding that the features of the given, which scientific research reveals and with which sensory experience acquaints us, are not equally 'there,' in which event the idealist implications of the views which I have discussed are erroneous.

II. Criticism of 'Faculty' View of Intuition

The views summarized in the last chapter presuppose the existence of a special faculty of intuitive or mystical insight, by means of which we apprehend the nature of reality as it really is. This faculty is regarded as sudden, penetrative and coercive; it carries immediate certainty and is explicitly and favourably contrasted with the slow and fallible study of the outward appearances of things by scientific method which, it is pointed out, is based ultimately upon the misleading experience derived from the senses. And the postulation of this faculty is at once the corollary and the presupposition of the view of the familiar world as in some sense unreal. On the one hand, the doubts concerning our common knowledge of the familiar world and the scientist's knowledge of the world of physics, at which I have glanced, prepare the way for the reception of what seems a higher wisdom; unless there is such higher wisdom, then, indeed, we have no certain knowledge of anything except perhaps ourselves. On the other hand, the assertion of a faculty by means of which this higher wisdom is obtained leads to, indeed it requires, the conception of a reality behind the worlds of appearance and utterly different in its nature from them. It is in the knowledge of this reality that the higher wisdom consists.

Common sense tells us that the familiar world exists and

is real; reason also tells us that in some sense the world of physics exists and is real. Any doubts which may be thrown upon the deliverances of reason and common sense in these respects would either be themselves suggested by reason or would be fundamentally non-rational. Instances of doubts suggested by reason are afforded by the arguments advanced by modern physicists for disbelieving in the objective reality of the worlds of science and of sense. I have tried to show that the reasons for these doubts are not more certain than the reasoned beliefs upon which they purport to throw suspicion, and that there is, therefore, so far as reason is concerned, no good ground for supposing that the science and sense worlds are not objectively real. If, therefore, their reality is to be successfully impugned, it must be in virtue of considerations of an entirely different and non-rational order.

Those who hold that reality is mental and is a unity, and that the worlds of science and of sense are appearances only, do, therefore, in the last resort, frequently invoke a faculty of a different order from reason, which assures them of these things. This is the intuitive faculty which, because it introduces us to reality of a higher order, is regarded as more worthy of respect than reason. Thus the view of reality as a unity underlying the worlds of appearance, and the belief that there is a special faculty by means of which the unity is known, logically imply each other.

This conception of a special intuitive faculty by means of which the fundamental nature of reality is known, and not only known but known to be different from the worlds of science and of sense, seems to me to be exposed to serious objections. Of these I will mention two, the first of which consists of several related objections.

(*a*) (i) The view that there are separate faculties or ways of knowing presupposes a conception of the mind not far removed from the old "faculty psychology," now very generally abandoned. If reality, which is, in fact, one, nevertheless appears to me under many different guises and aspects, the question arises, why does it so appear? It is difficult to avoid the answer, because it is by different faculties that it is known, the familiar world in sensory experience, the world of science by reason and the world of value by intuition. It is on these lines that, as we have seen, the question is actually answered by the scientists whose views I have summarized. But I cannot detect by introspection the operation of any such special faculty of 'intuiting,' which is other than an intellectual faculty of 'reasoning,' and other again than the faculty of 'sensing.' I can only discover an activity of knowing which makes me aware of different types of objects, and results in my having different experiences according to the nature of the objects upon which it is directed. I shall return to and elaborate this point in the next chapter.

(ii) Nor, I think, is it difficult to show that the opposition between intuition and reason, upon which those who advocate the view of intuition as a separate faculty set over against reality lay stress, is illusory. Against such opposition I should urge that all beliefs, both those which are usually called rational and those which are usually called intuitive, are formed as the result of that direct apprehension of reality for which apparently the advocates of this view wish to reserve the name of 'intuitive.' Intuition, I should hold, leads us to form views which reason subsequently confirms or rejects. But the confirmation is in the last resort brought about by agreement with other beliefs which are similarly intuitive in origin; the agreement is, moreover, itself intuitively perceived. This is not to say that reason is, as some of those who advocate the superior merits of intuition assert, a purely practical faculty, the product of evolution and incapable therefore of theoretical knowledge. Even in the purely abstract sphere of philosophical theory men frequently hold strong instinctive beliefs; from the fact that some of these are contradictory, it follows that some must be mistaken. Yet the fact that they are contradictory is established by reason which insists that beliefs shall be mutually compatible, and, when two of them conflict, endeavours to discover possible sources of error. Thus reason is a harmonizing and controlling force rather than a creative one; but in the exercise of its function of reconciliation and agreement, it can operate only within that framework of beliefs which intuition has constructed.

In the last event the distinction between intuition and reason appears to be one not of kind but of degree; all beliefs are reached by and founded upon intuition or insight; the demand that they shall be consistent no less than the perception that they are not is intuitive, and the process of harmonization which reason undertakes is effected as the result of an impulse which is again intuitive.

Reasoning, in other words, is merely the name we give to a series of linked intuitions each of which is seen to be self-evident. In the case of so-called intuitional beliefs the linking intuitions are left out. The point which I am making is not by any means a novel one. It is, indeed, a commonplace of textbooks on logic and need not be laboured here.

The intuitive character of the mind's apprehension of general propositions, for example, is generally conceded.

The intuitive character of the basis of induction and of the law of cause and effect can be shown by familiar methods.

It seems difficult in the light of these considerations to maintain an ultimate difference between an intellectual and an intuitive form of knowing. Yet it is precisely this difference that the theory of intuition as a special way of knowing reality, which reveals it to us under the aspect of value, presupposes.

(*b*) As I have already pointed out, most writers on theory of knowledge, however they conceive the relation of knowledge to its objects, maintain that this relation is the same in all types of knowing. Idealist philosophers, for example, hold that what is thought or judgeable is an inseparable content of the act of thinking or judging, in precisely the same way as what is sensed is an inseparable content of the act of sensory apprehension. They hold, in fact, some variant of the views (2) and (3) described at the beginning of Chapter VII.[1] The point which at the moment I am concerned to emphasize is that, whatever view they take of the knowledge relation, they maintain this view throughout. Similarly, those who take realist views and stress the independence of objects of consciousness maintain that the distinction between subject and object, which they regard as fundamental, characterizes all forms of cognitive experience. The writers on modern physics whose views I have described are, as we have seen, disposed to take an idealist view of theory of knowledge, and hold that the worlds of science and of sense are in some important respect dependent upon the minds of those who know them.

If, therefore, there are, as I believe and as is generally admitted, strong reasons for maintaining that the relation of consciousness to its objects is uniform, they ought to hold that the objects of the intuitional consciousness are similarly dependent upon the intuiting mind. I say 'dependent upon' because this is the most non-committal phrase that occurs to me to denote a relationship which is ill-defined and, as we have seen, variously described. In fact, however, this relation of mind 'dependence' is logically reducible, as I have tried to show, to a more extreme type of Idealism, in which the object which is dependent upon consciousness becomes an inseparable aspect of the consciousness upon which it depends. I should urge, then, as an objection to the view that there is a special faculty called intuition which immediately apprehends the characteristics of the real world, that in practice it is logically reducible to the view that the characteristics in question belong not to the world but to

[1] See pp. 156, 157.

the mind that intuits them. This, at least, seems to be the case where the view of the intuitive faculty as cognitive of reality as value is held in conjunction with a theory of knowledge, which gives an idealist account of the objects of scientific inquiry and sense experience.

If, on the other hand, the distinction of subject and object is maintained in regard to our knowledge of the worlds of science and of sense, there is no ground for supposing it to be transcended in aesthetic or religious experience. That the distinction is in fact transcended in the view of those who regard the ultimate nature of reality from the standpoint of the mystic is common knowledge, and I have given quotations to show that this view is in fact shared by Sir James Jeans and Professor Eddington. They hold, I think, although they do not clearly state, that the knowledge of the reality which underlies the world of appearance is a process in which mind becomes one with its object. Moreover, it is, as I have pointed out, an alleged characteristic of the intuitive way of knowing, upon which both lay stress, that it "seizes its object from within" and places itself "within an object in order to coincide with what is unique in it and therefore inexpressible."[1]

That Professor Eddington, at least, endorses this view, his insistence on self-knowledge and self-consciousness as the key to an understanding of the "underlying background," affords, I think, a strong presumption. For self-consciousness is regarded as the outstanding example of an identity between subject and object, which transcends and precedes the difference which is subsequently distinguished, and any form of knowledge which is conceived after the model of self-consciousness must bear witness to a similar identity. The implications of this view in their bearing upon a universe which bases itself upon the discoveries of modern physics are somewhat disconcerting.

However modern physicists may define the relation

[1] Bergson, *Introduction to Metaphysics*, p. 6.

between mind and the objects of its inquiry—and they define it, as we have seen, very variously—they do not, as far as I can see, at any time wish to suggest that it is one of complete fusion. Professor Eddington and Sir James Jeans, however they may stress the character of the objects of the scientific consciousness as symbolic or abstracted or constructed, do not at any point seem to assert that the mind *is* the atoms and electrons whose existence science asserts. There is, in other words, nowhere in their works any suggestion that by continued study of atoms and electrons one becomes oneself electric or even like electricity.

A similar point arises in connection with our knowledge of the familiar world. Even those who take an idealist view of perception, maintaining that the objects of everyday experience are aspects of the consciousness of the perceiver, do not, I think, wish to maintain that they *are* or *are identical with* the consciousness of the perceiver. Nor, so far as I can see, is there any disposition to hold this view in regard to aesthetic value. It is not, so far as I am aware, usually maintained that, when I appreciate a Beethoven quartet, I do in any sense become it, still less that the greater the aesthetic merit of the work of art the more irresistibly does it tempt me to transcend myself, and, entering into communion with it, become other than myself.

Yet it is precisely this that appears to be affirmed with regard to the knowledge of reality in religious and mystical experience by the intuitive consciousness. If such expressions as "fused with" or "merged in," "become one with," mean anything at all, they must, I think, mean that the experience of knowing reality is one in which the subject-object distinction is transcended and the knower becomes one with what is known. Yet this, surely, is a remarkable circumstance, that after behaving in one way when I know familiar objects, study science or appreciate beauty in a work of art, I begin to believe in an entirely different way when I enjoy religious experience, so that ceasing to be myself I become one with what I know.

For such a drastic change in the knowledge relationship some reasons should, I think, be given more cogent than the reasons which are actually brought forward. For it is difficult to see that any reasons are in fact brought forward for such a conclusion except such as are susceptible of analysis in terms of rationalization or wish fulfilment.

To conceive the universe as fundamentally of the same nature as our own spirits, to conceive it further as capable of fusion with us, is, I cannot help feeling, to give to our natures a cosmic importance which may be justified, but which no reasons are given for thinking to be justified.

The questions raised by this issue are more germane to the subject of the final chapter, and I do not wish to pursue them further here.

I find it difficult, however, to conclude this chapter without entering a protest against the implications of this view of reality conceived as value, which represents it as capable of becoming one with the apprehension of it. It seems to me that an object is worthy of reverence not because of its kinship with, but because of its difference from, myself. I believe that in aesthetic and mystical experience the mind is brought into contact with an extra-human reality, but that the contact remains that of knower and known. To go further and to insist that the mind is continuous, or even that it becomes one with that which it knows, would by implication degrade the object by infecting it with the partialities and imperfections of the subject. This view quickly degenerates in practice into an anthropomorphism which, by interpreting religious experience as an extension of the self in continuity or community of being with the not-self, imposes the nature of the self upon the not-self, and so limits our hopes and aspirations to what are, in the long run, purely human values.

I do not wish to suggest that a view is necessarily untrue

because it degrades the universe. But if the idealist attitude to reality, which modern science is held to support, does in fact, as I believe and in the last chapter shall try to show, encourage this view, then it would be idle to deny the satisfaction which one derives from the conviction not only that this attitude is itself mistaken, but that the belief that modern science supports it is mistaken no less.

CHAPTER X

A THEORY OF VALUE ADVANCED IN RELATION TO THE CONCLUSIONS OF MODERN SCIENCE

INTRODUCTORY

I propose in this chapter to try to elaborate the hypothesis, which I have called B[1], that reality is plural and contains a number of different orders or realms. This hypothesis I shall consider more particularly in its relation to the questions discussed in this book; I shall try to show that it is not only compatible with, but in some degree required by, the conclusions of modern science, and that it is capable of giving a satisfactory account of value. By the assertion that the conclusions of modern science require this hypothesis, I mean that it is only on the basis of a pluralistic metaphysic that we are entitled to claim an objective reference for the results of modern physics, and to assign to the world which physics studies a status other than that of an aspect of the consciousness of physicists. By the assertion that it is capable of giving a satisfactory account of value, I mean that it enables us to interpret the deliverances of the aesthetic, and more particularly of the religious consciousness as the responses of the human spirit to an external and extra-human reality; so interpreted they may be regarded as conveying information about that to which they respond. It is only on this supposition that, I should urge, what we call 'value' can be regarded as constituting an adequate object of aesthetic emotion, or an adequate goal of religious endeavour.

Use of the Word 'Reality'

Before I proceed further, I must endeavour to define the sense in which I propose to use the word 'reality.' On the

[1] See p. 192

monistic hypothesis considered and criticized in the last chapter, reality is a unity in the sense, at least, in which an organic system is a unity, and, being so, may appropriately be designated by a single word. Hence, when in preceding chapters I have used the word "reality," I have used it in the sense in which the scientists and philosophers, whose views I have been discussing, have used it, to mean the unity or the unified system which is the universe. If, however, the universe is, as I am now suggesting, a manifold in the sense that it contains different orders or realms of being, the use of a single word to designate what is more properly to be regarded as a collection than a unity may be questionable.

To employ the word "reality" to mean all that there is, when by "all that there is" no more is meant than a number of orders, or realms containing entities of different sorts, is, in view of the historical associations of the word, misleading, and I shall not, therefore, use it in this sense. When I wish to designate the sum total of existing things, I shall use the words "the universe," or the phrase "all that there is." I propose, however, to retain the word "reality" and to use it in a restricted and perfectly specific sense, to indicate one department or realm of what exists and one only. I hold that the universe contains at least three different orders or realms of being. There are the material constituents of which the physical world is composed, which, I believe, are analysable in terms of sense data; there are the minds which are aware of them; and there is a third order or realm which contains objects which are neither mental nor material, which I have designated by the word 'subsistent.' These objects are changeless; they are also, I should say, independent both of the physical world and of the minds that know them. In this realm, if in any of the three, I should be disposed to place those objects of value of which we are aware in religious, ethical and aesthetic experience. But I think it is at least possible that they belong to a fourth realm or order of which, with the possible addition of truth, they are the sole inhabitants of which we have knowledge.

Now I propose to reserve the use of the word 'reality' for the realm of changeless and eternal objects, truth, goodness, beauty, and, it may be, deity, which are neither mental nor material. As I do not wish to raise here the question whether this realm or order is the same as that which also contains subsistent objects, or whether it is a separate realm or order which lies beyond in the sense of being known at a later stage of evolution than the realm of subsistent objects, I shall use the word 'reality' to denote those constituents of the universe which fulfil the two conditions of being neither mental nor material and of possessing value.

I do not wish, however, to imply that these constituents are in any sense more real than the material world or than knowing minds. Whatever exists must in my view be equally real; I am merely proposing to appropriate the word "reality" for a particular department of what exists.

I ought also to explain that in this chapter my object is to state a position rather than to defend it. I have endeavoured to give elsewhere the reasons which seem to me to suggest that the universe is such as hypothesis B rather than such as hypothesis A asserts.[1] My present concern is merely to apply this hypothesis to the particular questions discussed in this book, and to show that it is not only compatible with but reinforced by the considerations derived from a study of modern science.

I propose to bring forward a number of considerations derived in the first place from epistemology, and in the second from metaphysics, in favour of the hypothesis; in a third section I shall endeavour to correlate the two sets of considerations. This process of correlation will enable me to indicate the status which, on my view, should be assigned to scientific objects and the function which scientific knowledge performs in the general development of the mind of

[1] See my *Matter, Life and Value*, especially Chapters VI–IX.

the race. In a concluding chapter I shall extend the same mode of treatment to the religious consciousness. A brief interpretation of mysticism as the mind's awareness of reality will lead to a sketch of the general conception of the universe to which the preceding lines of argument have seemed to point. In the light of this conception I shall offer certain observations with regard to the temper of mind from which the metaphysical views examined in this book spring. This temper is, in my view, different from that of science itself —it is more anthropomorphic and less impartial—and in emphasizing the difference I shall try to show that a true view of the universe, and also of the nature of scientific knowledge and the status of its objects, is likely to be reached by retaining and not abandoning the spirit of science when we proceed to philosophize about its results.

I. Knowledge and its Objects

The first point which I wish to emphasize is the non-contributory character of the act of knowing. Knowledge, I am convinced, does not in any way contribute to the nature of its objects. I am aware of the difficulties to which this view leads, and in particular to the undesirability of those unreal objects, golden mountains, red-hot snow and the like, with which it peoples the world. These cannot but be unwelcome in any philosophical view, although how far the objection which all must feel to the inclusion of such objects in the category of 'what is,' is based on logical grounds, and how far it is emotional, or, it may be, aesthetic, I do not know. So far at least as logic is concerned, it is difficult not to concede the force of Parmenides's aphorisms: "Thou canst not know what is not—that is impossible—nor utter it; for it is the same thing that can be thought and that can be." And again: "It needs must be that what can be thought and spoken of is; for it is possible for it to be, and it is not possible for what is nothing to be." It certainly seems to follow from these remarks that whatever can be thought of must in some sense be. Now I can certainly think of "red-hot snow"; moreover, the experience of doing so is quite different from the experience of thinking of a golden mountain. And it is, I think, very difficult to account for the admitted difference between these two experiences, except on the supposition that they are experiences of different things, that, in other words, the attention of the mind of which they are the experiences is, when it is enjoying the experiences, directed upon different objects. I do not, however, wish to pursue this point, which I have discussed elsewhere, because I am fully prepared to concede the difficulty which the postulation of so-called unreal objects must involve for any philosophy, if I may do so without committing myself to the view that the difficulty is final.

Whatever may be the force, and whatever the basis of the objection to these 'unreal' constituents of the universe, I am by no means indifferent to it. The importance, however, of maintaining the view that knowledge is in essence a process of revelation and not of construction seems to me to be so great as to outweigh the difficulties to which I have referred. On balance I prefer to try to meet these difficulties as best I can, rather than abandon the view of the knowing process which appears to involve them. And the importance of maintaining the view seems to me to be this, that, once we admit that mind may contribute to the objects it knows, that its capacity is, in fact, at least in part constructive, then I know of no method by which we can assign limits to the exercise of this capacity. It seems, in other words, to be impossible to assert of any object that is known or of any part of the object known, that it does *not* owe its existence as object or as part to the fact of our knowing it. If this impossibility be admitted, there is no longer any basis for maintaining a realist view of the universe. Hence, to admit that mind can "do" anything to what it knows is to open the flood-gates to the waters of Idealism.

I am not here arguing that Idealism is necessarily mistaken, although this is in fact my view. Moreover, I admit that if we are prepared to accept a wholeheartedly idealist view of the universe, then, whatever may be the other objections to which it is exposed, the particular difficulty I am here raising is a difficulty no longer.

In practice, however, those who as scientists are accustomed to insist on mind's abstractive or constructive activity in relation to the world of science are very far from admitting the full idealist implications of their view. In practice, as I have tried to show, modern scientists, while asking us to believe that the world of physics, and even the familiar world, owe their appearance, if not their being, to the activities of the knowing mind, and are to this extent subjective, wish to maintain that there is another world, the world of what they call "reality," which is independent of the mind that knows it, and is revealed to it in religious and mystical experience. The fact that this world may itself be mental does not for them imply that it is in any sense the product of *our* minds. It follows that the activity of knowing which our minds undoubtedly exercise is sometimes, as, for example, in sensory experience and scientific thought, an activity of construction or selection, and sometimes, as in religious and aesthetic experience, it is not. By what principle the differentiation is established I do not know; no principle, at any rate, is laid down. And the fact that the view is continually found, as I have shown, to involve a subjectivist attitude even to the world of religious experience, by testifying to the difficulty of maintaining on these premises the strict 'otherness' of the 'real' world revealed in such experience, is highly suggestive of the conclusion that the differentiation is inadmissible.

I have already had occasion to comment upon the fact that in the last resort the writers, whose views I have discussed, frequently speak of the mystic's world as if it, too, were continuous with, if not actually the product of, the mystic's mind; and this inconsistency, for inconsistency it is, springs, I think, inevitably from the admission of the constructional operations which mind is held to perform in relation to the worlds of science and of sense. It is *because* it is held that these worlds are in part subjective, that it is found so difficult in practice to resist the view that the so-called 'real' world is subjective too. This view is, nevertheless, distasteful so far as the underlying unity, the so-called real world is concerned, and it is not, so far as I can see, the view which any of the writers whose speculations I have considered really wish to take of it. Yet once the conception of mind as creative, or in part creative, of its objects is admitted, I do not see how the application of the conception to all the objects of mind's knowledge is to be evaded.

I myself believe that the world of which we are aware in aesthetic and religious experience is objective, and that in knowing it we discover and do not create what we know. It is for this reason among others that I am anxious to maintain that the worlds revealed to us in everyday experience and in scientific research are also objective. It is, indeed, partly because the subjective attitude to the world of science favoured by modern physics seems to me to be prejudicial to the objective status of the world of value that I have tried to show that this attitude is mistaken.

From the assertion that the activity of mind in knowing is non-contributory I should proceed further to assert that it is always the same. This second assertion does not, of course, necessarily follow from the first, since it is logically possible that there should be various forms of a non-contributory activity. I do not, however, believe that this in fact is the case. At the beginning of Chapter VII I summarized four views to which, as it seemed to me, the different theories actually advanced by philosophers with regard to the character of the mental activity involved in our knowledge of the external world could be reduced.[1] I mentioned objections to which the first three of these views were exposed, and gave reasons in favour of the fourth, according to which the mental activity of knowing was said to involve a relation between mind and its object which was unique and common to all mental acts. In saying that it is common to all mental acts I mean that whether we are sensing or imagining, intuiting or reasoning, the mental activity involved is the same activity, and the relation of the mind to what is sensed, imagined, intuited or reasoned about is the same relation. And this mental activity seems to me to be most appropriately represented as one of discovery; the mind 'discovers' what it knows. I do not mean that the word 'discovery' *completely* expresses the relation; if it did, the relation involved when a mind knows an object would not have the uniqueness which I am claiming for it. I do mean, however, that the activity of knowing or being aware approximates more closely to a process in which a world which is external to and independent of the mind may be thought of as being directly revealed to it, than to one in which the mind either projects, creates, constructs, selects or abstracts the objects which it then proceeds to know.

The simile which seems, then, most nearly to represent the nature of mental activity, as I conceive it, is that of the searchlight. The objects which the searchlight illuminates are found but not formed by it; and the searchlight has no choice but to reveal them. In this sense the mind is passive; it cannot avoid apprehending what is, in the particular direction in which it is, so to speak, pointing, *there*; and the character of its experience is determined by as much of what is there as, at the particular level of development which it happens to have reached, it is capable of apprehending. But, just as the searchlight may be turned in this direction or in that, so a mind may within limits direct itself to whatever area of reality it chooses. In this sense,

[1] See Chapter VII, pp. 156, 157.

the sense in which it may look *here* rather than *there*, the objects of which at any given moment it is aware are those of its own choice. In exercising this capacity of choice the mind is influenced by the interests, the hopes, the wishes, and in part, no doubt, by the past biography of the perceiver. In this sense, and in this sense alone, the mind is active and determines what objects it shall apprehend. And just as one searchlight may differ from another in point of scope and intensity, and one will illuminate a greater area of objects and illuminate it with greater clarity than another, so, I should hold, different minds are capable of being aware of quantitatively more extensive and qualitatively richer areas of the universe. Thus I should hold that in a perfectly literal sense the mind of a savage knows more of the universe, and also knows a more varied universe, than that of a dog, while in the same literal sense the mind of a civilized man knows more than the mind of a savage. I do not mean merely that the civilized mind apprehends more of the *physical* world—if, as is sometimes asserted, civilization blunts our senses, it is conceivable that it apprehends less—but it knows a greater variety of objects, and of objects belonging to different worlds. It can think, that is to say, it has the power to apprehend subsistents; it achieves the knowledge of scientific objects, and in religious and aesthetic experience it has intimations of objects possessing value. I shall return to this point and endeavour to elaborate it in the next section. I mention it here only in order to illustrate what is meant by the suggestion that minds at different levels of development illuminate different areas of the universe.

It follows from what has been said that, in so far as our mental life is qualitatively various, in so far as sensing and thinking, imagining and intuiting involve different experiences, the differences must be due to the nature of the objects upon which the activity of the mind which is said to be sensing, thinking, imagining or intuiting is directed.

The experiences are, in other words, felt to be different because the mental activity which results in the experiences is directed upon different objects. In so far as what are usually termed sensory experiences are concerned, this would, I think, be generally conceded. Consider, for example, the experiences which result from the visual apprehension of the physical world. The experience of seeing what is called a pen is, it is obvious, a different experience from that of seeing what is called an ink-pot, and most people would, I think, be prepared to agree that the sole and sufficient cause of this difference is the fact that the pen is a different object from the ink-pot; they would, that is to say, be disposed to agree that the two experiences were felt to be different simply because the apprehending mind was, if I may use a metaphorical expression, in contact with two different objects. Similarly in the case of thinking, it would, I think, be agreed both that the thinking of an electron was a different experience from that involved in thinking of a living organism, and that the difference between the experiences was due to the fact that the objects of the two mental acts were different objects.

Now I see no reason why what is regarded as a sufficient account of the admitted fact that the mental activity of awareness involves different experiences, when it is directed upon objects belonging to the same order of being, should not also be adequate to explain differences between the experiences which are involved when this activity is directed upon different orders of being. On this hypothesis, the difference between the experiences involved in perceiving a present fire and thinking of an absent one would be adequately explained as due to the fact that the fire which we "perceive" is a different object from the fire about which we "think." And if, as I have tried in Chapters V and VII to show, the fire we perceive is simply the name which we give to a number of sense data of varying colours and temperatures, while the fire we think about is a non-material object of thought, the sharpness of this difference would be readily explicable.

It is on these lines that I should seek to account for the admitted difference between the experiences involved in perceiving things and in imagining them. The activity of the mind when imagining is directed upon a different order of reality from that upon which it is directed when it is perceiving. It follows, if I may put the point colloquially, that man normally lives in two worlds. There is the physical world which we apprehend in sensory experience, a world which is composed of innumerable, changing, momentary data; and there is the invisible world about which we think, the constituents of which do not change. Both worlds can be described only from the human standpoint; they can be described, that is to say, only as they appear to us. But this affords no reason for supposing that their appearance to us is in any way illusory, or that we do not truly know them as they are. I have already tried to give reasons for supposing that the objects of scientific knowledge may be regarded as members of the "thought world." Among the other constituents of this world are physical objects, universals, and the realities which correspond to mathematical statements. To say that $7 + 5 = 12$ is a statement of fact, a statement, that is, about a fact which is as real as any fact in the so-called physical world. Moreover, unlike objects of which we are aware in sense experience, the fact is permanent and changeless. It was a fact before there were sense data, and it will be a fact after they have ceased to be.

I have further tried to indicate the way in which the mind's knowledge of the objects belonging to the first world may direct its attention to those belonging to the second. But the process by which mind's increasing knowledge of one world conditions the awareness of another may be repeated. As evolution proceeds and mind develops in scope and power, new levels of awareness continually emerge, and at these levels new types of objects begin to be known. One such level has emerged or is in process of emergence during the period of evolution known as human history. This is the level at which objects of value begin for the first time to be apprehended. This apprehension is at present fleeting and uncertain, nor should we perhaps be justified in postulating for it a special type of object, were it not for the unique characteristic of the experience in which the apprehension consists.

This unique characteristic is that to which we give the somewhat ambiguous name of "significance." The most conspicuous example of this type of experience at our present level of development is that which we call aesthetic experience. The apprehension of beauty in art and nature is certainly significant; so, it seems, is the experience of the mathematician establishing chains of reasoning, which are no less elegant than they are economical, and elegant because they are economical. So, too, it may be, is that of the scientist contemplating the laws of nature. I should further include in the category of 'significant' experiences the emotion which is sometimes evoked in us by good actions and noble characters, although I think this emotion in its pure form is comparatively rare, being in practice almost always alloyed with extraneous and inessential elements. Finally, there is religious experience, the emotion which the saint and the mystic feel for reality.[1] This is assuredly significant; significance is, indeed, its most noticeable characteristic.

On the analogy of the preceding argument, that persons apprehending objects of different types enjoy experiences which vary in virtue of the differences between the objects of apprehension, I should say that the fact that all these experiences possess this common element of "significance" presupposes that the mind is in contact with a particular

[1] I am speaking loosely here for the sake of brevity. I shall endeavour to expand this expression. See pp. 306–308, 314–316, and 322–324.

and unique department of what is; and that the character of "significance" which the experiences seem to have is due to the peculiar nature of the objects upon which the mind's awareness is directed.

We are, then, led to envisage another order of the universe, the objects of which share in common with those belonging to the world of subsistence the property of changelessness, but are distinguished by this further property that the experiences resulting from the apprehension of them by minds at a certain level of development possess the character of "significance." The general name by which I propose to designate this property is that of "value." I should say, then, that the universe contains an element or realm of value; that this realm may be merely a subsection of the world of subsistence, but that, if we may judge from the difficulty which besets the apprehension of it, and the comparatively recent date at which such apprehension has begun to be possible, it should more appropriately be regarded as a separate realm lying as it were behind and beyond the world of subsistence.

I must now endeavour to supplement this account of the development of the mental faculty of knowing as awareness, with a brief statement of the nature of the known universe which this account presupposes.

II. The World as a Plurality of Orders

The considerations advanced by Bergson to show that reality contains an element of ceaseless flux or change have always seemed to me impressive. This element is, I believe, exemplified by my own consciousness, which I recognize as a stream of pure becoming. To say that consciousness is pure becoming is to say that no account can be given of consciousness as such; it can only be described in terms of the objects upon which the stream of 'becoming,' which is consciousness, is at any moment directed. Upon the epistemological implications of this statement I have already commented.

Considerations drawn from biology seem to me to demonstrate fairly conclusively that the change and development of living organisms, which we call the process of evolution, is inexplicable on purely mechanical lines. The classical factors of natural selection and adaptation to environment, while able to explain the success of variations in establishing themselves, are totally unable to explain their occurrence, while the fact that evolution still continues after a large measure of purely *physical* adaptation has been achieved, and even seems at times to be in the direction of less rather than of more satisfactory *physical* adaptation, suggests that it must be regarded as the expression of a dynamic impulsion, a principle or force of life, which, developing in and through those individual currents of itself which are living organisms, moulds and uses matter in the process of its development.

Similarly psychology seems to me to have convincingly shown that the behaviour of the living organism is not explicable on the assumption that it is all body—that it is, in other words, a highly complicated automaton, but that such behaviour exemplifies or expresses a spontaneous, active and immaterial principle which in the raw we call life, and which in human beings emerges at the level of mind.

It is difficult to avoid bringing these three lines of thought into relation, and seeing in the stream of consciousness which constitutes the stuff of my experience, a particular expression of that principle of life, which biology seems increasingly driven to postulate to account for the development of the various species of living organisms, and psychology to account for the behaviour of particular individuals of the species. I am thus led to postulate the presence in the universe of a dynamic force or principle of change, which enters into association with matter to form living organisms, and is known to the biologist as life, to the psychologist as mind, and to myself as the stream of consciousness which constitutes my being.[1]

But the principle is not therefore to be identified with the whole of what is. The attempts which are made by philosophies of the *élan vital* type to account for matter in terms of the stream or flux of life have always seemed to me unconvincing. Bergson, for example, speaks of matter as being the result of an interruption of the vital flow. It is the "spent drops which fall back." But there can be no interruption without something to perform the function of interrupting, and the necessity for postulating an interrupting factor, which is other than the vital flow, is thus apparent. Again, Bergson speaks of matter as the view which the intellect takes of reality. The intellect makes cuts across the continuous flow which is the universe, articulating it and congealing it into separate, solid objects extended in space. But the criticism of which I have already made use in previous pages[2] may be applied with equal force to this conception. Either the cuts which the intellect makes are arbitrary, in which event we should be able to inhabit whatever kind of material world we please, or they are not, in which event reality must contain within itself the germs of all the distinctions which the intellect proceeds to discover. In this latter event the material world or the potentiality for it is no less part of reality than life itself.

Nor is it only Bergson's philosophy that raises this difficulty. Modern philosophy has been prolific of metaphysical views which seek to represent the universe as the expression of a dynamic, active principle. These views are monistic in the sense that they affirm that everything is ultimately one, that reality, in fact, is a unity, but unlike the monistic idealism of the Hegelians, they represent the unity as a 'becoming' rather than as a being. Schopenhauer's philosophy as elaborated in *The World as Will and Idea* affords a

[1] See my *Matter, Life and Value*, Chapter IV, for an elaboration of this view.

[2] See pp. 117, 118.

good example of this metaphysical type. For Schopenhauer the fundamental nature of reality is that of a changing, dynamic, unconscious Will. This Will is literally all-including; there is nothing else besides it. It is driven (presumably by the necessities of its own being) to objectify itself in various manifestations. All the variety and multiplicity of the world of existence, from chairs and tables to living beings, and from living beings to the objects of aesthetic contemplation, are different forms of its objectivation. The differences between them are as unreal as their appearance as separate and isolated entities; on a closer view they will be seen to be merely phenomenal expressions of an underlying unity. But if the unity is really a unity, how comes it to develop the differences which the expression of itself in various forms implies? Even if the apparent multiplicity be *merely* phenomenal, the potentiality for its development must have qualified the initial unity, just as the potentiality for development into a chicken is a characteristic of the egg. Nor can we stop at the potentiality for developed difference. The Will does not merely objectify itself; it objectifies itself in certain ways and not in others. We must start, therefore, not merely with a bare Will, but with a Will initially qualified by the capacity for developing either particular kinds of differences, namely, those which actually appear to exist in the world we know, or—for it comes to the same thing—the illusion of particular kinds of differences. But what does this mean, if it does not mean that the unity is not a unity at all; that there already exist in an incapsulated form within it all the diverse and finite individualities which it subsequently generates, and that it is not, therefore, one thing but many things? This difficulty is not in any monistic metaphysic with which I am acquainted resolved, nor, in my view, can it be resolved. It is a difficulty which besets the theological view of the world as the creation of an omnipotent being, and one with which all religious interpretations of the universe must contend.

Dualistic theologies of the Manichaean type are a testimony to the force with which it presents itself.

In the endeavour to maintain a theological monism, it has been from time to time suggested that the world is not a separate entity created by God, but an expression of God's overflowing goodness. As an illustration of this conception may be mentioned the view of the creation of the world common in Hindu theology which represents God, although perfect, as unable to contain Himself in His perfection. He feels a need to express Himself; so great is His joy, so perfect His goodness, that He overflows. Just as the artist inspired by beauty feels a need to express himself by creation, so also was God moved to create the world, not out of any deficiency or lack, but out of the very fullness and abundance of His goodness. The conception is similar to that of the Neo-Platonists, who thought of God as expressing His eternal purpose in a world other than Himself, by an act needing naught for its consummation save the intrinsic plenitude of his perfection. But, if we are to take the artist analogy seriously, the difficulty still remains. The artist does not merely create; he creates in a medium which is other than that which he creates. If there were no material medium, the artist's inspiration would be denied expression. Creation is always creation out of something; expression, expression in something; this, at least, is true of the creation and expression of the artist. Hence, if we are to retain the conception of the artist's self-expression as an analogy on which to conceive God's creation of the world, we must introduce a principle of objectivity which is other than God, in which, or through interaction with which, God expresses Himself. The necessity for this principle is in fact realized by Sankarachaya, and it appears in his work, and indeed in that of many Indian philosophers, under the name of 'Maya.' In my view this necessity is ultimate; we are, that is to say, however we conceive the creative principle, whether as mind, spirit, personal deity or blind impulse, driven to postulate the existence of some principle of opposition or obstruction in addition to the principle we affirm. If we stress the purposive aspect of the principle as mind, we must oppose to it a factor of chaos, of blankness and disorder, which mind orders and informs. If we emphasize its dynamic aspect as an impulsive stream of life, we must postulate the existence of an obstructive factor to condition the objectification of life in matter and provide a ground for the plurality of living units. Something in fact is required to break up the stream as a line of rocks disperses a wave. If I am asked what this factor is, I answer that since it is not such as can be deduced *a priori*, it must be such as is apprehended empirically. What I immediately apprehend in sensory experience is a world of related sense data, and the demand of theory of knowledge, that these sense data should be other than my apprehension of them, is thus endorsed by the demand of a metaphysical dualism that there should be some principle of otherness in the universe in which life may be manifested or expressed. Life in fact is both in the mind-body relation associated with and in sensory apprehension aware of the raw material of the world, which analysis shows to be sets of sense data.

The Goal of 'Becoming.'—Nor is this principle of obstruction, which I have called the raw material of the universe, the only one which in addition to life I feel driven to affirm. Life, I hold, is purposive; there is, in fact, a goal to the process of evolution, which life seeks to achieve, and which, in my view, must be other than the process itself.

Here again the philosophies which base themselves exclusively on the fact of evolution demur. These philosophies, even when they recognize the possibility of there being a goal which the process of becoming may be conceived as seeking to achieve, do not exempt it from the activity of the process itself. Like the process, it is conceived to change and to evolve, and it does so because in the last resort it is continuous with the process. A goal to which the world continually approximates is too static and aloof to command the admiration of these philosophies. Not only the degree of approximation which at any moment may be achieved, but the goal which it is sought to achieve must, therefore, change and develop. As mind changes, so inevitably does its conception of the goal. This conception is not set over against a reality outside time which life with increasing clearness apprehends; it determines a corresponding development in the goal which it affirms, from which, indeed, it is only by a falsifying act of thought that it is distinguished.

In this way the existence of a changeless world is denied; everything is part and parcel of the stream of becoming, and time is represented as a devouring tyrant of all that is.

This view is, I think, exposed to certain logical objections which I have endeavoured to set forth elsewhere.[1] The logical objections are, however, less important than what, to my mind, is the inability of this view to do justice to the facts of aesthetic and religious experience.

In aesthetic and religious experiences we certainly *seem* to make contact with a non-human reality, which is perfect as we are imperfect, and changeless and permanent as we are changing and ephemeral. That the existence of this element of perfection and permanence is a more or less constant intimation of *bona-fide* aesthetic and religious experience would, I think, be generally agreed. I see no reason to suppose that the suggestion of these intimations is misleading, or that the character of significance which the experience of beauty, for example, seems to carry with it as revelatory of an objective world, is not really its character. If, therefore, we are to do full justice to the significance which is generally agreed to attach to religious and aesthetic experience, we must, I should say, regard such experience in the light of a revelation of a reality, which stands outside the stream of flux which is our consciousness.

I am not here arguing that this must be so; I am merely

[1] See *Matter, Life and Value*, Chapters VI and VIII.

stating a view which I am not, except implicitly, seeking to defend. It is a view which requires us to postulate, in addition to the stream of becoming, a changeless element in the universe. This changeless element, while standing outside the stream, seems nevertheless to be able in some way which I do not know how to describe to enter into, or, at least, into relation with, the flux of becoming, stamping its impression upon material things and moulding them into forms which prefigure it. Thus we may think of pictures as reproducing its shapes and music as catching something of its rhythms, almost as though it actually informed the material medium which manifested it. Such expressions are, it is obvious, metaphorical, and must not be pressed. Since, however, our treatment must be of necessity metaphorical, it may be pointed out that two rather different metaphors suggest themselves, which express two different modes of conceiving the relationship. Both these modes may be distinguished in Plato's treatment of the relationship between the Forms and the particulars.

I spoke above of the reality as "entering into" the stream of becoming, and it is possible that this metaphor may contain a literal statement of the truth, so that, as Plato puts it, the work of art literally *participates* in the Form of beauty, and owes its being to the presence of the Form in it. The objection to this conception of the world of value as "entering into" the world of becoming is that it entails a causal relation between one department or order of being and another, in virtue of which the world of becoming is conceived to derive its properties from the world of Forms, which in its turn confers its characteristics upon the world of becoming. This conception bridges the gap of discontinuity between different orders of being, and is inimical to the pluralistic view of the universe that I am suggesting.

A second way of conceiving the relation which is more consistent with a pluralistic metaphysic is suggested by Plato's alternative view, that the work of art reflects or imitates reality, and in reflecting points the mind forward to the real world which it imitates. Even this view may seem at first sight difficult to fit into the epistemological framework which I sketched in Chapter VII. A work of art, in so far as it is a constituent of the physical world, is, according to the view there expressed, analysable into the series of sense data which are directly apprehended in sensory experience. It was, I suggested, the function of these sense data to direct the mind's awareness upon "the physical object," the picture, which was properly to be regarded as a member of the world of subsistence. The present discussion might seem at first sight to demand that this conception should be qualified by the assertion that *some* sets of sense data possess the property of directing the mind's awareness not upon the world of subsistence, but upon the world of value, so that in the sensory apprehension of a picture or a piece of music the mind, in so far as it enjoys aesthetic experience, might be conceived as "penetrating directly through" into the world of value.

I do not think, however, that it is necessary to introduce this qualification or to assert this direct connection between the world of sense data and the world of value. It is possible to maintain the view already elaborated that the function of sense data is limited to directing the awareness of the mind upon "the physical object," the picture, which belongs to the world of subsistence, supplementing it with the conception of the subsistent object, the picture, as further directing the mind's awareness upon the world of value. This view would entail that the property of imitating or reflecting beauty belongs not to sense data but to objects which are constituents of the realm of subsistence. The sense data concerned must, however, still be credited with a derivative relation to the world of value, a relation which they enjoy as it were at second hand, in virtue of the fact that they direct the mind's awareness not upon *any* subsistent object, but upon subsistent objects of a particular class, the particularity of which consists in the property which its members possess of copying or reflecting the world of value. There is thus a twofold "pointing forward" of the mind's awareness; the apprehended sense data direct it to a particular set of subsistent objects, which again "point it forward" to the world of value. Hence, the sense data, no less than the subsistent objects, are differentiated, though at second hand, by a particular relation to the world of value.

I do not wish to pretend that this account is satisfactory, but I do not know how better to describe the relation between so-called aesthetic objects which belong to the stream of becoming and the world of value from which they appear to derive their significance. Whatever view we take of it, however, it is, I feel convinced, to the existence of *some* relation of this type that the profoundly moving quality which we find in works of art is to be attributed. I am convinced, that is to say, that it is only on the supposition that in religious and aesthetic experience the mind is in contact with a different order of reality that the significance of these experiences can be adequately interpreted. That no account of them which is couched *exclusively* in terms of our knowledge of the familiar world is satisfactory is fairly generally agreed. They seem, moreover, to elude interpretation by the descriptive methods of science; so much, at least, I have argued in the preceding chapter. It seems to be a reasonable inference that the area or department of the universe upon which in aesthetic appreciation and religious experience mental activity is directed is different both from the flux of sense data which we know in sensory experience and from the realm of subsistence to which, I have suggested, the objects which science studies should properly be assigned.

Whatever may be the precise nature of the relation between the world of value and aesthetic objects, the mind's knowledge of value in aesthetic experience must, I suggest, be in some sense mediated and indirect. By the words "mediated and indirect," I do not mean that the value is known *through* the sense data and the subsistent object, but that these must in aesthetic experience be known first in order that by them the mind may be pointed forward. We must be aware of a picture as an ordinary physical object before we can cognize it as an aesthetic one. But the world which we know indirectly in aesthetic may be known, I conceive, directly in religious experience. In religious experience the sensuous element which seems inseparable from the awareness of beauty is absent. We know beauty as it informs paint or landscape, stone or sound; but in so far as deity is known, our knowledge is not of a copy or representation to which we have access only after we have *first* known sensory objects, but immediate and direct. It is to this knowledge that we give the name of mystical experience.

Summary of the View of Knowledge as Discovery of the Universe.

It may be desirable briefly to summarize this account, so far as I have taken it up to the present, of knowledge as the process of mind's discovery of the universe and of the different orders of the universe which in knowing are revealed to it.[1] The view for which I have contended is that the nature of mental activity is to be 'an awareness.' It is not creative but exploratory, revealing to the knower the nature of the universe upon which it is directed. The universe so revealed seems to consist of a number of orders or realms. These orders or realms of being constitute the objects which the activity of knowing reveals. Mental activity

[1] The view may be represented schematically as follows:—

Animals, and probably babies, aware of sense data.

Men, and perhaps some higher animals, aware of sense data and subsistent objects.

Some men (artists) aware of sense data, subsistent objects, and because of them of value.

Some men (mystics) directly aware of value.

which was directed upon nothing would be nothing. It is the universe outside us which provides the colour and content of our lives, by constituting the object of our knowledge. Moreover, it is in terms of the differences between these orders or realms that the differences between the various types of experience involved in the knowing of them are to be interpreted. There is, in the first place, the material world, which, I have suggested, is analysable in terms of sense data. Mind's apprehension of this world involves what is known as sensory experience. There is, in the second place, the world of objects, which we know otherwise than in sensory experience; it is of this world that the mind is aware in thinking, whether thinking takes the form of judging, of ratiocinating, of the ordering and arrangement of information, or of imagining. The forms of experience involved in these mental activities would be normally distinguished from the experience involved in what we call sensory apprehension, and they are, I suggest, to be so distinguished in virtue of the fact that the awareness of the mind which enjoys the experiences is directed upon objects of thought. These objects of thought include so-called "physical objects" and scientific objects.

The significance of aesthetic experience is to be interpreted in terms of the mind's awareness of objects which, belonging to the world of subsistence, nevertheless occupy a peculiar position in that world. Standing in a special relation to a further realm or world, the world of value, they direct the awareness of the mind that knows them upon value, just as sense data direct its awareness upon subsistent objects. The unique feeling which we experience in the presence of beautiful things is, therefore, not aroused by the apprehension of the sets of sense data, which is the starting-point of the aesthetic experience. It is evoked by the objects of which the sensory apprehension causes us to become aware, and it is felt because of the special relation of these objects to the world of value.

The peculiar quality of mystical experience, which is again to be distinguished from the quality of aesthetic experience, is similarly to be interpreted in terms of the mind's awareness of the realm of value, for which I have reserved the title of 'reality.' The admitted difference between the two types of experience is, I suggest, due to the fact that in religious experiences the mind knows directly the object or objects of which in aesthetic experience it knows only the copies. Thus religious experience is evoked by a direct awareness of the world of value, whereas in aesthetic experience the mind's awareness of value begins with the apprehension of sense data, and is mediated by the knowledge of subsistent objects. The two types of experience admittedly overlap, and sensory apprehension may equally be the starting-point of the religious experience.

This account is admittedly unsatisfactory, and I do not know how to improve it. As I said above, I do not know precisely in what terms to conceive the relation of the world of value to the world of subsistence or to the sensory world. I shall suggest in the last section reasons why it may not be possible to know. What is important is the realization of the fact that since the activity of knowing, which is life's expression at a certain level, and its object belong to two different orders or realms of reality, the relation between them cannot be that of community or continuity of being. It must, in other words, in all forms of experience and at all levels of evolution involve a distinction between knower and known. The vital process which expresses itself as cognition may change and evolve and develop fuller and more discriminating powers of awareness, but it can never become one with that of which it is aware. Thus the goal of the evolutionary process must remain outside the process which seeks to know it, the static and changeless element in the universe outside the stream of becoming.

On these lines the epistemological view of experience as taking colour and content from the nature of the objects upon which mental activity is directed, and the metaphysical view of reality as consisting of different orders or realms of objects may be brought into relation. The relation between them is one of logical implication; each view, if I am right, presupposes, and is presupposed by, the other.

III. Sketch of a Pluralistic Metaphysic

I am now in a position to sketch the general view of the universe to which the considerations enumerated seem to me to point. It can most conveniently be presented by outlining the five main positions which it embodies. I shall, therefore, say something about each of these positions in turn.

A. Mental Activity as an Expression of the Stream of Life.—I hold that individual minds are not, as they at first sight appear to be, isolated and separate activities, but are expressions of a universal force or principle of life. This universal force or principle is associated with matter, which constitutes a separate and distinct factor of the universe. Matter differentiates and disperses life into an infinity of separate living monads, much as a line of rocks will disperse into a cloud of spray the wave which dashes against them. Each individual monad is, therefore, a unit or current of life, temporarily insulated from the main stream by the matter with which it is associated. Individuality is thus conferred upon living organisms by matter, which interposes as it were a barrier between them and the vital principle which is their common source. This individuality is, however, temporary only; it is to be regarded as a device to further the realization of ends which transcend it. At death the individual is merged again in the main stream from which he took his rise. The view that the preparation of a certain number of individual souls conceived in the likeness of twentieth-century adults for eternal blessedness is the object for which the evolutionary process exists, seems to me to be the product of an anthropomorphism which is a legacy of man's past. In the light of what biology has discovered about the past of life it is difficult to resist the conclusion that the process which has led from the amoeba to man will lead from man to different and more complex types of life, and that our minds and individualities are, therefore, temporary and provisional forms which will be superseded.

The conviction that we are being used for a purpose which transcends our own, by a force or principle of which we are but temporary expressions, is thus the first factor upon which I wish to lay emphasis. And in this conception I desire specially to stress the fact that we are *means.* To say that we are means is to say that we are means to ends which are other than our own. This consideration may suggest a reason why the life which consists in the pursuit of purely individual ends is an unsatisfactory life, and the conduct which a hedonistic philosophy prescribes is never expedient even if it be practicable. Effort and endeavour are of the essence of the successful life. It is the efforts that we make to achieve our ends rather than the ends themselves which are valuable—so much, at least, we may on reflection and in retrospect admit—although, while the need for effort persists, the truth is one which it is the part of wisdom to ignore. On an impartial view of history it is difficult to resist the conclusion that those ends for which men have struggled hardest and endured most have not in the main been purely individual Men have suffered and endured to serve and to save their fellows. But the impulse to serve and to save mankind is an impulse which is heedless of individual good. Again, men have striven to achieve goodness, to create beauty, or to discover truth; but it is difficult to see that they have been the richer, the happier, or the more powerful as a result of their efforts. Yet wealth, happiness, and power are usually regarded as the appropriate ends of purely individual, human desire. Thus, through all the process which we call history, chaotic as it seems, there may, nevertheless, be discerned an urge compelling men, reluctant and hesitant though they may have been, towards a purpose which is both their own and yet greater than they. History, in fact, may be regarded as the expression of that urge. It is at once our privilege and our responsibility that our own lives should be cast at that stage of the evolutionary process at which an inkling of its purpose is for the first time beginning fitfully to dawn upon our consciousness.

B. Thinking as the Awareness of the Subsistent World.—In order to indicate what I conceive the nature of this purpose to be, I must revert to the preceding epistemological discussion of the nature of the activity of knowing and of the different objects upon which it is directed. I have already given reasons for the view that mental activity is essentially an awareness of something other than itself, that this relation to something other is both common to and peculiar to all forms of mental activity, and that the character and quality of the experience which results from the activity is determined by the nature of the objects upon which the mental activity is directed. With a view to bringing these statements into relation with the position outlined in (*A*) above, I proceed to the further assertion that the level at which the principle of life, which constitutes the being of individual organisms, expresses itself in human beings is that of cognitive activity. Experience, in other words, as we know it, is essentially cognitive. All experience is an experience of something, nor do I think that it is possible to make any affirmation about it except by reference to the nature of the objects upon which the mental activity, which results in the experience, is directed. An account of the evolution and development of life in the higher organisms will be, therefore, an account of the evolution and development of the cognitive activity of awareness, and changes in the quality of living experience will be interpretable in terms of changes in the types of objects upon which at different levels the mental activity of awareness is directed.

So far as human life is concerned, the changes in the quality of experience which, as we develop, accompany changes in the objects which we know are sufficiently obvious. These changes I have already described in Chapter VII.

I will here content myself by briefly recapitulating the main stages. There is considerable agreement among modern psychologists that a baby is conscious only of sense data. These sweep in disorderly, meaningless progress across the vista of his consciousness. Presently the sense data begin to fall into patterns or groups; they clot. As Professor Elliott puts it, "a visual sensation of brown colour is associated with tactual and muscular sensations of hardness, resistance, smoothness, and so on," and there emerges that which the baby will one day name "table." Read 'sense-data' for "sensations," and concede, in the light of the discussions in Chapters V–VII, that the table is neither a mentally constructed object nor a directly apprehended constituent of the physical world, and the description may be taken as adequately conveying the process which, as I suggest, takes place when we begin to think. In thinking the mind's awareness is directed upon objects which are not constituents of the physical world. These objects are of many different kinds, but they possess the common characteristic of being neither mental nor physical. Since they are not physical, they are outside space and time. Among objects of thought are so-called physical objects, universals and scientific objects. The advance in mind's cognitive capacity, which is known as education, or, more precisely, which is produced by education, is to be interpreted as an extension of its knowledge of these objects. Cæsar, for example, is not a physical existent, for he is dead, and, unless we are prepared to adopt some theory of a reincarnationist type, or to commit ourselves to a doctrine of personal survival, we must agree also that Cæsar is not a mind or a spirit. Yet to think of Cæsar is assuredly to think of something, if only because thinking of Cæsar is a different experience from thinking of Napoleon. We may, of course, hold that historical objects, and therefore, presumably, history itself, are merely aspects of our own consciousness. But in this case we should be committed to the view that each of us thinks of something different when he thinks about Cæsar, and it would be difficult to understand how historians could intelligibly communicate with each other, since they would never succeed in thinking or talking about the same thing. Moreover, this view would entail the conclusion that historical facts depended for their being facts upon the consciousnesses of which they were aspects or projections, from which it would follow that if, at any given moment, no conscious mind was thinking of the fact that the battle of Waterloo was fought in 1815, it would no longer be a fact that it was fought in that year. This conclusion seems to me to be distinctly unlikely. Hence I conclude that to think of an historical object, such as Cæsar, is not to be aware of an aspect of one's own consciousness, whether this aspect be conceived as an idea or a projection of the mind. But, if Cæsar is neither a material nor a mental existent, the only alternative seems to be that to think of Cæsar is to be aware of a non-mental, non-physical fact. The conclusion may be generalized to apply to all historical knowledge.

By similar arguments it can, I think, be shown that the knowledge of literature and languages, of geography and economics, of science and philosophy, may be analysed in terms of the mind's awareness of non-material, non-mental objects. Thinking, in short, is the awareness of objects of thought, and education, in so far as it produces an enlargement of the range and scope of the capacity for thinking, enlarges also the area of the universe which is revealed to the educated mind.

This capacity for being aware of objects of thought seems to be a specifically human faculty. The reasoning faculty, especially when it is employed in what is called scientific thought, is, in current parlance, frequently stigmatized as 'inhuman.' The epithet is a misnomer. This capacity for being aware of something other than the material things which crowd upon our senses, this 'cold' power of classification and abstraction, is the chief distinction of the human species. It is an emergent property in virtue of which mankind may be said to have evolved at a higher level than other organisms. There can be no reasonable doubt that our passions and emotions are experienced by the animals. Sheep feel fear, dogs the emotions of joy at a welcome and guilt at a misdeed, cats anger and disappointment. But the capacity to multiply seven by seven, to understand that the earth is round, that the battle of Waterloo was fought in 1815, the dynamic policy of Louis XIV and the meaning of such statements as "Civilizations pass through cycles of growth and decay," is our own; it is the distinguishing characteristic of the level at which, in our species, life has emerged.

But, as I have already suggested, intimations of a new level of vital development, definable in terms of the awareness of a new class of object, begin to appear. Objects belonging to this class I call objects of value, and the world to which they belong the world of value. The awareness of this world is at present fleeting and intermittent, and it is not possible to do more than indicate by means of metaphor and simile, by hint and suggestion, the nature of what it reveals. To the world of value there seem to be three main avenues of approach: the dispassionate, intellectual activity of thinking and reasoning which is characteristic of modern science, and more particularly of modern mathematics; the sensibility of the artist and the aesthetic appreciation by others of the qualities of his work; and the revelatory vision of the mystical consciousness. I will endeavour to say something about each of these in turn.[1]

C. Science and Value.—The treatment of science from this point of view enables me to indicate the special function in the hierarchy of knowing which, it seems to me, the scientific consciousness performs, and the status which should be accorded to scientific objects. I have already in Chapter VII suggested that scientific objects are apprehended by minds at a certain stage of evolutionary development inspired by interests of the kind which are regarded as non-practical. Minds so developed and inspired are, I suggested, directed by the apprehension of sense data to the awareness not of physical objects but of scientific objects. Thus, although physical objects and scientific objects are both members of that realm of subsistence which I have called the third order, scientific objects are known only by minds which have reached a higher level of evolutionary development, a level at which they are capable of interests such as that of intellectual curiosity, which only evince themselves when the pressure of immediate practical needs is no longer felt with the old insistence. The capacity of mental awareness to which they are revealed is, in other words, more subtle and profound than that which is exercised in the practical affairs of daily life; it is, with the possible exception of philosophical thought, the most subtle and profound of all the capacities which we are accustomed to describe as purely cognitive. Abstract scientific thought may, therefore, not inappropriately be regarded as exercised at the highest level of purely reasoning activity which the species has reached, and liable, therefore, at any moment to elevate the mind to a new and different level of awareness which is beyond reasoning. The objects upon which, in scientific

[1] It is possible, I think probable, that a fourth avenue is afforded by the moral consciousness (see Chapter VII of my *Matter, Life and Value*); but, as ethics falls outside the scope of this book, I shall not treat of it specifically here.

reasoning, our mental activity is directed may similarly be regarded as lying on the furthermost verge of the world of subsistence, and liable therefore to point forward the mind's awareness to a new type of object belonging to a different order of reality, just as I have suggested the apprehension of sense data may point forward the activity of the mind's awareness to objects of thought.

In this connection I should like to develop a hint which Plato lets drop in the *Symposium*, where the prophetess Diotima instructs Socrates in the pursuits which must be followed by those who wish to know the form of beauty. The Form of Beauty is, it will be remembered, apprehended after a process which, beginning with the appreciation of the beauty of single beautiful objects and persons, comes to recognize the common quality of beauty which distinguishes them as members of a class and so to appreciate classes of beautiful objects and persons, proceeds to the appreciation of abstract beauty in laws and morals, then to the sciences and a realization of the beauty of Science, and so at last reaches a knowledge of the Form itself.[1] The knowledge of science is thus ranked only below the knowledge of Beauty; it is the stage immediately before the apprehension of the Form, which, although different from it, leads directly to it. Further, in the *Republic* we are told that the proper education of the mind for a knowledge of the Forms is a training in the exact sciences of measuring, weighing and counting, namely, the Theories of Number, Geometry, Stereometry and Astronomy.[2] The mind, in other words, is to be trained in precision; it must observe accurately and reason correctly. The apprehension of the Form is, it seems, not lightly to be achieved, nor, indeed, is it possible except to minds which have been prepared by hard and continuous exercise in abstract pursuits. The apprehension of the Form itself is, in the *Symposium*, described in the language of a mystical vision; the Form will, we are told, 'shine forth.'

[1] Plato, *Symposium*, 210, 211. [2] Id., *Republic*, 525–8.

But the vision, though conditioned by, is logically divorced from the strictly intellectual process which leads up to it.

The hint of the *Symposium* is confirmed by the testimony of subsequent writers. That meditation and contemplation are the necessary preliminaries to the mystical vision, and that meditation and contemplation involve not merely or always a purely receptive state of intellectual passivity, there is ample evidence in the literature of mysticism. Some writers go further and insist upon the need for hard mental discipline and training.

If I do not at this stage dwell upon the point as it bears upon mysticism, it is because I am here concerned with the particular function performed by scientific observation and reasoning in conditioning the mind's awareness of a new type of object. A considerable amount of research into the conditions attending the process of creative thinking in the arts and the sciences has been carried out by psychologists in recent years, as a result of which it seems fairly clear that scientific thought of the first order involves a process analogous to what is called artistic inspiration and creation.

An interesting summary of this research will be found in Professor Graham Wallas's book *The Art of Thought.*[1] He distinguishes four stages in the process which goes to the making of a new generalization, the discovery of a new formula or the devising of a new invention. The first is that of Preparation, during which a particular problem is investigated in all directions; the second, that of Incubation, during which no conscious thinking is done in connection with the problem or work of art with which the creative thinker or artist is concerned; the third, consisting of the appearance of the 'happy idea,' together with the psychological events accompanying that appearance, is called Illumination; and the fourth, embodying the working out and application of the idea in thought or the execution of the work of art, Verification.

[1] See especially Chapter IV, pp. 79–101.

Particular stress is laid upon the importance of Preparation as a preliminary to Illumination. Professor Wallas speaks of the many men of genius who have done their best work after a period of idleness.[1] But the period of idleness must itself be preceded by a spell of hard thinking, during which the intellect is working at full pressure. To adopt the language of modern psychology, we may say that consciousness during the thinking stage propounds a problem, collects the relevant data and explores different avenues for a possible solution. A period of rest ensues during which the problem and relevant data are transferred to the unconscious. That the unconscious may work effectively, consciousness must so far as possible be unoccupied. The solution is worked out by the unconscious, and appears in due course in consciousness as the "happy idea" of the scientist and the inspiration of the artist. The conclusion that emerges bears out Plato's hint in the *Symposium*. The "happy idea" which succeeds the period of hard thinking is of an entirely different order from the thinking itself. It outruns the thinking, and, although it is led up to, is far from being necessitated by it. The mind, in other words, makes a definite jump, and it is for this reason that in the sphere of science a subsequent process of 'Verification' is necessary.

Translating into the language which I have used to describe the process of knowing, I should say that "the happy idea" with which the mind is illuminated is the mind's sudden awareness of a new object, possibly of a new type of object, and that the jump which occurs is a sudden extension in the range of the mind's awareness, an extension which may reveal an object of a new type. The jump is analogous to that which the mind makes from the direct apprehension of sense data to the knowledge of physical objects, and in both cases it is exercise and practice at the lower level of apprehension which conditions the functioning of mental activity at the higher.

[1] Wallas, *The Art of Thought*, pp. 88–91.

Thinking is, in my view, simply the living activity of awareness exercised at a certain level and directed upon a certain area of the universe. That effort and endeavour are the conditions of life's development on the biological plane is a commonplace, and, I suggest, the formula which they embody still holds good now that life's activity is mainly exercised in the sphere of thought. The formula is that effort and endeavour exercised at a particular level of thought not only perfect the mind's activity at that level, but facilitate its emergence at a higher level, or, translating again into epistemological terms, the continued and intensive exploration of one particular order of the universe prepares the mind for the apprehension of a new order.

Applied to the case of scientific knowledge, this doctrine would suggest that the scientist who follows scientific thought as far as it will take him, is liable at any moment to become more than a scientist. In pursuance of this suggestion, which cannot, of course, be more than pure hypothesis, I would hazard the view that the type of subsistent object with which contemporary science deals lies, if I may express myself figuratively, at the furthest confines of the world of subsistence and on the threshold of the world of value. I have already noted how scientific objects have gradually divested themselves of the qualities of the sensory world, until the most recent developments of wave mechanics postulate a world of objects which have completely emancipated themselves from the last traces of the world of sense. Modern science moves, in other words, in a world of what is popularly called pure abstraction. Is it, then, too venturesome to suggest that the scientist may be in touch with objects which, lying on the outermost confines of the realm of subsistence, may perform the 'propaedeutic' function which Plato postulates for the studies of counting, weighing and measuring, the function, namely, of directing the mind's awareness to a new type of object belonging to a different realm? In favour of this suggestion a number of considerations may be mentioned, which, although separately possessing but little weight, have a certain cumulative force.

There is, for example, the emotion which the mathematician is said to feel for certain abstract operations which belong to the higher reaches of mathematics. Chains of mathematical reasoning are described as being aesthetically satisfying; solutions have a certain elegance; proofs and explanations are admired because they are economical and do not introduce inessential factors. The expressions frequently used in reference to the performance of these mathematical operations are strongly reminiscent of the language in which a pictorial artist might describe his own technique, and the emotions which they appear to arouse in mathematicians seem to be analogous to the aesthetic emotion which is ordinarily felt for a good picture. It seems plausible, then, to suggest that the emotion is felt for the same type of object or objects, that is to say, for an object or objects of value.

Nor does the mathematician alone among thinkers evince this 'aesthetic' attitude to his work, although, as might perhaps be expected, in virtue of the purity of mathematics and its remoteness from the sensory realm of changing physical data, he evinces it more frequently than others. In proportion as his work becomes more abstract and the objects with which he deals more divorced from daily life, the physicist seems to experience something of the same satisfaction.

We are frequently told that the scale upon which the operations of contemporary science are conducted conduces to an attitude of aloofness from the affairs of the mundane world. The astronomer concerned with the incredibly large, the physicist with the incredibly small, are equally remote from the objects and interests of daily life. Moreover, the work upon which modern science, and especially modern physics, is engaged is, it is generally conceded, of the highest order, demanding the full stretch of the faculties of the mind.

If science were the only intellectual pursuit open to our species, it would suffice to employ the intelligence and the imagination of the keenest minds for thousands, perhaps millions, of years. The man of science looks out upon the universe in which he is an invisible speck, maps its geography, measures its motions, enumerates its contents. In the enormous ferment of the universe which he studies, his own life appears briefer than the most ephemeral of insects, frailer than that of the lightest butterfly. His cares, his hopes, his frets and pains raise but a bubble on the vast ocean of the universe. Yet he, knowing these things, is undismayed, and by the mere fact of his knowledge is elevated into a sphere in which his spatial and temporal insignificance become irrelevant. To return from such pursuits to the familiar world is not unlike the descent of the philosopher into the cave. Nor is an incursion into the atomic world, an examination of structures minutely small, less remote from the confused and muddled issues of daily life.

This continual sojourning in remote and abstract realms cannot but have its effect upon the mind, and, in revealing to it the size and complexity of the universe, predispose it to travel outside its own particular department of inquiry, and to seek for a cosmic principle of explanation which will embrace all the varieties of being. Thus is generated the psychological mood, from which springs, as I conceive, the increasing tendency to metaphysical speculation so noticeable in modern science. A desire is felt to understand the universe as a whole, in pursuance of which an endeavour is made to pass beyond the world of science and to penetrate through to the reality of which it is thought to be a phenomenal aspect. Such an endeavour involves, as we have seen, an abandonment of the methods of science. In my view this abandonment is inevitable,[1] being conditioned by a change in the nature of the objects with which the inquiry is concerned. The method of experiment and of observation

[1] Of method, but not of spirit (see Chapter XI, pp. 337–340).

gives way inevitably to that of philosophic thought, because the objects with which the scientist in his wider speculations is concerned declare themselves unamenable to experiment, and even, it may be, in the last resort, to reasoning.

For the scientist feeling wonder and awe at the size and immensity of nature, and seeking for a unifying principle whereby to interpret its multitudinous phenomena, is, it is obvious, no longer in contact with the ordinary objects of scientific inquiry. I would hazard the suggestion, without necessarily committing myself to the view that these objects of wider scientific speculation belong to the world of value, and that physics as well as mathematics may, in virtue of the degree of abstraction which it requires, be not inappropriately regarded as at least an avenue of approach to this world. Modern physics constitutes, it is obvious, one of the most important of those preliminary studies of weighing, counting and measuring which Plato specified as 'propaedeutic' to the knowledge of value, and, if Plato is right, it would seem natural to suppose that the emotion of reverence and wonder which the scientist is often said to feel may be an emotion felt for value.

It is this emotion which, I suggest, is responsible for the metaphysical bent of modern science, and in particular for the endeavours on the part of scientists to form a consistent view of reality as a whole, which I have traced in the earlier part of this book. The fact that there seem to be good reasons for regarding the general view which results from these endeavours as mistaken does not alter the significance of the fact that the endeavours are made. And the explanation of this significance which I am suggesting is that prolonged and arduous study of the world of subsistence points the mind forward to a further realm which lies beyond it, and prepares it for the apprehension of its contents.

The apprehension of this further realm, which I have called the world of value, involves experiences which are profoundly moving, so that by whatever avenue a man reaches it, he finds it impossible to retain that impartial and dispassionate temper of mind, that attitude of calm and disinterested contemplation which has always been regarded as the characteristic virtue of science. Science, in fact, cannot be maintained beyond a point; at the furthermost limits of scientific explantion the mind passes into another sphere which is not the world of science, but the world of value. Hence the importance of scientific knowledge at the present stage of mind's evolution lies in the fact that it prepares the mind for the revelation of a world beyond scientific knowledge.

It is this revelation which, I suggest, may have been the privilege of the eminent scientists whose views I have summarized; but I suggest also that they have been led by their lack of philosophic training to misinterpret the nature of the world so revealed.

D. Art and Value.—I have argued above[1] that aesthetic enjoyment is the emotion we feel on apprehending the images of reality, and that for the ordinary man art constitutes the easiest method of approach to the real world. To take up another hint of Plato's, Beauty among the Forms alone appears as she really is, and a knowledge of the real world is, I should say, more readily accessible through the avenue of art than by any other. The general view which I wish to suggest is, as I have already indicated, that objects that excite us aesthetically stand in some special relation, which I do not know how exactly to define, to the world of value, and possess therefore a unique capacity for turning the mind in the direction of value. The enjoyment of beauty, like the pursuits of mathematics, is in this sense also 'propaedeutic' to mysticism.

I now make the further suggestion that the aesthetic appreciation of beauty should be regarded as a foretaste of the experience which life as a whole is seeking to realize

[1] Pp. 277–279; see also my *Matter, Life and Value*, Chapter VI.

more fully, more freely and more continuously, and that in this general sense the drift of the evolutionary stream of life is towards a goal which may be conceived as the untrammelled and continuous apprehension of beauty. It is this goal which through the chances and changes of day-to-day existence we unalterably pursue, drawing beauty by pain and effort out of the heart of life, disentangling it with ever greater success from the confused welter of existence and making it clear to ourselves in a hundred varying forms, now as a quality of colour, now in shape, now in sound, now in the lines of a landscape, but always as beauty. The apprehension of beauty emerges more clearly with each decade in the life-history of the individual and each generation in the life-history of the race. Beauty is strictly indefinable; it is at once unique and ultimate, and because it is unique and ultimate it cannot be described in terms of any other thing. In writing of it one finds oneself dropping insensibly into the language of mysticism; for beauty may well be, as suggested above, a revelation because an aspect of deity.

I will endeavour to translate this general conception into the epistemological language appropriate to the theory of knowledge I have advocated. A person apprehending a work of art, a picture, say, or a statue, is primarily aware of a set of related data. These data direct his attention to the physical object, the picture or statue of which he believes himself to have *sensory* apprehension, but which, on the view I have suggested, is an object of thought.

Arguments were summarized in Chapter VIII which sought to show that aesthetic value is in an important sense a quality of a whole. For this reason, it was urged, no account of it can be given by the methods of science. These arguments seemed to me to state a truth; I dissented only when they were used as the basis of the inference that science does not give us objective truth, or that the objects which scientific method investigates are not objectively real. To say that aesthetic value is a quality of a whole is to say also that it is not a quality of sense data, since sense data are not wholes in the sense of the word 'whole' which was examined in Chapter VIII, but particulars. If beauty is not a quality of sense data, it follows that, when we apprehend a picture and call it beautiful, what we affirm to be beautiful must be, not the sense data, but the physical object, which is an object of thought. Beauty, therefore, is not, like colour or sound, an inhabitant of the physical world, but appears to be a property of objects which belong to the world of subsistence. Thus, when I speak of beautiful objects as standing in a certain particular relation to the world of value, the statement is intended to refer not to sense data, but to physical objects which are objects of thought. I have already reached the same conclusion by a different route in Section II of this chapter.[1]

My position is, then, that certain objects of thought, which are regarded as beautiful, are so regarded because they possess the property of directing the attention of minds at a certain level of development to the world of value. In this respect they are like the so-called abstract objects of scientific and mathematical thought, which I have spoken of as being situated as it were on the threshold of the world of value, and as liable in virtue of their position to induce the mind to cross it. And just as the cosmic emotion of the scientist may be conceived to be aroused not by the subsistent object upon which his thought is immediately directed, but by the world of value of which the presence is dimly sensed in abstract scientific thought, so aesthetic emotion is aroused not by the picture, which is a member of the world of subsistence, but by the world of value to which the picture introduces the apprehending mind. I am not, then, asserting that the beautiful picture is itself a member of the world of value; merely that it stands in a particular relation to it which I do not know how better

[1] See pp. 278, 279.

to describe than by saying that it turns the eye of the soul towards it. This function it performs in virtue of the fact that in some way, which I am unable to explain, it copies or reflects that world. The question of how it comes to possess this property of reflection must be answered by reference to the circumstances and conditions in which it came to be painted;[1] and this reference raises in its turn the further question of the nature of the artist's inspiration, from which the picture took its rise and to which its aesthetic value is said to be due.

In order the better to deal with this question, I should like to recall the conception suggested in Section II[2] of life as a dynamic, changing impulsion, of which living organisms are the individual expressions.

At every stage of the evolution of life there occur organisms which biologists call "sports." The outstanding characteristic of the "sport" that breeds true is that it anticipates some of the future characteristics of the species. In it first appear those qualities which will presently characterize the species as a whole; it is, in other words, an advance instalment of what the species is to become. The special characteristics of a "sport" may involve such radical novelties as to constitute what is in fact a difference of species. Thus the view is now generally taken that it is through the occurrence of "sports," the results of fortuitous mutations in the germ plasm, that new species arise.

The method of life's progression is still, I suggest, essentially the same as it was at the strictly biological level. Its developments are still announced by the appearance of "sports"; but the "sporting" now takes place primarily at the mental level. Any marked and sudden enlargement of the capacity for awareness in individuals may, therefore, be

[1] The "painting" of the picture is, of course, a colloquialism. What the artist actually 'does' is to engender certain arrangements of data, which cause the person apprehending them to become aware of a particular 'physical' object.

[2] See pp. 270–272.

diagnosed as the harbinger of a development which may sooner or later characterize the species as a whole. It is such an enlargement which, I suggest, is the peculiar and essential characteristic of the great artist. And the enlargement expresses itself in the form either of a direct awareness of the world of value or of a quickened perception of the significance of the "physical object" (which is a subsistent object) which reflects it.

Whatever may be the precise epistemological explanation of the artist's vision, we must, I think, concede that it implies in some sort and in some degree the presence of value. Its presence is implied whether the artist is said to commune with value, to be fertilized by it, to create it, to express it, or, as I am suggesting, to be merely aware of it. I suggest, further, that it is in virtue of his quickened capacity for awareness that the artist stands in advance of the average of the species, pointing the way to a level of development which for most of us has still to be attained. But although the artist, in view of his "precocity of vision," is enabled to penetrate further into the world of value than the average man, possibly even on occasion to attain to a direct vision of value itself,[1] his apprehension is precariously achieved and is with difficulty maintained.

The awareness of value cannot at our present stage of evolution be more than a fleeting and uncertain experience; like thinking in a dog, it is a mode of apprehension to which the species has only just attained. It is still an abnormal capacity, exercised not continuously at the level of everyday experience, but enjoyed in fleeting and tantalizing glimpses of a world not normally accessible to consciousness. The soul of man, if I may resort to metaphor, is like a chrysalis maturing in the cocoon of matter, from which one day it will burst forth and spread its wings in the sun of pure reality. In the appreciation of art which is a fore-

[1] E.g. as I have urged elsewhere, as Beethoven does in the music of his last period.

taste of our knowledge of reality, the soul is, as it were, torn prematurely from its cocoon and subjected to experiences of a quality and intensity for which it is as yet insufficiently prepared.

For the world of value is a shining glory, the direct vision of which man is unable as yet to endure. Yet the glory shines through the veil of sense and the alert and receptive mind catches its reflection in common things. The artist and the musician are seekers after that glory, and the haunting beauty that they pursue is the reflection of its light. At times they may even catch a glimpse of the original itself, and, seeing it, are transported with delight. But their vision, if indeed they have it, is never more than a fleeting glimpse. For a continuous vision the soul of man is not as yet prepared. Faced with a direct view of reality, it falters and falls back, and, were not the veil of matter mercifully interposed, it would be stunned and blinded by the force and glory of reality; thus it must content itself with images. It is this inability of the soul to prolong or to maintain the awareness of value that suggests a clue to the interpretation of much that is puzzling in aesthetic experience, whether regarded as creative or appreciative.

It may, for example, be cited in answer to the question I raised above, the question why the artist comes to create at all. It is inconceivable that a mind, enjoying a continuous and direct awareness of the world of value, should interrupt its vision in order to reproduce its images in matter. In this connection it is significant that it is the artist, not the mystic, who 'creates.' The mystic's vision is, as I suggest and shall try to show, at once more continuous and more satisfying, and, although the mystics in the intervals of contemplation can be active enough, their activity does not seem to arise directly from their vision in the same way as does that of the artist. For the activity of the artist is, I conceive, prompted by his desire to perpetuate a vision which he cannot retain, to perpetuate it, that is to say, in memory, since he cannot do so in fact. Finding that his vision fades, and filled with a feeling of indefinable longing and regret for that which he has seen but can see no longer, he sets to work, while the memory of it is still with him, to make a copy of it in matter, which will have such semi-permanence as the things of the material world possess, so that, contemplating it, his memory may be stirred, and he may again enjoy, albeit faintly, the emotion which he felt for reality, contemplating its reflection in stone or paint or sound.

Thus the artist creates not because he enjoys but because, although he has enjoyed once, he cannot enjoy still. His work is a witness not to the inspiration which he has, but to the inspiration which he has had, and has no longer. In this sense every work of art is testimony to a failure, a failure to retain the vision of reality. We cannot suppose, to revert to Plato's simile, that the philosopher will return to the cave when he can stay in the sunlight, and a man will not waste his time in making images while he enjoys a vision of the original. This is not to say that the artist is satisfied with the image that he makes. It is, indeed, a characteristic which has frequently been noted of the great artist that he loses interest in his work so soon as he has completed it. And the loss of interest arises, I suggest, from the realization that the image does not satisfy the need for which it was made. It is because it is so poor and faulty, so ridiculously inadequate as a representation of that which has moved him that the artist turns away from it in disgust, and immediately sets to work to make a better. Thus he will paint picture after picture in the effort to do justice to the memory which haunts him, hoping, though vainly, to recapture the form of the original.

I turn now to consider the question of the appreciation as opposed to the creation of works of art and to the aesthetic experience of the ordinary man. The artist, I have suggested, is one who in virtue of his more developed capacity of awareness is enabled to discern those among "physical objects" which reflect the world of value. This capacity for recognition further suggests that fleeting intimations of the world of value itself are from time to time vouchsafed to him. In virtue of this same developed capacity his attention is directed by the sense data of the material world to those subsistent objects which stand in the special relation, a relation to which I have frequently referred but do not know how to define, to the world of value.

At each stage of apprehension the mind is directed by the reflection to that which it reflects, by the sense data to the subsistent object, by the subsistent object to beauty, or aesthetic value. But the reflections are only for those who have eyes to see, and, I should say, normally escape the notice of ordinary men. The road that leads from physical data through the world of subsistence to the world of value is not one which we at our present stage of evolution are fitted to take; or not, at least, to take unaided. For it is here that the artist comes to our assistance, and exhibiting to us works of art awakens in us the awareness of value which material objects have first aroused in him. These works are, I have suggested, the outcome of the artist's inability to hold his vision; nevertheless they enshrine his memory of it, and, being stamped, as it were, in the likeness of the world of value by his informing hand, possess in a marked degree the power of turning the mind in the direction of that world which confers their significance upon them. It is as though the beautiful objects made by artists focussed together features of the universe at once too vast and too subtle for ordinary human comprehension.

In this way the artist acts as a midwife to value, bringing to birth in the work of his hands the patterns or reflections of the real world. In the work of art that property of objects in virtue of which their special relation to value consists, a property which is usually denoted by the word significance, is thrown into high relief so that it is discerned by the less sensitive and evolved awareness of the ordinary man. Thus the work of art performs for the ordinary man the function which the ordinary sense object[1] performs for the artist, that, namely, of awakening in him an apprehension of value. But the apprehension of beauty in the copy, although it exalts and excites, is no less evanescent than the artist's apprehension of the original.

It is, indeed, characteristic of the apprehension of beauty in whatever form it comes to us that against our will it passes and fades. We cannot, the fact, alas, is obvious, contemplate beauty long. Taken as a statement of literal fact, the first line of Keats's *Endymion* is simply not true. The sensation which a thing of beauty bestows is, indeed, magical; but having acknowledged the magic the mind quickly begins to wander. The contact with beauty is an ecstasy, a momentary thrill, which because it is momentary refuses to be pinned down for description and dissection. Freeze it into a psychic state to analyse it, and what you analyse is no longer the feeling you experienced.

Also, beauty is meaningless; there is nothing to be said about it. You can smell the perfume of a rose; you can listen to the theme of a fugue, but, having smelt and listened, the limit of your appropriate reactions has been reached. That is why pictorial and musical criticism is almost always irrelevant. All that the critic can tell you with regard to Bach's twelfth prelude is to listen to it carefully and not to let your mind wander. What else he has to say is history, biography or technical explanation; it is an account of the means which have been employed that the effect may be produced; it is in no sense an account of the effect.

And just because the feeling for beauty is momentary and does not last, just because beauty is meaningless, and there is nothing to say about it, while yet it seems right to say something, people do commonly read other qualities into beauty, pathos and tenderness, humanity or grandeur, and proceed

[1] By sense objects I mean the sense data which direct the mind of the artist upon the subsistent objects which reflect value.

to speak at length of these. Dwelling upon them they prove that beauty is this or that, that it is noble or refining, that it spiritualizes our nature or brings us nearer to the infinite. Yet it is not of beauty that they speak, but of considerations which have nothing to do with beauty, which they have imported into beaùty. For this reason too beauty is, and must remain, meaningless to one who has not experienced it. We can convey the meaning of a sentence in a foreign language or the appearance of a foreign land to a person ignorant of both, because both can be translated in terms of things with which the listener is familiar. But so to translate beauty is to falsify it; seeking to speak of it, one finds to one's discomfiture that one has described something quite different, sensations connected with it no doubt, but not the actual feeling which beauty itself has aroused. Beauty is not for description or understanding, but for enjoyment.

E. The Function of Mysticism.—The inadequacy of mystical literature is, I suspect, due to the same cause.

The mystic, to whose position in the hierarchy of knowing I now turn, is, I conceive, one in whom life has emerged at the highest level which it has yet reached; the mystic's faculty for awareness is, in other words, keener and more sensitive than that of any other living organism. In the first place his vision of reality is direct, direct, that is, in the special sense in which the artist's is indirect. Whether the vision of the artist is confined to those subsistent objects which, as I have suggested, stand in a special relation of imitation or reflection to the world of value, whether reality is, as Plato suggested, in some way literally manifested in the objects which the artist apprehends, or whether his vision may on occasion break through into the world of value itself, we must, I think, deny to him that direct view of reality which the mystic achieves. On the ladder whose rungs are the stages of our developing awareness of the universe, the mystic has attained to a higher rung than the artist, standing on which he passes behind the image or reflection of reality which the artist makes in paint or sound or stone, to a vision of the original which the image reflects. In the second place, he can, we must suppose, retain this vision for considerable periods of time, and is not, therefore, under the artist's necessity of making for himself as souvenirs copies of the reality which he can no longer apprehend.

But for this very reason, because he has achieved a direct vision of the world of value as it is in itself, he is unable to describe it. Language was invented to serve the uses of the familiar world; it may not readily be invoked to convey the meanings appropriate to another. Thus the mystics with their talk of a "dazzling darkness" and "a delicious desert" seem to those who have no tincture of mystical experience merely to babble. Yet the fact that the mystic cannot describe to us what he experienced is no ground for supposing that his experience did not occur, or that it did not possess the tremendous significance with which, on the view I am suggesting, only a direct view of the world of value could be held to invest it. The emotion is what matters, the written or spoken word is simply an attempt to express emotion, which is itself inexpressible, in terms of intellect and logic. If mysticism could give an account of itself, it would cease to be mysticism.

The world, I am suggesting, contains an element that we may point to but cannot describe. Language, indeed, is only significant in so far as it is able to indicate something beyond language. The minimum prerequisite of the possibility of mysticism is thus a view of the world as containing ineffable and alogical elements which cannot be described, although they may be known.

Nor are we entitled to suppose that the knowledge even of the most advanced mystic is clear. The race, after all, is still in its childhood, and there is no reason to think that a complete understanding of the universe, still less a complete vision of reality, is vouchsafed to children. The eyes of children, if I may resort to my metaphor, are dazzled by too close a view; hence their vision is blurred, and what they seek to tell of it in stammering words would, perhaps, be false even if we could understand what they tell. There is something dreamlike in mysticism, and its stories of wonder and mystery are of the nature of a dream, even if it be a true one. The most that we can say is that life has now reached a stage of its journey at which to a few here and there, there shoot down from the place where there is light, flashes and gleams which, though they blind and dazzle, reveal to them a shining glory which makes the things of familiar life seem drab and grey, robbing our mundane achievements of their triumph and our mundane pursuits of their interest.

The only language in which we can convey a hint of the nature of this world is that of art, for great art embodies and conveys fleeting memories of the artist's vision of it. Yet even so the artist has rarely seen it face to face, but for the most part only its reflections in other things. Yet art, not words, is the language of reality conveying to us so much of its meaning and nature as at our present stage of development we are able to apprehend. Art is a window, misty and blurred, through which men look out upon the reality which the mystic has seen direct. Thus, although this section purports to deal with the knowledge of the mystic, I find myself compelled to revert to the message of art.

I commented in a previous chapter on the significance of the fact that, whereas the notes which constitute the theme of a Bach fugue struck at random on the piano constitute merely a series of noises of which physics and physiology could give a complete account, the same notes played in the right order could thrill to ecstasy.

And not only thrill but, if I may make use of a word which suffers from a not wholly undeserved unpopularity, edify. For what is striking in works of art of the highest order, Bach's Well-Tempered Clavichord, for example, or

Beethoven's posthumous Quartets, is not so much that we enjoy them as that we are edified by them. They constitute a world view which is both new and noble.

Joy, sorrow, tears, lamentation, to all these they give expression, but in such a way that we are transported from the world of unrest to a world of peace, and, glimpsing a vision of a reality that we have not known before, are released and refreshed because released in its contemplation. This quality of serenity in great art is perhaps its most universal characteristic. It is a quality which Bach's music possesses from the first, but which Beethoven achieves only in the music of his last period, and achieves then but intermittently. Listening to the music of Bach one is raised to an eminence from which the concerns of everyday life are suddenly seen to be unimportant. It is exactly as if a voice had reached one from another world: and it is from just this fact of otherworldliness that the sense of release, the serenity and security which I have noted as characteristics of all great art are derived. Human lives, I have suggested, are to be regarded as individual expressions of a force or principle of life which evolves towards the apprehension of a static and perfect world. They are the instruments which life has made to further the process of its own development. As instruments of evolution we are in our day-to-day existence mere channels through which flows restlessly and unceasingly the current of life. We are a surge of impulses, a battlefield of desires, over which we can only at length and after a lifetime of setbacks and of struggle obtain a degree of mastery through the achievement of self-discipline, which is itself the outcome of desire made rational. Wishing, fearing, craving, hoping, and willing, we may never, except in rare moments of aesthetic enjoyment, be at rest. We must for ever be doing and stirring, improving and making better, meddling and changing. It is one of the paradoxes of our nature that we cannot even love a thing without seeking to change it, and by changing it to make it other than what we love. The greatest lovers of mankind have been those who have spent their lives in the endeavour to save mankind; and, since they have always insisted that mankind could not be saved except it repented, to save man was to alter him. A man cannot love a woman without seeking to mould her nearer to his heart's desire, or a child without trying to form it upon himself. We cannot love the countryside without pruning and clipping, smartening and tidying, making meaningful and useful what has achieved beauty by haphazard, and imposing order upon the sweet disorder of nature. We cannot love a tree or a stone even, but sooner or later we must be pruning the tree or chipping a piece off the stone. We do these things because of the overmastering impulsion of our wills; yet were it not for our wills we should cease to be. Thus, for so long as we live, we must conform to the bidding of life, so that however we love and whatever we love, it can be for a few moments only, and to buy off our will for these moments we have to relinquish what we love to it, to change and alter as it needs must for the rest of our lives.

This, then, is the law of our being as units of the stream of life, that we should be for ever changing ourselves, and seeking to change the world around us. But this law, which is the law of life as evolving to an end, is not the law of life which has achieved the end. And so there is even now an exception to the law, in virtue of which we partake, if only for a moment, of the rest and freedom which it is the object of life to win permanently and to win for everything that is living. In the appreciation of music and of pictures we get a momentary and fleeting glimpse of the nature of that reality to a full knowledge of which the movement of life is progressing. For that moment, and for so long as the glimpse persists, we realize in anticipation and almost, as it were illicitly, the nature of the end. We are, if I may so put it, for the moment *there*, just as a traveller may obtain a fleeting glimpse of a distant country from a height passed on the way, and cease for a space from his journey to enjoy the view. And since we are for the moment *there*, we experience while the moment lasts that sense of liberation from the drive of life which has been noted as one of the special characteristics of aesthetic experience. We who are part and parcel of the evolutionary stream stand for the time outside and above the stream, and are permitted for a moment to be withdrawn from the thrust and play of impulse and desire, which are our natural attributes as evolutionary tools. For so long as we enjoy our vision of the end, life lets us alone. We feel neither need not want, and, losing ourselves in contemplation of the reality beyond us, we become for the moment selfless. It is of this, I take it, that Schopenhauer spoke, when he said that the will uses the intellect always as its servant except in aesthetic contemplation. When we experience those significant combinations of forms or sounds to which we give the name of beautiful in art, our contemplation is Will-less in its character. The object of aesthetic contemplation is something framed apart by itself, and regarded without memory or expectation simply as itself, as end not means, as eternally self-sufficient and universal. In so far as we are able to view it, we cease for the moment to be mere tools or expression of the Will, and take on a character of universality from the universal nature of that which we contemplate.

This interpretation of the emotion aroused by great art rests upon two assumptions. First, the beauty with which we are brought into contact must be a real, objective entity which is independent of ourselves. This will be true even if, as I have suggested, all that most of us ever perceive is its shadow and beauty itself is revealed to creatures of finer sense than ours, in intellect more enlarged and brighter and clearer in vision. That such creatures already exist is possible; that we shall ourselves become such as they are is, I conceive, some part, at least, of the purpose of life as it rises to higher levels of awareness in and through human consciousness. Beauty then, on this view, resides in reality, and it is the shimmer of it, faintly reflected in the things of this world, that gives its value to what we call aesthetic experience. Variations in aesthetic taste are due to the fact that men's differing capacities for vision cause them to see differently some more and some less clearly its faint and glimmering effulgence.

Secondly, this beauty can never become one with us. We may contemplate it, but never over-pass the gulf between ourselves and what we know. To this point I now turn in a final chapter.

CHAPTER XI

CONCLUSION. PHILOSOPHY AND THE TEMPER OF SCIENCE

I AM aware that the view suggested at the end of the preceding chapter, that the value which is revealed to us in aesthetic experience is and must remain other than the mind that apprehends it, is contrary to the theory of reality and of mind's place in reality accepted by many philosophers at the present time. I am also conscious that the connection of the discussion of value which has occupied the last two chapters with the theme of the earlier part of the book may seem obscure. What bearing, it may be asked, has the nature of aesthetic experience upon the validity of the metaphysical speculations inspired by modern physics? My object in these concluding pages is to establish this connection, while at the same time endeavouring to illustrate and to defend the conception of the impassable gulf which, I have suggested, separates knowing and object known, mind and reality. I will begin with a short discussion of this second point.

For the purpose of this discussion it will be necessary to take up the threads of the treatment of mysticism with which I concluded the last chapter. My object in doing so will be to consider the bearing of mystical experience upon epistemological issues. I have maintained that the awareness of the artist and of the mystic remains distinct from the value which it apprehends. I have also suggested that this value is an objective element in the universe, a factor in a world or order of reality to which goodness, truth, and, it may be, deity also belong. As to whether deity is other than these values or their sum, whether God transcends them as a whole transcends its parts or is the unity of their aspects, I do not venture to hazard any suggestion. That there is an important connection between the three elements of value, goodness, truth and beauty, I am convinced; that they may point forward to a unity within which they are contained as the movements of a symphony are contained within the whole, seems to me to be at least possible; it may even be probable. But, for the reasons at which I have already glanced, in so far as the human mind has developed an awareness of the world of value, it can give no account of what it knows, and it does not, therefore, seem to me to be possible either to make statements purporting to describe the relations between the factors constituting the world of value, or to deny those which may be made by others. But, if my general conception is valid, it will follow that aesthetic experience, which is experience of a part or aspect of value, will be an awareness of the same order of reality as mystical experience, which may be interpreted as a consciousness of the unity of value; and art a portrayal of the same thing as mystics study, glimmering somehow through the forms of the sensible world.

I have spoken of the artist in the last chapter as a biological 'sport.' But the term should, perhaps, have been reserved for the mystic. The mystic is a precocious child of evolution in whom the capacity of awareness has reached a level at which it is capable of direct, albeit intermittent, experience of the world of value, and, it may be, of that world as a unity in which goodness, truth and beauty are somehow fused. It is as though in the case of the mystic an envelope, which shuts most of us off from the world of reality, were torn or frayed, so that the mystic's consciousness filters through into a region which is normally inaccessible. And the significance of the conception of this world as consisting of a *person* lies in the suggestion that the mystic's personality may be fused with or absorbed in that person. There is authoritative backing for the view that the human soul which "penetrates through" into the real world transcends itself and becomes one with that which it apprehends.

Reinforced by a strong vein of direct testimony from the Eastern religions, this may be regarded as the orthodox Oriental view. The language in which, for example, Al Ghazzali, the Persian Sufi, seeks to describe the final stage of the mystic's ascent identifies it with a complete absorption in God. "The end of Sufism," he says, "is total absorption in God. This is at least the relative end to that part of their doctrine which I am free to reveal and describe." Again, the state of *Samadhi* which certain people in India are believed to attain, while it is regarded as completely indescribable, is commonly spoken of as the complete merging of the self in the infinite. Into the question of the authority of this testimony I do not propose to enter, nor do I wish to embark upon a general discussion of the nature of the mystical experience. As I have pointed out, there is good reason to distrust the language in which mystics speak of their experiences, though little to distrust the validity of the experiences themselves, nor should much weight be attached to one particular account rather than to another. It is pertinent, moreover, to point out that, taken at their face value, the accounts of mystical experience are frequently contradictory. For example, Al Ghazzali himself, after describing "total absorption in God" as the "*relative* end" of Sufism, goes on to say that it is "but the beginning of the Sufi life." As to the nature of the *real* end, he is not explicit, but he goes out of his way to stigmatize the view of it as "amalgamation" with God, or "identicality" with God as "sin."

And the reason why he so regards it appears to be his conviction that the final stage is not so much one of absorption or identification as of annihilation. "It is right," says Mrs. Underhill, "to state that Oriental Mysticism insists upon a further stage beyond that of union, which stage it regards as the real goal of the spiritual life. This is the total *annihilation* or re-absorption of the individual soul in the Infinite. Such an annihilation is said by the Sufis to constitute the

'Eighth stage of Progress,' in which alone they truly attain to God. Thus stated it appears to differ little from the Buddhists' Nirvana."

The steps from union to absorption, from absorption to annihilation are, to my mind, almost inevitable. To admit the possibility of fusion between the finite and the infinite is in fact to annihilate the finite. The only logical alternative to such annihilation of the individual soul is to maintain its complete otherness from that which it contemplates. It is, however, pertinent to point out that the Oriental view of the mystical experience as testifying to the soul's oneness with God may be confronted by equally strong testimony from the great Christian mystics, to the effect that the soul, although it may aspire to a vision of God, remains outside and distinct from the divinity which it knows.

While, however, no good purpose can in my view be served by examining the precise import of the language in which mystical visions are described, comment may, I think, usefully be offered upon the temper of mind from which the conception of the oneness of subject and object in mystical experience is derived. It is clear that if the possibility of an ultimate unity of being between mind and reality is to be granted, reality must be conceived as essentially of the same nature as mind. It is inevitable, therefore, that a metaphysical view which postulates a reality behind the world of appearance, with which in mystical experience the mind is fused, should postulate also a kinship between reality and the human spirit.

It is thus characteristic of those metaphysical and theological views which impugn the reality of the familiar world, as a mere appearance, that the real world which they affirm should be at once more spiritual and more tractable. The world of everyday life thwarts our desires and disappoints our hopes. It contains evil, pain and imperfection; it is also a chaotic manifold. So far from spirit triumphing over matter, matter on all hands contracts and degrades spirit. The world, then, is not such as we should choose, and it is not such as we should have made. What, therefore, more natural than for aspiring souls, outraged by the imperfections and bewildered by the irrationality of the familiar world, to insist that reality must differ from it in precisely those respects in which it is found to be unsatisfactory. And it is, in fact, a noticeable feature of all those theories of the universe which assert a distinction between the world of appearance and the world of reality that they do affirm this difference; that is to say, the latter world, however it may be envisaged, always possesses the characteristic of being more congenial than the former. In general it is like a mind, and, since the human mind is the most advanced mind that we know, to say that it is like a mind is to imply that it is like a human mind. Religion personifies the reality which is like a mind into a deity who is like a person; and, since the human person is the most advanced personality that we know, to say that the Deity is like a person is to imply that He is like a human person.

With a reality so conceived the human spirit may in its highest development aspire to merge, just because the fundamental nature of this reality is not really different from that of the human spirit. Thus the metaphysical conception of the soul's fusion with or absorption in ultimate reality presupposes that the reality is akin to the human spirit, and therefore spiritual, that it is friendly to human nature and therefore personal, and that it is all-pervasive and therefore a unity. As for the familiar world, it is only a phenomenal appearance, and in most views less real than that of which it is an appearance.

It is interesting to notice how closely the metaphysical speculations which are based upon modern science agree. The views which I have traced in this book, the views of Eddington, of Jeans and of Russell, as also, I am led to understand, those of Einstein and Planck, all uphold the traditional distinction between appearance and reality.

Known reality, they suggest, is mere phenomenon or appearance; but behind the appearance there must be a real essence; behind the phenomenal manifestation there must be an ultimate force; beneath the outer phenomenon there must be an inner reality. And essence, force and inner reality are not, they hold, to be known by an intellectual faculty, since what our reasons and our senses know is always the spatially and temporarily limited phenomenon to the making of which our minds have contributed. Nevertheless, since they are in some sense known, they must be known by process of revelation to an intuitive faculty of direct insight. So revealed, reality is seen to be spiritual and even personal. Thus, with regard to the most fundamental issues of metaphysics, the speculations of modern physicists seem to bear out and to support what is, perhaps, the main traditional mystic view.

Reality, it is agreed, is in some sense mental or spiritual, and in some sense personal; reality is known by a non-intellectual faculty, which identifies the knower with what is known, and the familiar world of everyday life is only an appearance of the real world. But while their general outlook on the universe is one which has been common to a certain school of philosophers and mystics in all ages, the scientists introduce two apparent novelties. There are, they assert, two worlds of appearance, the world of science as well as the world of sense; and physics is invoked to reinforce the testimony of the mystical consciousness and the speculative reason.

In Chapter IX I have suggested certain logical criticisms of this general view of the universe as divided into a real world of spirit and into semi-real manifolds of sense and science. In this concluding chapter I propose to offer a few observations upon the temper of mind from which, in scientists no less than in philosophers or mystics, it appears to me to spring. This temper, to borrow a convenient word from Mr. Santayana, is "malicious" in regard to the familiar world and also to the world of science. Springing as it does from an impulse to regard the universe as a whole which is both spiritual and all-embracing, it is driven to convict these worlds, which are neither spiritual nor all-embracing, of unreality in the interests of the harmony it postulates. It is because of this temper of mind which is born not of logical necessity but of impulse that scientists are, I venture to suggest, led to ignore the confusions and inconsistencies which I have sought to point out, and to ignore in particular the inconsistency of basing a theory of reality upon the study of a world which is "maliciously" regarded. To read the book of Nature in the conviction that it is misleading may be a permissible, although I see no reason to suppose that it is a necessary, proceeding; but, if the results of your reading are used as the basis for a theory of the universe, then the superstructure will inevitably be infected with the character of the foundations upon which it is based.

Nor is it only on logical grounds that this procedure is open to question; it may, I think, fairly be urged that the temper of mind from which these metaphysical speculations spring, and in which they are conducted, is fundamentally unscientific.

It lays itself open to the charge of arriving at conclusions which are merely a rationalization of the wishes of its authors, and it derogates from the dignity of the universe by assimilating it to the human spirit. The two charges raise different issues, and I will briefly consider each of them in turn.

I. The Impulse to Rationalize

I have already commented upon the significance of the fact that the world of reality differs from the familiar world in being such as we should wish to exist. It conforms to our wishes and satisfies our hopes. This, it is obvious, is true of the reality affirmed by those philosophies which define it as a personal deity, an absolute mind or an all-pervading spirit; other philosophies again, while affirming the universe to be in essence a flux or progression, regard the ultimate perfectibility of the human spirit as the end which the progression is seeking to achieve. This perfected human spirit takes the place of the all-pervading thought structure of the monists and the deity of the theologians.

For example, in philosophies of the Bergsonian type, which regard evolution as the key to metaphysical truth, the conception of goal takes the place of that of reality. A goal is a "reality" conceived in time; "reality," a timeless goal. It is difficult not to see in such philosophies a projection of human wishes upon the screen of reality. They bear upon them the marks of an essential anthropomorphism. That plurality is appearance and evil unreal, that reality is fashioned after our heart's desire and in our spirit's likeness and that the universe shares our ethical preoccupations, is affected by an interest in our mundane affairs, and is concerned for our future destiny: these beliefs spring from the heart rather than from the head. In the light of the discoveries of science, the fact can no longer be denied. Science shows that man is a comparatively late arrival upon the cosmic scene. For thousands of millions of years the universe, so far as we know, was lifeless. Then on one little "speck of burnt-out ash," slowly and hesitatingly living organisms appear. In the vast immensities of astronomic space and geologic time their life seems a tiny glow flickering uncertainly, and, so far at least as the teaching of science goes, destined in the end, under the action of blind material forces, to be frozen out of the one corner of the world in which it has appeared.

But if life is recent in time and insignificant in space, human life is incomparably more recent and more insignificant. For twelve hundred million years has there been life; for only a million human life. During only a very small part of these million years have human beings been able to think; and the minds, by means of which their thinking is conducted, are lately developed products, makeshift and imperfect, bearing upon them the unmistakable marks of the transitional. As they have been evolved from an animal consciousness which was below the level of the human mind, so in all probability will they be succeeded by a form of intelligence which is as unlike our minds and as superior to them as our minds are unlike and superior to the consciousness of protozoa. Our species itself will, indeed, in all probability, be superseded, and the universe will know our longings and our aspirations no more.

Is it not, in the light of such facts as these, the height of presumption for human minds to assert not only that human minds so lately evolved, so imperfectly developed, can comprehend the reality of the universe, but that this reality has a unique and special relation with, nay more, a unique and special interest in and concern for themselves; to affirm further that reality is itself mind or spirit modelled in their own image, and to conclude in virtue of this alleged kinship of reality with themselves that it is even now continuous with them, so that they may ultimately aspire to enter into it and, becoming one with it, assure themselves of perpetual being? The philosophies of evolution arose historically as a reaction from the theological conceptions current at the end of the nineteenth century. But they are vitiated no less by the anthropomorphism against which they protest. For, it may well be asked, what presumption could be greater than to hold that the universe is a process in time, seeking the perfection of the human spirit as its goal, and that the preparation for this perfection of a certain number of individual souls, conceived in the likeness of twentieth-century men, is the object for which the whole creation travails?

Nor, if we feel disposed to reject these conceptions on the ground of the crude anthropomorphism which inspires them, need we be deterred by the mystics' report of the reality revealed in their vision. The view of the mystical vision as implying an absorption of the mystic in the reality presupposes, as I have already pointed out, that reality is ultimately of the same nature as the mystic. Thus to take at its face value the strong vein of tradition which represents absorption of being as the goal of the mystical experience, would imply a consent to the view of reality as in some sense both spiritual and in some sense personal.

But is there, in fact, any obligation to accept literally the interpretations which mystics place upon their vision? In trying to appraise the metaphysical significance of mystical testimony, it is important to distinguish between the fact of the mystic's vision and the account which he subsequently gives of it. Of the authenticity of the former I am convinced. The contemptuous dismissal of the mystic's vision as subjective feeling, the babbling of men beside themselves with solitude and fasting, exciting as intoxication is exciting, but conveying no information with regard to the object that excites, seems to me to be born of the prejudices of common sense. For the mystic, as for the artist, his revelation is a psychological fact; like colour, or sound, heat, or shape, it is undeniably a part of his experience; it is there; it is real. Admittedly his experience is different from that of most of us; but so is an artist's—obviously, since he records it—or a dog's. And what claim, after all, has the world revealed to the eye of twentieth-century common sense to be the sole type of reality? It is negligible! Science and philosophy combine to discredit the physical reality of objects of everyday experience, dissolving chairs and tables into a whirl of dancing electrons, mathematical events in a spatio-temporal continuum, colonies of souls, sets of sense data or ideas in the mind of the observer. The external world of common sense is a conventional construction, a legacy from man's philosophical past; common sense itself is a mass of dead metaphysics. Most of us, admittedly, conceive the common-sense world alike because we have similar interests and similar sense organs. But slightly change the condition of our sense organs, and how differently it appears. We have only, for example, to raise the temperatures of our bodies five degrees, for sights and sounds, tastes and smells, to acquire a new significance. Above all, the world we touch, or rather that touches us, is radically changed; it is richer, more insistent and more varied. Yet, because a man's temperature is temporarily above normal, nobody would say that his sensations are not really felt, or that the world they reveal to him has not as much right to be called real as that which is experienced by bodies with temperatures at 98·4 degrees Fahrenheit. It would, indeed, be a feat of parochialism to which even common sense should be unequal to maintain that only that kind of world which is perceived by the sense organs of human bodies heated to a temperature of 98·4 degrees Fahrenheit is real. Even a counting of heads discredits it; most organisms, after all, are cold-blooded, and a frog's world is certainly not ours. As with the frog's world, so with the mystic's. Most mystics have been ascetics. Ascetic practices are methods for inducing artificially a certain kind of psychological and physiological condition. The condition modifies the perceiving apparatus, and the mystic's universe is accordingly changed. Changed, and, it may be, deepened, widened and enriched. For men have found that the particular kind of abnormality that ascetism induces is one that enables them to perceive not only a quantitatively larger, but a qualitatively richer world. It is to them a more exciting world because of the things it contains—goodness, for example, and beauty, and, it may be, God. Hence they seek to retain and continually to enjoy it.

This experience that the mystic enjoys may, I have suggested, be interpreted as a direct awareness of reality conceived as value. This awareness is the highest level at which life has emerged, as it is the latest faculty which it has succeeded in evolving. Because of its recent acquirement, its exercise is precarious, and the mystic is accordingly able to enjoy it only intermittently. He can achieve the vision but he cannot retain it. It is not, indeed, a mere fleeting glimpse like that of the artist, but a prolonged contemplation deliberately enjoyed and in some cases, it seems, deliberately commanded. Nevertheless, the vision fades and the mystic's consciousness sinks back to the normal level at which his awareness is directed upon the familiar worlds of thought and of sense. In the artist this failing of the vision leads to the creation of works of art, in which what has been glimpsed is recorded, that it may be the better remembered. In the mystic it prompts the impulse to explain and describe. Thus the account of mystical experience springs from a mood very different from that to which it testifies. The vision convinces the seer of a reality different from that of everyday life, different and more exciting. It is natural, then, that he should conclude that the world of everyday life is less real, at any rate less important, and invoke his reason to justify his belief. Hence arises the logic of the philosophies which seek to make a distinction between appearance and reality. Again the vision carries with it a feeling of self-transcendence; the mystic is transported by the sublimity of what he contemplates. It is natural, then, that in the mood of explanation he should seek to persuade himself and others that he has ceased for a time to be himself and become one with what was other than himself; that, in other words, he has achieved a temporary identity with reality.

If I am right in my suggestion that mystical experience is the awareness of a new order of reality, then the essence of it is incommunicable. Nor, if he were wise, would the mystic seek to communicate it. Language, as I have already pointed out, was invented to convey the meanings of the familiar worlds, the worlds of sense and of thought. Words may point to a realm of being deeper and wider than either, but they cannot describe it. Hence any attempt to give an account of the object of the vision must necessarily falsify that which it purports to describe. It follows that there is no need to suppose either that the familiar world is unreal, or that the mystical experience implies self-transcendence, merely because mystics have supposed that only on the basis of these beliefs could full justice be done to the uniqueness of that experience. In fact, as I have tried to show, both beliefs involve a faulty logic; while neither is necessarily entailed by the conception of the mystical experience as a direct awareness of a supra-sensible reality.

II. The Status of Reality

In the second place, the view of reality as in some sense akin to our nature and amenable to our wishes seems to me to degrade reality, and by consequence the mind that apprehends it. That the human mind is neither an epitome of the universe nor even a clue to its character I have already tried to show. It remains to point out that the conception of reality as continuous or akin is derogatory to the very value which it seeks to assign, and that human life is dignified not by its kinship with reality but by its isolation in face of an indifferent universe, which assumes grandeur from its very indifference to human life.

It is interesting to notice the marked difference between the temper of mind from which the conceptions of the universe favoured by modern scientists spring, and the mood of science itself. Science has not legislated to the universe; it has been content to catalogue it. Its triumphs have been gained as the result of an impartial outlook upon the universe which has sought to maintain a modest attitude towards objective fact. Instead of prescribing to things what they must be, it has been the object of the scientific method to discover what things are. It was only when science divorced itself from ethical preoccupations that it advanced. The early sciences, for example, astrology and alchemy, were dominated by utilitarian considerations. It was thought that the movements of the stars had an important influence on human beings, and that certain combinations of elements would bring untold material benefits to human lives; for these reasons the movements of the stars and the nature of chemical combinations were studied. The early physicists were dominated by the desire to prove that the universe had a purpose and was therefore ethically admirable, and psychology is still to some extent influenced by the need to arrive at similar conclusions about human nature. It was only when astrology and alchemy divested themselves of utilitarian considerations that they developed into astronomy and chemistry; only when physics emancipated itself from the need to show that the universe it studied possessed this or that ethical characteristic, that it was found possible to discover how the physical universe worked. Psychology is only now beginning to reach a certitude of result as it emancipates itself from the necessity of illustrating preconceived notions about the rationality or ethical desirability of human nature.

The same principle holds in the realm of artistic endeavour. There is a theory of aesthetics which regards beauty as a quality of human apprehension, not as an objective character of what is apprehended. Beauty, in so far as the word on this view has any meaning, is a character of human responses or of the relation between human responses and the external world. Many artists, especially in recent times, have been dominated by this view, art having on the whole developed in a reverse direction to that of science, and, instead of advancing from the subjective and the human to the impartial and the neutral, become more personal and more human in its interests and more subjective in its treatment. Hence the vogue of portrait painters, who concentrate upon the human face as expressive of character and emotion, and the emergence of the school of Expressionism which, instead of trying to reproduce the non-human beauty of external forms portrayed for their own sake, seeks to express human emotions in arrangements of lines and colours. It will, I think, be generally conceded that the art which has sprung from this attitude has rarely achieved greatness, nor has it succeeded in arousing the most intense aesthetic emotions in those who come into contact with it. To achieve beauty in art as to achieve truth in science, it is necessary to divest oneself of preoccupations with the human, and to try, as far as one may, to achieve a pure receptivity to objective fact. The mind which would know beauty and reproduce it should be sensitive to the impress of beauty in the world, rather than seek by the act of its own self-expression to impose beauty upon the world.

Nor is it only for the sake of utilitarian considerations that this ethical neutrality of view is to be advocated. Perpetually to appraise the universe, to seek to find in it an embodiment of human ideals, or a guarantee of human aspirations, is by assimilating it to the human to destroy the very value with which it is sought to endow it. Art tends to be successful in so far as it succeeds in reproducing non-human values. The conception of aesthetic value, in other words, is deepened and broadened in proportion as value is recognized as a character of the universe which is independent of the human spirit.

Logic and mathematics illustrate the same point in regard to truth. Many philosophers have held that the laws of logic are laws of thought which prescribe the operations of our minds. This conception lowers the dignity of reason by circumscribing its scope. It requires us to suppose that thinking is not an investigation into the inner nature of things, an activity by which the evanescent human may become acquainted with the eternal and non-human, but is an enquiry into, because it is an enquiry prescribed by, the human, unable to transcend itself by contact with what is greater than man. It may be objected that it does not follow from the belief that the laws which the enquiry reveals are laws which the consciousness of the enquirer has prescribed, that the object of the enquiry is itself human; nor, I think, does it. Yet the difficulty experienced by systems of the Kantian type, which hold that the laws of logic are laws of the limitations of our minds, in escaping a reduction to the Solipsist conclusion that the *objects* of enquiry are the categories imposed by our own minds, from which it follows that all that thought can do is to introduce us to ourselves, is evidence of the close affinity between the two positions. Modern illustrations of this affinity, and of the ease with which the one position breaks down into the other, are afforded, as I have tried to show, by the speculations of Sir James Jeans and Professor Eddington.

In opposition to this attitude I should urge that the chief glory of the human mind lies in its ability to comprehend the nature of what is other than itself, and not only other but vaster and more valuable. The sense of impotence which attends the realization of the vastness of the external space world, a vastness in which no flicker of the human is anywhere apparent, is mitigated by the very fact that minds should have been able to discover and to explore it. The vaster and the more alien the physical world, the greater the dignity of the mind that can map it. But logic and mathematics take us into an alien world of a different kind, a world imposing by virtue not of size but of necessity. It is a world ruled by laws such that not only itself but all possible worlds must conform to them, so that, contemplating it, mind is ennobled and enriched by its realization of a necessity foreign to itself. This world of necessity is the dwelling-place of truth; it is also touched by beauty. Although to know it is, therefore, to know what is alien to ourselves, it is to know also what is nobler than ourselves. To discover that the universe contains a value to which, though we may contemplate it, we ourselves can never aspire, is surely a more exhilarating experience than to suppose that it contains only such poor values as those with which our minds can endow it. To recognize that the world which reason finds is an embodiment of values such as truth and beauty, while recognizing at the same time its entire independence of ourselves, is to see these values in their proper perspective. It is only by purging them of every element of human consciousness that we can properly regard them as goals of human endeavour. At the same time the mind achieves a nobility from its capacity to be swayed by reverence for that into which there enters no element of self. This is the attitude which underlies the great religions of the past.

All deeply religious views of the world have borne witness to the presence in the universe of a non-human element of perfection and eternality, which affords a standard by which the human and the changing is seen to be faulty. To it religion advocates submission in thought. To assimilate the element to ourselves, to regard it as sensitive to our wishes and responsive to our hopes, as akin to our spirit and ultimately continuous with our nature, is to degrade it to our level. So degraded it is bereft of just that character of value in virtue of which it inspires our wishes and awakens our hopes. That an anthropomorphically conceived deity is a degraded deity is matter of agreement; what is not so generally recognized is that an anthropomorphic conception of value, postulating a value which, although not made in man's image, is continuous with his nature, suffers from a degradation no less profound because less easily discerned.

The same criticism may be offered of those philosophies of evolution which substitute for a value which is an idealized version of the human spirit, a value which is brought to birth by human endeavour. The notion of a God whom we by our own efforts have brought into being, or of a goal which is a higher emergent level of the same life stream as ourselves, is infected, to my mind, with a certain triviality. Dominated by the same preoccupation with human aspirations and the same necessity of satisfying them, it is rendered by the very circumstance of its preoccupation incapable of giving the satisfaction for which they are invoked. If God is, indeed, the goal of evolution, He must be outside, not part of its stream; He must be independent of the process which seeks to achieve Him, and not a phase of that process.

The Mystical Experience.

Also He must be unreachable. By unreachable I do not mean unknowable; on the contrary, I should regard the object of evolution as the attainment of a complete and untrammelled knowledge of that reality, a fleeting and uncertain intimation of which is, in mystical experience, vouchsafed to the most advanced members of our species. But to know is not to be one with. Knowing, I have suggested, is the name that we give to life's activity as directed upon an external universe. Living experience is life's awareness of that universe. One experience differs from another not by virtue of any intrinsic mode of differentiation, but because of the different objects upon which in different experiences and forms of experience life's activity of knowing or awareness is directed. Just as knowing remains fundamentally the same activity throughout, so does the relation of the activity to the object which it knows remain the same.

I believe this statement to be as true of life's knowledge of value in aesthetic and mystical experience as it is of the apprehension of sense data, the knowledge of history, or the understanding of mathematics. I have also given reasons for supposing that life and value belong to different orders or realms of reality. Hence, although life may know value, it cannot become one with that which it knows.

Life is a dynamic impulsion, whose nature is to change and evolve, and whose activity is to know. Driven by the inherent urge of its nature to supersede itself, it manifests itself at ever higher levels of development, which, I have suggested, are to be interpreted in terms of an increasing scope and sublety of awareness. Life at a higher level is life aware of a greater area of the universe. Essentially, then, life is conscious of need and imperfection, the effort to transcend which is the impulsion which drives it forward. The world of value, on the other hand, is static and eternal. It neither changes nor feels the need of change, nor can we, without the risk of grave anthropomorphism, attribute to it anything of the nature of mind as we know mind. If it is without mind, it is also without will or purpose, and, since the vague intimations in terms of which we know it carry with them a suggestion of ineffable beauty and goodness, we must, I think, conceive it to be perfect.

If, then, there are these two orders of reality, life and value, radically opposed, as I conceive them to be, in every particular, a unity or communion between them which implies an identity of what, for want of a better word, I must call "substance," is inconceivable. Nor should it be desired. I have tried to show that the artistic and intellectual consciousnesses are exalted, not degraded, by the otherness of their objects. The point applies with even greater force to the religious consciousness. A Deity who, conceived as permanent and perfect, yet enters into relation with a world which is changing and imperfect, with the changing and imperfect living beings that inhabit it, or with the principle of life that animates them, is diminished in respect of the qualities for which He is venerated. Like goodness and beauty, Deity, if Deity exists, must be a non-human value, whose significance consists in His very unlikeness to the life that aspires to Him. He may be known by life, and, as life evolves and develops, he may be known increasingly, the first fleeting intimations of the saints and mystics reaching their consummation in the continuous joy of unclouded contemplation, but God Himself is unaffected by such contemplation, and, although to achieve it may be the end and the purpose of life's evolution, He is unaware of the movement of life towards Him. Nor can life enter into communion with Him. God, it is obvious, if He is to be an object worthy of our adoration, must be kept unspotted from the world that adores Him. To suppose that the mystic can enter into communion with Him is to suppose Him infected with the frailties and imperfections of the mystic; to suppose that the saint can become one with Him is to suppose that He can become one with the saint. But, I repeat, the permanent and perfect cannot be continuous with the imperfect and the changing; nor could it, without ceasing to be itself, enter into communion with the imperfect and the changing. For this reason, though the religious consciousness may hope to know God, the religious man cannot aspire to become one with that which he knows. That a Being so conceived exists the mystics have borne unanimous testimony.

But if we accept the fact to which that testimony bears witness, we cannot, I suggest, without degrading both self and God, accept the monistic implication of the language in which it is frequently described. It may be objected that this conclusion strikes at the essence of the religious consciousness, the aim of which is to transcend self in unity with God. I do not myself think that this is so. God, if He is such as we can worship, must be at once mysterious and aloof. He loses in holiness as He gains in accessibility. The most beautiful thing we can experience is the mysterious. It is the source of all true art and, I should add, of all true science. It is a direct insight into the mystery of the world which, though suffused with fear, has given rise to religion. To know that what is impenetrable to and unreachable by us really exists, manifesting itself as the highest wonder and the most radiant beauty, which our faculties can comprehend only in their most primitive forms, this knowledge and the feeling to which it gives rise are the core of the religious consciousness. That it should abandon the belief in a God who rewards and punishes the objects of His creation, whose purposes are modelled after our own, who is, in short, but an enlarged embodiment of human frailty and weakness, is the first requirement of a mature intelligence. To substitute for it the sense of a divine mystery manifesting itself in truth, goodness and beauty, and to most men known only in these forms, yet on occasion directly, albeit obscurely, revealed to the most advanced representatives of our species in the most exalted of human experiences, is not to degrade but to dignify the religious consciousness.

Nor is this view unsupported by the opinion of those who have reflected most deeply upon the testimony of the mystics. Von Hugel, to mention one who in modern times has written with an insight as keen as his interpretation of it was sane upon the nature of mystical experience, protests again and again against a monistic interpretation of that experience. It was his deliberately expressed opinion that religion had no more deadly or subtle enemy than Monism. Because it sought to transcend the distinction between knowing and known, Monism reduced itself, in his view, to a variety of Pantheism in which the element of value in the universe, instead of being kept pure and undefiled in unapproachable isolation, was made continuous with and thereby infected by the particularities and imperfections of human thinking. God, in short, in impregnating the activity which was the apprehension of God, became in His turn impregnated by it. A God so conceived could never, in von Hugel's view, evoke the true religious feeling, could never satisfy the hunger of the soul.

From a variety of similar passages I select two in which this position is plainly stated. In the Second Series of his *Essays and Addresses on the Philosophy of Religion*,[1] after describing God as supreme Goodness, Love, and Joy, von Hugel proceeds:

"All this Goodness and Joy God does not become, does not acquire. He simply *is* it. We will be watchful against the blurring over of the contrast between ourself, as experienced by us, and other contingent things always experi-

[1] Chapter VII, p. 209.

enced by us at the time; these things and we are not identical, never were and never will be. How much more, then, will we be on our guard against any real blurring of the contrast between God and ourselves. His Otherness is as essential a part of the facts and of religion as His Likeness can ever be."

Religion is here presented as at once the expression and the satisfaction of the soul's thirst for reality, the point of von Hugel's declaration being that it is only on the assumption that this reality is other than ourselves, that the *power* of the religious feeling can be explained.

"Religion," he continues, "presupposes and reveals man as inevitably moved by and in travail with the sense of and thirst after truth, *the* truth, reality, *the* reality. Man cannot renounce this sense and thirst as an illusion; the very dignity and passion that accompany or foster, at any time, his declaration of such illusion, ever imply such ontology—that there somehow exists a more than human truth and reality, and that man somehow really experiences it."[1]

It is of the essence of this doctrine that the reality which man experiences in moments of mystical illumination is not only other-worldly, but is unaffected by the travailing of this world. It is for this reason that von Hugel pronounces so strongly against the current modern view that ascribes to God a share in the world's pain. God is above pain, simply because He is above and other than the whole process which in travail and suffering seeks to approach and to apprehend Him. He may be in a sense responsible for the goodness of the world, in the sense, that is, in which He may be said to evoke and condition an awareness of Himself; but in no sense can we make Him responsible for its evil.

In mystical experience man has achieved in my view the fullest knowledge of the world of value of which he is as yet capable. But, like the prisoner emerging from the

[1] Von Hugel, *Essays and Addresses on the Philosophy of Religion* (Second Series), Chapter III, p. 59.

cave, he is dazzled and blinded by the light which flashes down to him. What he can tell of his vision in stammering words is false, since he did not see clearly, yet true for something that he saw. Mystical experience is thus a vision of the perfect by the imperfect, a vision which we may one day hope to become an untrammelled and continuous contemplation; but it is a vision in which the seer, though lifted out of himself by that which he sees, never transcends the gulf of pure otherness between them.

The Metaphysical Temper of Modern Physicists

The question may be raised as to the relevance of this discussion to the examination of the metaphysical claims of modern scientists with which this book has been chiefly concerned. The connection is, I submit, not far to seek. I have endeavoured to sketch and to criticize an attitude of mind which in one way or another affirms the fundamental kinship of an underlying world of reality with the human spirit. I have indicated the implications of this view in art, in logic and mathematics, and in theology, and have criticized it on two grounds. I have suggested that it rests upon a false theory of knowledge, and springs from an anthropomorphic temper of mind, which in seeking to liken reality to the self, degrades both the known and the self that knows it. I have also contrasted this temper with the impartial attitude to objective fact which has characterized science in the past, and by virtue of which the triumphs of science have been won.

Applying these conclusions to the thought of modern scientists, I would venture to suggest that it is precisely in the degree of their departure from this attitude, an attitude which is strictly maintained in their scientific work, that their metaphysics go astray. I have already pointed out how closely the conclusions of thinkers such as Jeans and Eddington approximate to those of the school of monistic

Idealism. Among these shared conclusions I have noted the distinction between the world of reality and the worlds of appearance, the insistence on the mental and even personal nature of the world of reality, an affirmation of man's capacity for self-transcendence in union or communion with that world, and a 'malicious' attitude to the world of appearance which leads to a denial of objective reality to the familiar world and even to the world of science.

It is, of course, possible that a metaphysic which embodies these conclusions may be true. Yet it is difficult to avoid being struck by the difference in quality between the main corpus of the work of Jeans and Eddington, which lies within the field of scientific experiment, investigation and deduction, and the metaphysical speculations with which the strictly scientific work concludes. The philosopher, no doubt, is apt to be unduly impressed by the quality of technical scientific work which his lack of scientific equipment renders it difficult for him to understand, but, even when I have made such allowance as I can for this limitation on my own part, I cannot resist the conclusion that the science of these writers is immeasurably more impressive than the philosophy, the foundations more worthy of respect than the superstructure which is reared upon them.

Modern physics is, admittedly, in a state of uncertainty and confusion; the uncertainty springs from the embarrassing abundance of data, the confusion from a natural inability to assess the significance of data, many of which seem at present to contradict each other. Both are pardonable; indeed, given the limitations of the human mind, they are in a large degree inevitable. It is not to be supposed that any large measure of truth, even such truth as relates to the world which science studies, is likely to have been discovered by the mind of twentieth-century man. The future of human life upon our planet, the period, that is to say, which must elapse before the sun grows too cold any longer to maintain the conditions suitable for living organisms, is estimated at about twelve hundred thousand million years, which is a thousand times as long as the whole past history of life. In the light of this immense tract of time, it is difficult to resist the temptation of asking how our remote descendants are to employ their intellectual energies, if the major part of the truth about even the material universe has already been discovered. But the fact that what has been found out is small in comparison with what remains, does not imply that it is not, therefore, true, nor does it suggest that the method which has been followed is mistaken.

This method is the slow and patient accumulation of evidence collected in a spirit of impartial acceptance of objective fact. The study of this evidence has been conducted in a mood of impersonal disinterestedness and freedom from utilitarian preoccupations, which is not alien to the spirit of the great religions. It is by such methods and in such a spirit that the triumphs of science have been won, and of these methods and of this spirit the scientific work of the writers discussed in this book affords an admirable illustration.

The Scientific Temper in Philosophy

But when, upon the basis of their scientific work, they proceed to metaphysical speculation, the case is different. Ethical neutrality, achieved with difficulty in the sciences, is harder of achievement in philosophy. When we seek to determine the nature of the whole, it is harder to expel self than when we are engaged in analysing the structure of the atom, and it is not easy for the philosopher to maintain that aloofness from mundane hopes and fears which now characterizes the best work of pure science. Man has always found it difficult not to distort evidence to suit his ends; it is the achievement of science to have triumphed to some extent over this difficulty. But when he seeks to pass beyond the evidence collected by the special sciences and asks himself the question, what sort of universe must it be in which such evidence occurs, self-forgetfulness is hard indeed. Unperceived, his mind will insist on legislating to the universe, and, instead of recognizing it to be such as the evidence suggests, pronouncing it to be such as his wishes would have it. That we cannot entirely transcend our nature is true; some subjective bias, if only the bias which causes us to pay attention to certain things rather than to others, must determine the direction of our thought, and the scope and subtlety of mind's awareness is in any event conditioned by the level of evolution which it has reached.

But some emancipation from the grosser and more primitive hopes and fears is now at least possible, and is a prerequisite of successful philosophizing. That man should no longer regard reality as friendly or hostile, mindlike or mindless, like or unlike a human spirit, that he should cease to define it in reference to any imagined relation to himself, is the first requirement of the scientific temper in philosophy. If it is urged that this condition makes the ultimate nature of reality unintelligible and, therefore, indescribable, the possibility is one that must be faced. Metaphysics provides us, so far as I know, with no *a priori* reason why metaphysical speculation *must* be successful, and it may be the case, as I think it is, that reality, even if it may be known, cannot be described. The modern realist movement in philosophy seems to me to have been inspired by something of this attitude. Modern Realism is a movement of metaphysical renunciation. It reconciles itself to the view that philosophy cannot hope to pronounce upon the nature of the universe as a whole, if, indeed, the universe can be said to be in any sense a whole of which a nature may be affirmed, and contents itself with a piecemeal investigation of certain particular problems. I am inclined to think that this cautious attitude to the possibility of metaphysical knowledge errs on the side of over-caution, although if it does so err, the fault is at least on the right side.

The suggestion I have made is that the facts of aesthetic and mystical experience do, in fact, entitle us to go beyond the purely agnostical attitude of most realists.

But if the nature of reality is revealed to us, albeit fleetingly and uncertainly, in aesthetic and mystical experience, if we are entitled to conceive it as the artist conceives the beauty that excites, or the mystic the Deity that awes him, our conception of it must be governed by two conditions. We must not conceive it in the likeness of ourselves, and we must not conceive it as capable of oneness of being with ourselves.

Man, as I envisage him, is a being very young, very simple, very little capable of insight. His knowledge of the world of value is but a fledgling's knowledge; his admiration is apt to be a nestling's admiration for the things which are kindly to his own nature. Nevertheless, he may, I believe, pass in thought beyond this fledgling condition, and view the world as indifferent to his aims and alien to his nature, and yet as supremely worthy of his admiration. It is on these lines that, I conceive, the scientific spirit may be introduced into the realm of metaphysical speculation.

It is perhaps superfluous to point out that the philosophizing of Sir James Jeans and Professor Eddington is inspired by a different purpose. Their object has been to present the reality at the back of things not only as worthy of man's admiration, but as friendly and even akin to his nature. In so doing they have remembered their wishes but have forgotten their science. When the scientist leaves his laboratory and speculates about the universe as a whole, the resultant conclusions are apt to tell us more about the scientist than about the universe. Possessing value as psychology, they possess little as metaphysics. In particular, they have led him, as we have seen, to a 'malicious' attitude to the world of familiar things. Many modern scientists have adopted a logic which requires them to regard not only the familiar world as unreal, but even the world of science on the study of which their conclusions purport to be based. Yet it is difficult to resist the application of the same logical method to the so-called real world which they believe to underlie the familiar world and the world of science. It, too, if we are prepared to push their mode of reasoning to its logical conclusion, turns out to be nothing more than an externalization of the human mind. Religious meditation becomes, therefore, not a method of making contact with a non-human reality, but an overhauling of one's own experience, or at most the expression of the will to make one's experience coherent. The conclusion is one which, I cannot help thinking, militates against the dignity both of religion and of science.

At this juncture, then, it seems to be the business of philosophy to intervene and to point out the logical difficulties involved in the view of the relation of knowledge to its objects which scientists seem disposed to adopt. In so doing it is enabled to safeguard not only the common world but the world of science itself from the tendency to make it dependent upon, if not a mere phase of, the consciousness of the scientist. It is, no doubt, something of a paradox that philosophy should have thus to step in to rehabilitate the method of science, by conceding to it a revelatory and not a purely constructive function; that it should be the philosopher and not the scientist who is prepared to believe that science can tell us something about the nature of an objective world. Yet the paradox is seen on reflection to arise inevitably from the nature and function of philosophy. The function of philosophy, as I conceive it, is the endeavour to understand every aspect of universe. Philosophy, that is to say, takes cognizance not, like physics or biology, of a special department of the universe, but of the whole mass of data to which the moral intuitions of the ordinary man, the religious consciousness of the saint, the aesthetic enjoyment of the artist, and the history of the human race, no less than the discoveries of the physicist and the biologist, contribute.

Philosophy is thus, in the first place, a bar to which the various methods of obtaining information about the universe may be called to give an account of themselves; in the second, it is a clearing-house in which different forms of experience may be pooled. And it is in performance of these, the historical functions of the philosopher, that I have presumed to criticize the metaphysical structures which modern scientists have erected, and the logic with which they seek to support them.

Herein lies the significance of the discussion of value which I have attempted in the last two chapters. Philosophy considering, as it must needs do, the bearing of modern theories of the physical world upon art and religion cannot but regard their implications as derogatory both to the knowing mind and to the universe that it contemplates. Seen in the wider perspective of philosophy the theories of the universe sponsored by modern physics have an appearance of triviality, making the universe smaller by assimilating it to the nature and subordinating it to the wishes of man. Apart, therefore, from the logical difficulties to which they are exposed, philosophy, concerned for the integrity of the universe which it studies, must start with a presumption against theories which belittle it.

And considering the instrument with which they have been wrought, the instrument of science, it cannot but be impressed with its novelty. Science is still a new thing, and because it is new, man is still inapt in its use. Science is a match which man has just got alight. Reading by that light scientists have written as if man were in a room—in moments of devotion they have thought it a temple—and his light were reflected from walls covered with writings in his own hand, writings which told him comforting truths and assured him of a universe in which he could feel at home. They have even in moments of exaltation suggested that he built the temple himself. It is only to a deeper view that the universe is revealed, now that the preliminary splutter is over and the flame burns up clear, as an immense void in which nothing of the human can be discerned. Man by the light of science can see his hands, and can catch a glimpse of himself, his past, and the patch upon which he stands; but around him in place of that known comfort and beauty he had anticipated, and in the first few moments falsely thought that he saw, is darkness still.

It is an experience strange but exhilarating, a stimulus to brace man's courage and to call him to new endeavours.

INDEX